PLACE IN RETURN BOX to remove this checkout from your record.
TO AVOID FINES return on or before date due.

DATE DUE	DATE DUE	DATE DUE
————	————	————
————	————	————
————	————	————
————	————	————
————	————	————
————	————	————
————	————	————

MSU Is An Affirmative Action/Equal Opportunity Institution
c:\circ\datedue.pm3-p.1

THE IMPERIAL CULT
IN THE
LATIN WEST

II, 2

ÉTUDES PRÉLIMINAIRES
AUX RELIGIONS ORIENTALES
DANS L'EMPIRE ROMAIN

PUBLIÉES PAR

M.J. VERMASEREN †

M.E.C. VERMASEREN-VAN HAAREN ET **MARGREET B. DE BOER**

TOME CENT HUITIÈME

DUNCAN FISHWICK

THE IMPERIAL CULT IN THE LATIN WEST II, 2

DUNCAN FISHWICK

THE IMPERIAL CULT
IN THE
LATIN WEST

Studies in the Ruler Cult
of the Western Provinces of the Roman Empire

VOLUME II, 2

E.J. BRILL
LEIDEN • NEW YORK • KÖLN
1992

The paper in this book meets the guidelines for permanence and durability of the Committee on Production Guidelines for Book Longevity of the Council on Library Resources

Library of Congress Cataloging-in-Publication Data

Fishwick, Duncan, 1929-
    The imperial cult in the Latin West.

    (Etudes préliminaires au religions orientales dans
l'Empire romain, 0531-1950 ; t. 108)
    Includes bibliographical references.
    1. Rome—Kings and rulers—Religious aspects.
2. Rome—Religion   I. Title,   II. Series.
BL805.F58   1987   292.2'13   87-6363

ISSN 0531-1950
ISBN 90 04 09495 4

PRINTED IN THE NETHERLANDS

Volume II, 2 comprises Abbreviated Titles, Select Bibliography, Indices and Corrigenda to Volumes I, 1-2 and II, 1 (Introduction, Books I-II), which together make a unit. The volume completes the preliminary set of studies and, by coincidence, brings the *EPRO* series to a conclusion. The individual volumes of Book III (provincial, municipal, private, military cult) and Book IV (theology of the Roman Emperor) will be published as independent monographs, each with its own apparatus, except that a consolidated bibliography is reserved for Book IV. Volumes III, 1-4 and Volume IV will now appear in a new series, *Religion in the Later Roman World*, to be edited for Brill by H. Drijvers and R. van den Broek.

CONTENTS

I. Abbreviated Titles 627

II. Select Bibliography 638

III. Indices 673
  1. Names and Subjects 673
  2. Places and Localities 748
  3. Literary Authorities 767
  4. Inscriptions................................. 790
  5. Coins 840
  6. Papyri 845
  7. Bas-Reliefs 846
  8. Gems 847
  9. Greek and Latin Words 847

IV. Corrigenda 866

I. ABBREVIATED TITLES

In addition to the short list of standard abbreviations given at the beginning of each volume, the following abbreviated titles have been used in Volumes I, 1-2; II, 1. Collections of inscriptions, coins, etc. are abbreviated according to standard conventions (below, pp. 790 ff.).

Alföldi, *Studien* = Alföldi, A. *Studien über Caesars Monarchie,* Lund, 1953.

Alföldi, *Repräsentation* = Alföldi, A. *Die monarchische Repräsentation im römischen Kaiserreiche,* Darmstadt, 1970.

Alföldi, "Divinisation" = Alföldi, A. "La divinisation de César dans la politique d'Antoine et d'Octavien entre 44 et 40 avant J.C.," *RN* 15 (1973), 99-128.

Alföldi, "Aufsteig" = Alföldi, A. *Octavians Aufstieg zur Macht* (Antiquitas 1), Bonn, 1976.

Alföldi, *Lorbeerbäume* = Alföldi, A. "Die zwei Lorbeerbäume des Augustus" in A. Wlosok (ed.), *Römischer Kaiserkult* (WdF 372), Darmstadt, 1978, 403-422.

Alföldi, *Vater* = Alföldi, A. *Der Vater des Vaterlandes im römischen Denken,* Darmstadt, 1978.

Alföldy, *Hilfstruppen* = Alföldy, G. *Die Hilfstruppen der römischen Provinz Germania Inferior* (EpigStud 6), Düsseldorf, 1968.

Alföldy, *Fasti* = Alföldy, G. *Fasti Hispanienses,* Wiesbaden, 1969.

Alföldy, *Noricum* = Alföldy, G. *Noricum,* London, 1974.

Alföldy, "Tarraco" = Alföldy, G. *RE* Suppl. 15 (1978), 570-644 s.v. Tarraco.

ANRW = Temporini H. *Aufstieg und Niedergang der römischen Welt,* Berlin, 1972-89, Vols. 1, II.

Audin, *Essai* = Audin, A. *Essai sur la Topographie de Lugdunum³.* Lyon, 1964.

Audin, *Lyon, Miroir* = Audin, A. *Lyon, Miroir de Rome dans les Gaules,* Paris, 1965.

Axtell, "Deification" - Axtell, H.L. *The Deification of Abstract Ideas in Roman Literature and Inscriptions* (Diss. Chicago), Chicago, 1907.

Badian, "Deification" = Badian, E. "The Deification of Alexander the Great" in *Ancient Macedonian Studies in Honor of Charles F. Edson* (Publ. Inst. Balkan Studies 158), Thessaloniki, 1982, 27-71.

Balsdon, "Divinity" = Balsdon, J.P.V.D. "The 'Divinity' of Alexander," *Historia* 1 (1950), 363-388.

Bastiaensen, *Atti* = Bastiaensen, A.A.R. *et al, Atti e Passioni dei martiri,* Milan, 1987.

Bayet, *Histoire* = Bayet, J. *Histoire politique et psychologique de la Religion romaine,* Paris, 1957.

Bayet, "Prodromes" = Bayet, J. "Prodromes sacerdotaux de la divinisation impériale" in *La Regalita Sacrà,* Leiden, 1959, 418-434.

Beaujeu, "Politique religieuse" = Beaujeu, J. "Politique religieuse et propagande numismatique sous le Haut-Empire" in R. Chevallier (ed.), *Mélanges d'Archéologie et d'Histoire offerts à André Piganiol,* Paris, 1966, 1529-1540.

Bellido, *Esculturas* = Bellido, A. Garcia y, *Esculturas romanas de España y Portugal,* Madrid, 1949.

Berlinger, *Beiträge* = Berlinger, L. *Beiträge zur inoffiziellen Titulatur der römischen Kaiser* (Diss. Breslau), Breslau, 1935.

Bickerman, "Consecratio" = Bickerman, E. "Consecratio" in den Boer (ed.), *Le Culte* 3-25.

Bieler, ΘΕΙΟΣ 'ΑΝΗΡ = Bieler, L. ΘΕΙΟΣ 'ΑΝΗΡ, Vienna, 1935, Vol. 1.

Bikerman, *Institutions* = Bikerman, E. *Institutions des Séleucides,* Paris, 1938.

Birley, *Septimius Severus* = Birley, A.R. *Septimius Severus the African Emperor,* London, 1971.

Birley, *Fasti* = Birley, A.R. *The* Fasti *of Roman Britain,* Oxford, 1981.

den Boer, "Ex-voto's" = den Boer, W. "Heersercultus en ex-voto's in het Romeinse Keizerrijk," *Mededel. der Konink. Nederl. Akad. van Wetensch., afd. Letterkunde* 36 (1973), 99-115.

Bömer-Herz, "Untersuchungen" = Bömer, F. and Herz, P. *Untersuchungen über die Religion der Sklaven in Griechenland und Rom,*[2] Wiesbaden, 1981.

Brilliant, *Arch* = Brilliant, R. *The Arch of Septimius Severus in the Roman Forum* (MAAR 29), Rome 1967.

Broughton, *Romanization* = Broughton, T.R.S. *The Romanization of Africa Proconsularis,* Baltimore, 1929.

Burkert, *Griechische Religion* = Burkert, W. *Griechische Religion der archaischen und Klassischen Epoche,* Stuttgart, 1977.

Burr Thompson, *Oinochoai* = Thompson, B.D. *Ptolemaic Oinochoai and Portraits in Faience,* Oxford, 1973.

Chantraine, *Freigelassene* = Chantraine, H. *Freigelassene und Sklaven im Dienst der römischen Kaiser*, Wiesbaden, 1967.
Charlesworth, "Observations" = Charlesworth, M.P. "Some Observations on Ruler-Cult, especially in Rome," *HThR* 28 (1935), 5-44.
Charlesworth, "Virtues" = Charlesworth, M.P. "The Virtues of a Roman Emperor: Propaganda and the Creation of Belief," *Proceedings of the British Academy* 23 (1937), 105-133.
Chevallier, "Gallia Lugdunensis" = Chevallier, R. "Gallia Lugdunensis. Bilan de 25 ans de recherches historiques et archéologiques," *ANRW* 2, 3 (1975) 860-1060.
Classen, "Gottmenschentum" = Classen, C.J. "Gottmenschentum in der römischen Republik," *Gymnasium* 70 (1963), 312-338.

Dar.-Sag. = Daremberg Ch. and Saglio E. *Dictionnaire des Antiquités grecques et romaines*, Paris, 1877-1919 (1962-1963), Vols. I-V.
Degrassi, *Fasti consolari* = Degrassi, A. *I Fasti consolari dell' Impero romano*, Rome, 1952.
Deininger, "Begründung" = Deininger, J. "Zur Begründung des Provinzialkultes in der Baetica," *MDAI(M)* 5 (1964), 167-179.

Diz. *Epig* = De Ruggiero E. *Dizionario Epigrafico di Antichità Romane*, Rome, 1895-1906 (1961-1962), Vols. I-III.
Dobesch, *Caesars Apotheose* = Dobesch, G. *Caesars Apotheose zu Lebezeiten und sein Ringen um den Königstitel*, Vienna, 1966.
Duthoy, "*Augustales" = Duthoy, R. "Les *Augustales," *ANRW* 2, 16, 2 (1978) 1254-1309.

Eitrem, "Apotheose" = Eitrem, S. "Zur Apotheose," *SO* 10 (1932), 31-34; 15/16 (1936), 111-137.

Fayer, *Dea Roma* = Fayer, C. *Il Culto della Dea Roma. Origine e diffusione nell'Impero*, Pescara, 1976.
Fears, *Princeps* = Fears, J.R. *Princeps a diis electus: The Divine Election of the Emperor as a Political Concept at Rome* (Papers and Monographs of the American Academy in Rome 26), Rome, 1977.
Fears, "Cult of Jupiter" = Fears, J.R. "The Cult of Jupiter and Roman Imperial Ideology," *ANRW* 2, 17, 1 (1981) 3-141.
Fears, "Virtues" = Fears, J.R. "The Cult of Virtues and Roman Imperial Ideology," *ANRW* 2, 17, 2 (1981) 827-948.

Fears, "Theology of Victory" = Fears, J.R. "The Theology of Victory at Rome: Approaches and Problems," *ANRW* 2, 17, 2 (1981) 736-826.
"Fer. Dur." = Fink, R.L., Hoey, A.S., and Snyder, W.F. "The Feriale Duranum," *YCS* 7 (1940), 1-222.
Final Report - Welles, C.B., Fink, R.O., Gilliam, J.F., *The Excavations at Dura-Europus, Final Report V, 1: The Parchments and Papyri*, New Haven, 1959.
Fishwick, "Annexation" = Fishwick, D. "The Annexation of Mauretania," *Historia* 20 (1971), 467-487.
Fraenkel, *Horace* = Fraenkel, E. *Horace*, Oxford, 1957.
Fraser, *Ptolemaic Alexandria* = Fraser, P.N. *Ptolemaic Alexandria*, Oxford, 1972, Vols. 1-3.
Fredricksmeyer, "Divine Honors" = Fredricksmeyer, E.A. "Divine Honors for Philip II," *TAPA* 109 (1979), 39-61.
Fredricksmeyer, "Deification" = Fredricksmeyer, E.A. "Three Notes on Alexander's Deification," *AJAH* 4 (1979), 1-9.
Fredricksmeyer, "Background" = Fredricksmeyer, E.A. "On the Background of the Ruler Cult" in *Ancient Macedonian Studies in Honor of Charles F. Edson* (Publ. Inst. Balkan Studies 158), Thessaloniki, 1982, 190-201.

Gagé, *Apollon* = Gagé, J. *Apollon Romain* (BEFAR 182), Paris, 1955.
Gagé, "Apollon impérial" = Gagé, J. "Apollon impérial, garant des "Fata Romana"," *ANRW* 2, 17, 2 (1981) 561-630.
Gascou, "Politique municipale" = Gascou, J. "La politique municipale de Rome en Afrique du Nord. I. De la mort d'Auguste au début du IIIe siècle," *ANRW* 2, 10, 2 (1982) 136-229.
Gayraud, *Narbonne* = Gayraud, M. *Narbonne antique des Origines à la Fin du IIIe siècle* (Rev. Arch. de Narbonnaise, Suppl. 8), Paris, 1981.
Gesche, *Vergottung* = Gesche, H. *Die Vergottung Caesars* (Frankfurter Althistorische Studien 1), Kallmünz, 1968, 40-53.
Gesche, *Caesar* = Gesche, H. *Caesar* (Erträge der Forschung 51), Darmstadt, 1976.
Grant, *Aspects* = Grant, M. *Aspects of the Principate of Tiberius: Historical Comments on the Colonial Coinage issued outside Spain* (Numismatic Notes and Monographs 116), New York, 1950.
Grant, *Anniversary Issues* = Grant, M. *Roman Anniversary Issues, An Exploratory Study of the Numismatic and Medallic Commemoration of Anniversary Years 49 B.C.-A.D. 375*, Cambridge, 1950.

Grant, *RIM* = Grant, M. *Roman Imperial Money*, Edinburgh, 1954.

Grenier, *Manuel* = Grenier, A. *Manuel d'Archéologie gallo-romaine*, Paris, 1960, Vol. IV.

Gros, "Fonction symbolique" = Gros, P. "La fonction symbolique des édifices théâtraux dans le paysage urbain de la Rome augustéenne" in *L'Urbs. Espace urbain et Histoire (1er siècle av. J.C. - IIIe Siècle ap. J.C.)* (Coll. de l'Ecole franç. de Rome 98), Rome 1987, 319-346.

Gros, "Remarques" = Gros, P. "Remarques sur les fondations urbaines de Narbonnaise et de Cisalpine au début de l'empire," *Quaderni* 10, 11, 12 (Atti del Convegno "Studi Lunensi e prospettive sull' Occidente romano," Lerici, settembre 1985), 1987, 73-95.

Gros, *Urbanistica* = Gros, P. and Torelli, M. *Storia dell' Urbanistica. Il mondo romano*, Rome-Bari, 1988.

Haase, "Voraussetzungen" = Haase, W. "Voraussetzungen und Motive des Herrscherkultes von Kommagene," *Antike Welt: Zeitschrift für Archäologie und Urgeschichte* 6 (1975), *Sondernummer Kommagene*.

Habicht, *Gottmenschentum* = Habicht, Chr. *Gottmenschentum und griechische Städte*² (Zetemata 14), Munich, 1970.

Habicht, "Augusteische Zeit" = Habicht, Chr. "Die augusteische Zeit und das erste Jahrhundert nach Christi Geburt" in den Boer (ed.), *Le Culte* 41-88.

Hammond, "Transmission" = Hammond, M. "The Transmission of the Powers of the Roman Emperor from the Death of Nero in A.D. 68 to that of Alexander Severus in A.D. 235," *MAAR* 24 (1956), 63-133.

Hammond, "Elements" = Hammond, M. "Imperial Elements in the Formula of the Roman Emperors during the first two and a half centuries of the Empire," *MAAR* 25 (1957), 17-64.

Hammond, *Ant. Mon.* = Hammond, M. *The Antonine Monarchy* (Papers and Monographs of the American Academy in Rome 19), Rome, 1959.

Hasebroek, *Untersuchungen* = Hasebroek, J. *Untersuchungen zur Geschichte des Kaisers Septimius Severus*, Heidelberg, 1921.

Hansen, *Attalids* = Hansen, E.V. *The Attalids of Pergamon*², Ithaca and London, 1971.

Heinen, *Begründung* = Heinen, H. "Zur Begründung des römischen Kaiserkultes," *Klio* 11 (1911), 129-177.

Henig, *Gemstones* = Henig, M. *A Corpus of Roman Engraved Gemstones from British Sites* (BAR 8), Oxford, 1978.

Hermann, "Antiochus" = Hermann, P. "Antiochus der Grosse und Teos," *Anadolu* 9 (1965), 29-159.

Hermann, "Götteraltäre" = Hermann, W. *Römische Götteraltäre*, Kallmünz, 1961.

Herz, *Festkalender* = Herz, P. *Untersuchungen zum Festkalender der römischen Kaiserzeit nach datierten Weih- und Ehreninschriften* (Diss. Mainz), Mainz, 1975.

Herz, "Kaiserfeste" = Herz, P. "Kaiserfeste des Prinzipatszeit," *ANRW* 2, 16, 2 (1978) 1135-1200.

Hesberg, "Archäologische Denkmäler" = von Hesberg, H. "Archäologische Denkmäler zum römischen Kaiserkult," *ANRW* 2, 16, 2 (1978) 911-995.

Hirschfeld, *Verwaltungsbeamten* = Hirschfeld, O. *Die kaiserlichen Verwaltungsbeamten bis auf Diokletian*², Berlin, 1905 (1963).

Hölscher, *Victoria* = Hölscher, T. *Victoria Romana*, Mainz, 1967.

Hopkins, *Conquerors* = Hopkins, K. *Conquerors and Slaves* (Sociological Studies in Roman History 1), Cambridge, 1978.

Hull, *Roman Colchester* = Hull, M.R. *Roman Colchester*, London, 1958.

Jones, *Studies* = Jones, A.H.M. *Studies in Roman Government and Law*, Oxford, 1960.

Koestermann, *Annalen* = Koestermann, E. *Cornelius Tacitus. Annalen*, Heidelberg, 1963.

Kornemann, *Doppelprinzipat* = Kornemann, E. *Doppelprinzipat und Reichsteilung im Imperium Romanum*, Leipzig and Berlin, 1930.

Kraft, *Der goldene Kranz* = Kraft, K. *Der goldene Kranz Caesars und der Kampf um die Entlarvung des Tyrranen*, Darmstadt, 1969.

Krascheninnikoff, *Einführung* = Krascheninnikoff, M. "Über die Einführung des provinzialen Kaisercultus im römischen Westen," *Philologus* 53, n.F. 7 (1894), 147-189.

Kunkel, *Genius* = Kunkel, H. *Der römische Genius*, (MDAI[R] Ergänzungsheft 20), Heidelberg, 1974.

Ladage, *Städtische Priester* = Ladage, D. *Städtische Priester- und Kultämter im lateinischen Westen des Imperium Romanum zur Kaiserzeit* (Diss. Köln), Cologne, 1971.

Lambrechts, "Politique 'apollinienne'" = Lambrechts, P. "La politique 'apollinienne' d'Auguste et le culte impérial," *La Nouvelle Clio* 5 (1953), 65-82.

Larsen, *Representative Government* = Larsen, J.A.O. *Representative Government in Greek and Roman History* (Sather Classical lectures 28), Berkeley and Los Angeles, 1955.

Le Glay, "Hadrien" = Le Glay, M. "Hadrien et l'Asklépieion de Pergame," *BCH* 100 (1976), 347-372.

Liebeschuetz, *Continuity* = Liebeschuetz, J.H.W.G. *Continuity and Change in Roman Religion*, Oxford, 1979.

L'Orange, *Apotheosis* = L'Orange, H.P. *Apotheosis in Ancient Portraiture*, Oslo, 1947.

MacMullen, *Paganism* = MacMullen, R. *Paganism in the Roman Empire*, New Haven and London, 1981.

Mastino, *Titolature* = Mastino, A. *Le Titolature di Caracalla e Geta attraverso le Iscrizioni (Indici)* (Studi di Storia Antica 5), Bologna, 1981.

McCann, *Portraits* = McCann, A.M. *The Portraits of Septimius Severus* (MAAR 30), Rome, 1968.

Mellor, PΩMH = Mellor, R.J. ΘEA PΩMH *The Worship of the Goddess Roma in the Greek World* (Hypomnemata 42), Göttingen, 1975.

Mellor, "Goddess Roma" = Mellor, R.J. "The Goddess Roma," *ANRW* 2, 17, 2 (1981) 950-1030.

Merten, *Zwei Herrscherfeste* = Merten, E.W. *Zwei Herrscherfeste in der Historia Augusta* (Antiquitas 5), Bonn, 1968.

Mundle, *Untersuchungen* = Mundle I. *Untersuchungen zur Religionspolitik des Septimius Severus (Herkules, Bacchus, Jupiter, Juno)*, Diss. Freiburg, 1957 (unpublished).

Musurillo, *Acts* = Musurillo, H. *The Acts of the Christian Martyrs*, Oxford, 1972.

Nash, *Pictorial Dictionary* = Nash, E. *Pictorial Dictionary of Ancient Rome*, New York, 1981.

Niemeyer, *Studien* = Niemeyer, H.G. *Studien zur statuarischen Darstellung der römischen Kaiser* (Monumenta Artis Romanae 7), Berlin, 1968.

Nilsson, "Pagan Divine Service" = Nilsson, M.P. "Pagan Divine Service in Late Antiquity," *HThR* 38 (1945), 63-69.

Nilsson, "Lampen" = Nilsson, M.P. "Lampen und Kerzen im Kult der Antike" in *Opuscula Selecta*, Lund, 1960, 189-214.

Nock, "Studies" = Nock, A.D. "Studies in the Graeco-Roman Beliefs of the Empire," *JHS* 45 (1925), 84-101.

Nock, "Notes" = Nock, A.D. "Notes on Ruler Cult, I-IV," *JHS* 48 (1928), 21-43.

Nock, "Synnaos" = Nock, A.D. "Σύνναος Θεός," *HSCP* 41 (1930), 1-62.

Nock, "Heroes" = Nock, A.D. "The Cult of Heroes," *HThR* 37 (1944), 141-173.

Nock, "Comes" = Nock, A.D. "The Emperor's Divine *Comes*," *JRS* 37 (1947), 102-116.

Nock, "Julian" = Nock, A.D. "Deification and Julian," *JRS* 47 (1957), 115-123.

Nock, "Son of God" = Nock, A.D. "'Son of God' in Pauline and Hellenistic Thought," *Gnomon* 33 (1961), 581-590.

Nock, "Essays" = Nock, A.D., [ed. Z. Stewart], *Essays on Religion and the Ancient World*, Oxford, 1972, Vols. 1-2.

Oliver, *Gerusia* = Oliver, J.H. *The Sacred Gerusia* (Hesperia Suppl. 6), Baltimore, 1941.

Pekáry, *Kaiserbildnis* = Pekáry, T. *Das römische Kaiserbildnis in Staat, Kult und Gesellschaft* (Das römische Herrscherbild: Abt. 3; Bd. 5), Berlin, 1985.

Pflaum, *Procurateurs équestres* = Pflaum, H.-G. *Essai sur les Procurateurs équestres sous le Haut-Empire romain*, Paris, 1950.

Pflaum, *Carrières* = Pflaum, H.-G. *Les Carrières procuratoriennes équestres sous le Haut-Empire romain*, Paris, 1960.

Pflaum, "Chevaliers" = Pflaum, H.-G. "La part prise par les chevaliers romains originaires d'Espagne à l'administration impériale" in *Les Empereurs romains d'Espagne* (Actes du Colloque International du Centre National de la Recherche Scientifique, Madrid-Italica, 31 mars-6 avril), Paris, 1965, 87-121.

Pflaum, *Fastes Narbonn.* = Pflaum, H.-G. *Les Fastes de la Province de Narbonnaise* (Gallia Suppl. 30), Paris, 1978.

Platner-Ashby, *Topog. Dict.* = Platner, S.B. and Ashby, T. *A Topographical Dictionary of Ancient Rome*, London, 1929.

Pleket, "Nine Inscriptions" = Pleket, H.W. "Nine inscriptions from the Cayster-Valley in Lydia: A re-publication," *Talanta* 2 (1970), 55-88.

Pollini, *Augustan Reliefs* = Pollini, J. *Studies in Augustan "Historical" Reliefs* (Diss. California), Berkeley, 1978.

Porte, "Romulus-Quirinus" = Porte, D. "Romulus-Quirinus, prince et dieu, dieu des princes," *ANRW* 2, 17, 1 (1981) 300-342.

Price, "Sacrifice" = Price, S.R.F. "Between Man and God: Sacrifice in the Roman Imperial Cult," *JRS* 70 (1980), 28-43.

Price, *Rituals* = Price, S.R.F. *Rituals and Power. The Roman Imperial Cult in Asia Minor*, Cambridge, 1984.

Radke, "Augustus" = Radke, G. "Augustus und das Göttliche" in *Antike und Universalgeschichte* (Festschrift H.E. Stier), Münster, 1972, 257-279.

Radke, *Götter* = Radke, G. *Die Götter Altitaliens*² (Fontes et Commentationes. Schriftenreihe des Instituts für Epigraphik an der Universität Münster 3), Münster, 1979.

Radke, "Quirinus" = Radke, G. "Quirinus. Eine kritische Überprüfung der Überlieferung und ein Versuch," *ANRW* 2, 17, 1 (1981) 276-299.

Rainer, *Bild* = Rainer, A. *Das Bild des Augustus auf den frühen Reichsprägungen. Studien zur Vergöttlichung des ersten Prinzeps* (Schriftenreihe der Numismatischen Gesellschaft Speyer 21), Speyer am Rhein, 1981.

Robert, "Cultes royaux" = Robert, L. "Sur un decret d'Ilion et sur un papyrus concernant des cultes royaux" in *Essays in Honor of C. Bradford Welles* (American Studies in Papyrology 1), New Haven, 1966, 175-211.

Robert, *Gladiateurs* = Robert L. *Les Gladiateurs dans l'Orient grec*, Amsterdam, 1971.

Romanelli, *Stori* = Romanelli, P. *Storia delle Province romane dell' Africa*, Rome, 1959.

Roscher, Lexicon = Roscher, W.H. (ed). *Ausführliches Lexicon der griechischen und römischen Mythologie*, Leipzig, 1884-1937, Vols. I-X.

Scott Ryberg, *Rites* = Scott Ryberg, I. *Rites of the State Religion in Roman Art* (MAAR 22), Rome, 1955.

Sherwin-White, *Letters* = Sherwin-White, A.N. *The Letters of Pliny*, Oxford, 1966.

Snyder, "Anniversaries" = Snyder, W.F. "Public Anniversaries in the Roman Empire," *YCS* 7 (1940), 225-317.

Soechting, *Porträts* = Soechting, D. *Die Porträts des Septimius Severus* (Habelts Dissertationsdrücke: Reihe Klassische Archäologie 4), Bonn, 1972.

Squarciapino, *Leptis* = Squarciapino, M.F. *Leptis Magna*, Basel, 1966.

Strack, *Untersuchungen* = Strack, P.L. *Untersuchungen zur römischen Reichsprägung des zweiten Jahrhunderts*, Stuttgart, 1931, Vol. 1.

Sutherland-Kraay, *Catalogue Ashmolean Museum* = Sutherland, C.H.V. and Kraay, C.M. *Catalogue of Coins of the Roman Empire in the Ashmolean Museum, Part I, Augustus (c. 31 B.C. - A.D. 14)*, Oxford, 1975, Vol. I.

Taeger, *Charisma* I = Taeger, F. *Charisma. Studien zur Geschichte des antiken Herrscherkultes,* Stuttgart, 1957, Vol. 1; 1960, Vol. 2.

Talbert, "Biographies" = Talbert, C.H. "Biographies of Philosophers and Rulers as Instruments of Religious Propaganda in Mediterranean Antiquity," *ANRW* 2, 16, 2 (1978) 1619-1651.

Tarn, *Alexander* = Tarn, W.W. *Alexander the Great,* Cambridge, 1948.

Torelli, *Typology* = Torelli, M. *Typology and Structure of Roman Historical Reliefs* (Jerome Lectures 14), Ann Arbor, 1982.

Tuchelt, *Denkmäler* = Tuchelt, K. *Frühe Denkmäler Roms in Kleinasien I: Roma und Promagistrate* (MDAI[I] Beiheft 23), Tübingen, 1979.

Turcan, *Religions* = Turcan, R. *Les Religions de l'Asie dans la Vallée du Rhone* (EPRO 30), Leiden, 1972.

Turcan, "Autel" = Turcan, R. "L'autel de Rome et d'Auguste 'Ad Confluentem'," *ANRW* 2, 12, 1 (1982) 607-644.

Versnel, "Heersercultus" = Versnel, H.S. "Heersercultus in Griekenland," *Lampas* 7 (1974), 129-163.

Veyne, "Honneurs" = Veyne, P. "Les honneurs posthumes de Flavia Domitilla et les dédicaces grecques et latines," *Latomus* 21 (1962), 49-98.

Veyne, *Pain et Cirque* = Veyne, P. *Le Pain et le Cirque,* Paris, 1976.

Vitucci, "Origini" = Vitucci, G. "Alle origini del culto della dea Roma," *C & S* 65 (1978), 71-74.

Wardman, *Religion and Statecraft* = Wardman, A. *Religion and Statecraft among the Romans,* Baltimore, 1982.

Weaver, *Familia Caesaris* = Weaver, P.R.C. *Familia Caesaris,* Cambridge, 1972.

Weinstock, "Treueid" = Weinstock, S. "Treueid und Kaiserkult," *MDAI(A)* 77 (1962), 306-327.

Wilcken, "Entstehung" = Wilcken, U. "Zur Entstehung des hellenistischen Königskultes," *SPAW* 28 (1938), 298-321.

Wilcken, *Chrestomathie* = Wilcken, U. *Grundzüge und Chrestomathie der Papyruskunde,* Leipzig, 1912 (1963), Vols. I-II.

Wilcken, *Griechische Ostraka* = Wilcken, U. *Griechische Ostraka aus Aegypten und Nubien*, Leipzig and Berlin, 1899 (1970).

Wlosok, *Kaiserkult* = Wlosok A. (ed.), *Römischer Kaiserkult* (*WdF* Vol. 372), Darmstadt, 1978.

Wlosok, "Einführung" = Wlosok, A. "Einführung" in *eadem* (ed.), *Kaiserkult*, 1-52.

Wuilleumier, *Lyon, Métropole* = Wuilleumier, P. *Lyon, Métropole des Gaules*, Paris, 1953.

Zehnacker, *Moneta* = Zehnacker, H. *Moneta. Recherches sur l'Organisation et l'Art des Emissions monétaires de la République romaine (289-31 B.C.)* (BEFAR 222), Rome 1973.

II. SELECT BIBLIOGRAPHY

The following list is restricted to items that relate directly to the central topics of Volumes I, 1-2 and II, 1.

Abaecherli, A.L. "The Dating of the Lex Narbonensis," *TAPA* 63 (1932), 256-268.

Abaecherli, A.L. "Imperial Symbols on certain Flavian Coins," *CPh* 30 (1935), 130-140.

Abaecherli, A.L. "The Institution of the Imperial Cult in the Western Provinces of the Roman Empire," *SMSR* 11 (1935), 153-186.

de Alârcao, J., Étienne, R. and Fabre, G. "Le culte des Lares à Conimbriga (Portugal)," *CRAI* (1969), 213-236.

de Alârcao, J. and Étienne, R. *Fouilles de Conimbriga I, L'Architecture,* Paris, 1977.

de Alârcao, J. and Étienne, R. "Archéologie et idéologie impériale à Conimbriga (Portugal)," *CRAI* (1986), 120-132.

Alföldi, A. *Studien über Caesars Monarchie,* Lund, 1953.

Alföldi, A. "Porträtkunst und Politik in 43 v. Chr." in *Nederlands Kunsthistorisch Jaarboek* 5 (Festschrift A. W. Bijvanck), Bussum, 1954, 151-171.

Alföldi, A. "Der Einmarsch Octaviens in Rom., August 43 v. Chr.," *Hermes* 86 (1958), 480-496.

Alföldi, A. "Ein Festgeschenk aus den Töpfereien des römischen Rhonetals," *Helvetia Antiqua* (Festschrift Emil Vogt), Zurich, 1966, 247-52.

Alföldi, A. *Die monarchische Repräsentation im römischen Kaiserreiche,* Darmstadt, 1970.

Alföldi, A. *Die zwei Lorbeerbäume des Augustus* (Antiquitas 14), Bonn, 1973.

Alföldi, A. "La divinisation de César dans la politique d'Antoine et d'Octavien entre 44 et 40 avant J.C.," *RN* 15 (1973), 99-128.

Alföldi, A. *Octavians Aufstieg zur Macht* (Antiquitas 1), Bonn, 1976.

Alföldi, A. *Der Vater des Vaterlandes im römischen Denken,* Darmstadt, 1978.

Alföldi, A. "Die zwei Lorbeerbäume des Augustus" in A. Wlosok (ed.), *Römischer Kaiserkult* (WdF 372), Darmstadt, 1978, 403-422.

Alföldi-Rosenbaum, E. "Kaiserpriester" in H. Beck and P.C. Bol (edd.), *Spätantike und frühes Christentum* (Ausstellung im Liebighaus Museum alter Plastik, Frankfurt-am-Main), Frankfurt-am-Main, 1983, 34-39.

Alföldy, G. "Ein hispanischer Offizier in Niedergermanien," *MDAI(M)* 6 (1965), 105-115.

Alföldy, G. *Die Hilfstruppen der römischen Provinz Germania Inferior* (EpigStud 6), Düsseldorf, 1968.

Alföldy, G. *Flamines Provinciae Hispaniae Citerioris* (Anejos de Archivo Español de Arqueologia 6), Madrid, 1973.

Alföldy, G. *Noricum*, London, 1974.

Almagro Basch, M. *Mérida, Guía de la Cuidad y de sus Monumentos*, Mérida, 1957.

Almagro Basch, M. "La topografia de Augusta Emerita" in *Symposion de Ciudades Augusteas I, Universidad de Zaragosa, Departamento de Prehistoria y Arqueologia, Zaragosa*, 1976, 203-206.

Amy, R. "L'inscription de la Maison Carrée de Nîmes," *CRAI* (1970), 670-686.

Amy, R. and Gros, P. *La Maison Carrée de Nîmes* (Gallia Suppl. 38), Paris, 1979.

Audin, A. "L'omphalos de Lugdunum," *Hommages Grenier* (Coll. Latomus 58), Brussels, 1962, 1, 152-164.

Audin, A. and Quoniam, P. "Victoires et colonnes de l'autel fédéral des Trois Gaules: données nouvelles", *Gallia* 20 (1962), 103-116.

Audin, A. and Binsfeld, W. "Médaillons d'applique rhodaniens du Musée de Cologne," *KJ* 7 (1964), 14-18.

Audin, A. *Essai sur la Topographie de Lugdunum*[3], Lyon, 1964.

Audin, A. *Lyon, Miroir de Rome dans les Gaules*, Paris, 1965.

Audin, A. "Les martyrs de 177," *CH* 11 (1966), 343-367.

Audin, A. *Les Fouilles de Lyon*, Lyon, 1968.

Audin, A. and Le Glay, M. "L'amphithéâtre des Trois-Gaules à Lyon: première campagne de fouilles," *Gallia* 28 (1970), 67-89.

Audin, A. "Lugdunum: colonie romaine et capitale des Gaules" in A. Latreille (ed.), *Histoire de Lyon et du Lyonnais*, Toulouse, 1975, 23-59.

Audin, A. "L'amphithéâtre des Trois Gaules à Lyon: nouvelles campagnes de fouilles (1971-1972, 1976-1978)," *Gallia* 37 (1979), 85-98.

Aurigemma, S. "Sculture del foro vecchio di Leptis Magna raffiguranti la dea Roma e principi delle casa dei Giulio-Claudi," *Africa Italiana* 8 (1940), 1-94.

Axtell, H.L. *The Deification of Abstract Ideas in Roman Literature and Inscriptions* (Diss. Chicago), Chicago, 1907.

Aymard, A. "Du nouveau sur un Toulousain et sur Toulouse à l'époque romaine," *Bull.Soc.Archéol. du Midi de la France,* 3e série, 1 (1942-1945) (1947), 513-528.

Aymard, A. "Flamen Primus," *REA* 50 (1948), 414-17.

Badian, E. "The Deification of Alexander the Great" in *Ancient Macedonian Studies in Honor of Charles F. Edson* (Publ. Inst. Balkan Studies 158), Thessaloniki, 1982, 27-71.

Balil, A. "Representación de la dea Roma en la decoración de la terra sigillata Hispanica," *Revista de Archivos, Bibliotecas y Museos* 69 (1961), 286-94.

Balsdon, J.P.V.D. "The 'Divinity' of Alexander," *Historia* 1 (1950), 363-388.

Balsdon, J.P.V.D. "Sulla Felix," *JRS* 41 (1951), 1-10.

Balsdon, J.P.V.D. "The Ides of March," *Historia* 7 (1958), 80-94.

Balty, J.C. *Etudes sur la Maison Carrée de Nîmes* (Collection Latomus 47), Brussells, 1960.

Balty, J.C. "Le prétendu Marc-Aurèle d'Avenches" in *Eikones. Studien zum griechischen und römischen Bildnis* (Festschrift H. Jucker), Bern, 1980, 57-63.

Barnard, L.W. "The Emperor Cult and the Origins of the Iconoclastic Controversy," *Byzantion* 43 (1973), 13-29.

Barnes, T.D. "Pre-Decian Acta Martyrum," *JThS* 19 (1968), 509-531.

Barnes, T.D. "Eusebius and The Date of the Martyrdoms" in *Les Martyrs de Lyon* (177) (Colloques internationaux du centre national de la recherche scientifique, no. 575), Paris, 1978, 137-141.

Barrett, A.A. "The Career of Tiberius Claudius Cogidubnus," *Britannia* 10 (1979), 227-242.

Barton, I.A. "Capitoline Temples in Italy and the Provinces (especially Africa)," *ANRW* 2, 12, 1 (1982) 259-342.

Bassignano, M.S. *Il Flaminato nelle Province romane dell' Africa,* Rome, 1974.

Bastiaensen, A.A.R. et al., *Atti e Passioni dei Martiri*, Milan, 1987.

Bayet, J. "Les sacerdoces romains et la prédivinisation impériale," *BAB* 5e sér. 41 (1955), 453-527.

Bayet, J. *Histoire politique et psychologique de la Religion romaine,* Paris, 1957.

Bayet, J. "Prodromes sacerdotaux de la divinisation impériale" in *La*

Regalita Sacrà, Leiden, 1959, 418-434.

Beard, M. "A British Dedication from the City of Rome," *Britannia* 11 (1980), 313-314.

Beare, R. "Ptolemy's Daimon and Ruler-Cult," *Klio* 62 (1980), 327-330.

Beaudoin, E. "Le Culte des Empereurs dans les Cités de la Gaule Narbonnaise," *Annales de l'Enseignement Supérieur de Grenoble* 3 (1891), 31-102, 253-341.

Beaujeu, J. *La Religion romaine à l'Apogée de l'Empire,* Paris, 1955.

Beaujeu, J. "Politique religieuse et propagande numismatique sous le Haut-Empire" in R. Chevallier (ed.), *Mélanges d'Archéologie et d'Histoire offerts à André Piganiol,* Paris, 1966, 1529-1540.

Beaujeu, J. "Les apologètes et le culte du souverain" in den Boer (ed.), *Le Culte* 103-136.

Bell, H.I. *Jews and Christians in Egypt,* Westport, Connecticut, 1924.

Bellen, H. "Die 'Verstaatlichung' des Privatvermögens der römischen Kaiser im 1. Jahrhundert n. Chr.," *ANRW* 2, 1 (1974) 91-112.

Bellen, H. "Das Drususdenkmal apud Mogontiacum und die Galliarum Civitates," *JRGZ* 31 (1984), 385-396.

Belloni, G.G. "Significati storico-politici delle figurazioni e delle scritte delle monete da Augusto a Traiano," *ANRW* 2, 1 (1974) 997-1144.

Beltran, A. "Los monumentos romanos en las monedas hispano-romanas," *AEA* 26 (1953), 39-66.

Beltran, A. "Las monedas romanas de Mérida: su interpretación historica" in *Augusta Emerita* (Actas del bimilenario de Mérida), Madrid, 1976, 93-105.

Benario, H.W. "The Date of the Feriale Duranum," *Historia* 11 (1962), 192-196.

Benoit, F. "La statue d'Auguste au Musée d'Arles," *MMAI* 36 (1938), 67-80.

Benoit, F. "Le sanctuaire d'Auguste et les cryptoportiques d'Arles," *RA* 39 (1952), 31-67.

Béranger, J. *Recherches sur l'Aspect idéologique du Principat* (Schweizerische Beiträge zur Altertumswissenschaft 5, 6) Basel, 1953.

Béranger, J. "La 'prévoyance' (providentia) impériale et Tacite, Annales I, 8" in *id., Principatus. Etudes de notions et d'histoire politiques dans l'Antiquité gréco-romaine,* Geneva, 1973, 331-352.

Béranger, J. "L'expression de la divinité dans les panégyriques latins" in *id., Principatus. Etudes de notions et d'histoire politiques dans l'Antiquité gréco-romaine,* Geneva, 1973, 429-444.

642   SELECT BIBLIOGRAPHY

Berlinger, L. *Beiträge zur inoffiziellen Titulatur der römischen Kaiser* (Diss. Breslau), Breslau, 1935.

Bernard, A. *Le Temple d'Auguste et la Nationalité Gauloise*, Lyon, 1863.

Berni Brizio, L. "Una *dedicatio* delle *imagines* di Gaio e Lucio Cesari da parte degli Augustales di Trebula Suffenas," *CSDIR* 4 (1972-73), 149-160.

Beurlier, E. *Le Culte impérial. Son histoire et son organisation depuis Auguste jusqu' à Justinien*, Paris, 1891.

Bickel E. "Die politische und religiöse Bedeutung des Provinzialoberpriesters im römischen Westen," *BJ* 133 (1928), 1-27.

Bickerman, E. "Consecratio" in den Boer (ed.), *Le Culte* 3-25.

Bickerman, E.J. "Diva Augusta Marciana," *AJPhil* 95 (1974), 362-376.

Bieler, L. ΘΕΙΟΣ 'ANHP, Vienna, 1935, Vol. 1.

Birley, E. "Senators in the Emperor's Service," *Proc. Brit. Acad.* 39 (1953), 197-214.

Birley, E. "Beförderungen und Versetzungen im römischen Heere," *Carnuntum Jahrbericht* (1957), 3-20.

Birley, E. "The Equestrian Officers of the Roman Army" in *Roman Britain and the Roman Army*, Kendal, 1961, 133-153.

Birley, E. "Cohors I Tungrorum and the Oracle of the Clarian Apollo," *Chiron* 4 (1974), 511-513.

Birley, E. "The Religion of the Roman Army: 1895-1977," *ANRW* 2, 16, 2 (1978) 1506-1541.

Birley, E. "The Deities of Roman Britain," *ANRW* 2, 18, 1 (1986) 3-112.

Blawatsky, W. "Le culte des empereurs romains au Bosphore" in R. Chevallier (ed.), *Mélanges d'Archéologie et d'Histoire offerts à André Piganiol*, Paris, 1966.

Blázquez, J.M. "Propaganda dinástica y culto imperial en las acuñaciones de Hispania," *Numisma* 23/24 (1973-74), 311-329.

Blumenthal, F. "Der ägyptische Kaiserkult," *APF* 5 (1913), 317-345.

von Blumenthal, A. "Zur römischen Religion der archäischen Zeit II," *RhM* 90 (1941), 310-334.

den Boer, W. (ed), *Le Culte des Souverains dans l'Empire romain* (Fondation Hardt, Entretiens 19), Geneva, 1972.

den Boer, W. "Heerscultus en ex-voto's en het Romeinse Keizerrijk," *Mededelingen der Koninklijke Nederlandse Akademie van Wetenschappen, Afd. Letterkunde* 36, 4 (1973), 99-115.

den Boer, W. "La 'damnatio memoriae' des empereurs et la religion romaine" in *Transformation et Conflits au IVᵉ Siècle ap. J.-C.:*

Antiquitas 29 (1978), 217-224.

Bogaers, J.E. "King Cogidubnus in Chichester: Another Reading of *RIB* 91,"*Britannia* 10 (1979), 243-254.

Bömer, F. "Vergil und Augustus," *Gymnasium* 58 (1951), 26-55.

Bömer, F. "Der Eid beim Genius des Kaisers", *Athenaeum* 44 (1966), 77-133.

Bömer, F. and Herz, P. *Untersuchungen über die Religion der Sklaven in Griechenland und Rom,*[2] Wiesbaden, 1981.

Borriello, M.R. "L'edificio degli Augustali di Miseno" in E. Pozzi (co-ord. gen.), *Domiziano-Nerva. La Statua equestre da Miseno; una proposta di recomposizione*, Naples, 1987, 13-24.

Bosworth, A.B. "Vespasian and the Provinces: Some Problems of the Early 70's A.D.," *Athenaeum* 51 (1973), 49-78.

Bosworth, A.B. "Augustus and August: Some Pitfalls of Historical Fiction," *HSCP* 86 (1982), 151-170.

Bousquet, J. "Inscriptions de Rennes," *Gallia* 29 (1971), 109-122.

Bowersock, G.W. *Augustus and the Greek World,* Oxford, 1965.

Bowersock, G.W. "The Imperial Cult: Perceptions and Persistence" in B.F. Meyer and E.P. Sanders (edd.), *Jewish and Christian Self-Definition,* Philadelphia, 1983, 3, 171-241.

Bowersock, G.W. "Greek Intellectuals and the Imperial Cult in the Second Century A.D." in den Boer (ed.), *Le Culte,* 179-206.

Brehier, L. and Battifol, P. *Les Survivances du Culte impérial romain,* Paris, 1920.

Bremer, J.M. "Greek hymns" in H.S. Versnel (ed.), *Faith, Hope and Worship,* Leiden, 1981, 193-215.

Bruhl, A. and Audin, A. "Inscription du Lyonnais Tiberius Aquius Apollinaris," *Gallia* 23 (1965), 267-72.

Brunn, P. "Notes on the Transmission of Imperial Images in late Antiquity" in K. Ascani et al. (edd.), *Studia Romana in Honorem P. Krarup Septuagenarii,* Odense, 1976, 122-131.

Brunt, P.A. "Charges of Provincial Maladministration under the Early Principate," *Historia* 10 (1961), 189-227.

Brunt, P.A. "The 'Fiscus' and its Development," *JRS* 56 (1966), 75-91.

Brunt, P.A. and Moore, J.M. *Res Gestae Divi Augusti,* Oxford, 1970.

Buchner, E. "Solarium Augusti und Ara Pacis," *MDAI(R)* 83 (1976), 319-365.

Burdeau, F. "L'empereur d'après les panégyriques latins" in F. Burdeau, N. Charbonnel, M. Humbert, *Aspects de l'Empire romain,* Paris, 1964, 1-60.

Burkert, W. "Caesar und Romulus-Quirinus," *Historia* 11 (1962), 356-376.

Buttrey, T.V. "Vespasian's Consecratio and the Numismatic Evidence," *Historia* 25 (1976), 449-457.

Buttery, T.V. *Documentary Evidence for the Chronology of the Flavian Titulature* (Beiträge zur klassischen Philologie 112), Meisenheim am Glan, 1980.

Cagnat, R. "Un temple de la Gens Augusta à Carthage," *CRAI* (1913), 680-686.

Canto, A.M. "Notas sobre los pontifices coloniales y el origen del culto imperial en la Bética" in *La Religión romana en Hispania. Symposio organizado por el Instituto de Arqueología Rodrigo Caro del 17 al. 19 de diciembre de 1979*, Madrid, 1981, 141-153.

Carson, R.A.G. "Caesar and the Monarchy", *G & R* 4 (1957), 46-53.

Castillo, C. "Un triennio de epigrafia latina en Hispania: logros y perspectivas" in *Unidad y Pluralidad en El Mundo Antiguo* (Actas del VI Congresso Español de Estudios Clásicos), Madrid, 1983, 105-125.

Castillo Garcia, C. "Städte und Personen der Baetica," *ANRW* 2, 3 (1975) 601-654.

Castro, A.D. *Tacitus and the "Virtues" of the Roman Emperor: The Role of Imperial Propaganda in the Historiography of Tacitus* (Diss. Indiana), Fort Wayne, 1972.

Catalano, P. "Aspetti spaziali del sistema giuridico-religioso romano. Mundus, templum, urbs, ager, Latium, Italia," *ANRW* 2, 16, 1 (1978) 440-553.

Cels, J. "Un problème controversé. L'origine d'un flamine de Narbonnaise, Sextus Fadius Secundus Musa," *Eos* 66 (1978), 107-121.

Cels-Saint-Hilaire, J. "Numen Augusti et Diane de l'Aventin: le témoignage de l'ara Narbonensis" in *Les grandes Figures religieuses* (Lire les polythéismes 1): *Fonctionnement pratique et symbolique dans l'Antiquité* (Annales littéraires de l'Université de Besançon 329), Paris, 1986, 455-502.

Cerfaux, L. and Tondriau, J. *Le Culte des Souverains dans la Civilization gréco-romaine* (Bibl. de Théol., ser. 3,5), Tournai, 1957.

Chante, D. *Le Culte impérial en Narbonnaise sous le Haut Empire* (D.E.S. Montpellier), 1967 (unpublished).

Chantraine, H. *Freigelassene und Sklaven im Dienst der römischen Kaiser*, Wiesbaden, 1967.

Chantraine, H. "Zur Nomenklatur und Funktionsangabe Kaiserlicher Friegelassener," *Historia* 24 (1975), 603-613.

Charles-Picard, G. "Civitas Mactaritana," *Karthago* 8 (1957), 1-166.

Charlesworth, M.P. "Deus Noster Caesar," *CR* 39 (1925), 113-115.

Charlesworth, M.P. "Some Observations on Ruler-Cult, especially in Rome," *HThR* 28 (1935), 5-44.

Charlesworth, M.P. "ProvidentiaandAeternitas,"*HThR* 29(1936),107-132.

Charlesworth, M.P. "Flaviana," *JRS* 27 (1937), 54-62.

Charlesworth, M.P. "The Virtues of a Roman Emperor: Propaganda and the Creation of Belief," *Proceedings of the British Academy* 23 (1937), 105-133.

Charlesworth, M.P. "The Refusal of Divine Honours. An Augustan Formula," *PBSR* 15 (1939), 1-10.

Charlesworth, M.P. "Pietas and Victoria: the Emperor and the Citizen," *JRS* 33 (1943), 1-10.

Chastagnol, A. "Aspects concrets et cadre topographique des fêtes décennales des empereurs à Rome" in *L'Urbs. Espace urbain et histoire (Ier siècle av. J.C. - IIIᵉ siècle ap. J.C.)* (Coll. de l'Ecole franç. de Rome 98), Rome 1987, 491-507.

Chevallier, R. "Dea roma Nicephore sur une intaille" in *Mélanges A. Bruhl I: RAE* 24 (1973), 361-374.

Chevallier, R. "Gallia Lugdunensis. Bilan de 25 ans de recherches historiques et archéologiques," *ANRW* 2, 3 (1975) 860-1060.

Chevallier, R. "Gallia Narbonensis. Bilan de 25 ans de recherches historiques et archéologiques," *ANRW* 2, 3 (1975) 686-828.

Christe, Y. "A propos de la thêka," *MH* 35 (1978), 335-340.

Christol, M. and Gascou, J. "Volubilis, cité fédérée?," *MEFRA* 92 (1980), 329-345.

Christopherson, A.J. "The Provincial Assembly of the Three Gauls in the Julio-Claudian Period," *Historia* 17 (1968), 351-366.

Clark, M.E. "Spes in the Early Imperial Cult: "The Hope of Augustus"," *Numen* 30 (1983), 80-105.

Classen, C.J. "Gottmenschentum in der römischen Republik," *Gymnasium* 70 (1963), 312-338.

Coello, J. Muñiz "Un flamen de la Provincia Baetica," *Habis* 7 (1976), 387-390.

Colin, J. "Martyrs grecs de Lyon ou martyrs galates?," *AC* 33 (1964), 108-115.

Colin, J. *L'Empire des Antonins et les Martyrs gaulois de 177* (Antiquitas 1), Bonn, 1964.

Collingwood, R.G. and Richmond, I.A. *The Archaeology of Roman Britain*, London, 1969.

Crawford, M.H. "Roman imperial coin types and the formation of public opinion" in C.N.L. Brooke et al. (eds.), *Studies in Numismatic Method presented to Philip Grierson*, Cambridge, 1983, 47-64.

Cumont, F. "L'éternité des empereurs romains," *Rev. d'Hist. et de la Lit. Relig.* 1 (1896), 435-452.

Cuss, D. *Imperial Cult and Honorary Terms in the New Testament* (Paradosis 23), Fribourg, 1974.

Daicoviciu, C. "Sévère Alexandre et la Dacie," *Acta Musei Napocensis* 3 (1966), 153-163.

Daicoviciu, C. "Un nou sacerdos Arae Augusti în Dacia," *Acta Musei Napocensis* 4 (1967), 469-470.

Dareggi, G. "Il ciclo statuario della "basilica" di Otricoli: la fase guilio-claudia," *Bolletino d'Arte* 14 (1982), 1-36.

Daut, R. Imago. *Untersuchungen zum Bildbegriff der Römer* (Bibl. d. Klass. Altertumswiss., n. F. 2, R. 56), Heidelberg, 1975.

Dayet, M. "Quelques remarques au sujet des monnaies de bronze romaines portant au revers l'autel de Rome et d'Auguste," *Bull. Soc. franc. de Numismatique* (1965), 426-427.

Dedet, B., Garmy, P., Pey, J. "Découverte d'une enciente de l'Antiquité tardive ou du Haut Moyen Age à Nîmes (Gard)," *Ecole Antique de Nîmes*, n.s. 16 (1981), 147-163.

Degrassi, A. *I Fasti consolari dell' Impero romano*, Rome, 1952.

Deininger, J. "Zur Begründung des Provinzialkultes in der Baetica," *MDAI(M)* 5 (1964), 167-179.

Deininger, J. *Die Provinziallandtage der römischen Kaiserzeit von Augustus bis zum Ende des dritten Jahrhunderts n. Chr.* (Vestigia 6) Munich, 1965.

Deininger, J. "Numinibus Augustorum. Anmerkung zur Datierung der Trierer Bronzeprora," *Germania* 44 (1966), 138-42.

Deissman, A. *Licht vom Osten*, Tübingen, 1923.

Desanges, J. "Les territoires gétules de Juba II," *REA* 66 (1964), 33-47.

Desanges, J. "Le statut des municipes d'après les données africaines," *Rev. Hist. de Droit français et étranger* 50 (1972), 353-373.

Devijver, H. "The Career of M. Porcius Narbonensis," *AncSoc* 3 (1972), 165-191.

Devijver, H. *Prosopographia Militiarum Equestrium quae fuerunt ab Augusto ad Gallienum*, Louvain, 1976-1980, Vol. 2.

Di Vita, A. "Gli *Emporia* di Tripolitania dall' età di Massinissa a Diocleziano: un profilo storico-istituzionale," *ANRW* 2, 10, 2 (1982) 515-595.

Di Vita-Evrard, G. "Municipium Flavium Lepcis Magna," *BCTH* n.s. 17B (1984), 197-210.

Di Vita-Evrard, G. "En feuilletant les 'Inscriptions Antiques du Maroc, 2'," *ZPE* 68 (1987), 193-225.

Dobesch, G. *Caesars Apotheose zu Lebezeiten und sein Ringen um den Königstitel*, Vienna, 1966.

Domaszewski, A. von "Die Familie des Augustus auf der Ara Pacis," *JOAI* 6 (1903), 57-60.

Domaszewski, A. von and Dobson, B. *Die Rangordnung des römischen Heeres*, Cologne, 1967.

Dörner, F.K. *Kommagene. Götterthrone und Königsgräber am Euphrat*, Bergisch Gladbach, 1981.

Dörrie, H. *Der Königskult des Antiochos von Kommagene im Lichte neuer Inschriften-Funde* (Abhand. Akad. Wiss. Göttingen, phil.-hist. K1.60), Göttingen, 1964.

Dragendorff, H. "Der Altar der Roma und des Augustus in Lugdunum," *JDAI* 52 (1937), 111-119.

Drinkwater, J.F. "A Note on Local Careers in the Three Gauls under the Early Empire," *Britannia* 10 (1979), 89-100.

Duchemin, J. "Personification d'abstractions et d'éléments naturels: Hésiode et l'Orient" in *eadem* (ed.), *Mythe et Personnification* (Actes du Colloque du Grand Palais: Paris, 1977), Paris, 1980.

Dumézil, G. "Encore Genius" in H. Zehnacker and G. Henz, (edd.), *Hommages à Robert Schilling* (Coll. d'Et. lat. Sér. scient. 37), Paris 1983, 85-92.

Duncan-Jones, R.P. "Costs, Outlays and Summae Honorariae from Roman Africa," *PBSR* 30 (1962), 47-115.

Duncan-Jones, R.P. "Equestrian Rank in the Cities of the African Provinces under the Principate: An Epigraphic Survey," *PBSR* 35 (1967), 147-186.

Duncan-Jones, R.P. "The Chronology of the Priesthood of Africa Proconsularis under the Principate," *EpigStud* 5 (1968), 151-158.

Dury-Moyaers, G. *Énée et Lavinium: à propos des découvertes archéologiques récentes* (Coll. Latomus 174), Brussels, 1981.

Duthoy, R. "Recherches sur la répartition géographique et chronologique des termes sevir Augustalis, Augustalis et sevir dans l'empire romain," *EpigStud* 11 (1976), 143-214.

Duthoy, R. "Les *Augustales," *ANRW* 2, 16, 2 (1978) 1254-1309.

Eck, W. *Senatoren von Vespasian bis Hadrian: Prosopographische Untersuchung mit Einschluss der Jahres- und Provinzialfasten der Statthalter* (Vestigia 13), Munich, 1970.

Edson, C.F. "Legitimus Honor. A Note on Hellenistic Ruler-Worship," *HThR* 26 (1933), 324-325.

Egger, R. "Die Ausgrabungen auf dem Magdalensberg 1960 und 1961," *Carinthia* 1, 153 (1963), 3-297.

Ehrenberg, V. "Caesar's Final Aims," *HSCP* 68 (1964), 149-161.

Eitrem, S. "Zur Apotheose," *SO* 10(1932), 31-43;15/16 (1936), 111-137.

Ensslin, W. "Der Einfluss Karthagos auf Staatsverwaltung und Wirtschaft der Römer" in J. Vogt (ed.), *Rom und Karthago*, Leipzig, 1943, 262-296.

Ensslin, W. "Gottkaiser und Kaiser von Gottes Gnaden," *SBAW* 6 (1943), 71-74.

Erkell, H. Augustus, Felicitas, Fortuna: Lateinische Wortstudien (Diss. Göteborg), Gothenburg, 1952.

Espérandieu, E. *Recueil général des Bas-Reliefs de la Gaule Romaine*, Paris, 1907-31, Vols. I-II.

Étienne, R. *Le Culte impérial dans la Péninsule ibérique d'Auguste à Dioclétien* (Bibl. des Ecoles franç. d'Athènes et de Rome 191), Paris, 1958.

Étienne, R., Fabré, G., Lévêque, P. and M. *Fouilles de Conimbriga II, Épigraphie et Sculpture*, Paris 1976, 235-247.

Étienne, R. "Culte impérial et architecture. A propos d'une inscription de Lacipo (Bétique)," *ZPE* 43 (1981), 135-142.

Étienne, R. "Un complexe monumental du culte impérial à Avenches," *Pro Aventico* 29 (1985), 5-26.

Étienne, R. "Aeternitas Augusti-Aeternitas Imperii" in *Les grandes Figures religieuses* (Lire les polythéismes 1): *Fonctionnement pratique et symbolique dans l'Antiquité* (Annales littéraires de l'Univ. de Besançon 329), Paris, 1986, 445-454.

Étienne, R. "A propos de quelques basiliques de Gaule et de la péninsule ibérique," *Quaderni* 10, 11, 12 (Atti del Convegno "Studi Lunensi e prospettive sull' Occidente romano" Lerici, settembre 1985), 1987, 37-52.

Euzennat, M. "Une dédicace Volubilitaine à l'Apollon de Claros," *AntAfr* 10 (1976), 63-68.

Farnoux, Combet B. "Mercure romain, les 'Mercuriales' et l'institution du culte impérial sous le Principat augustéen," *ANRW* 2, 17, 1 (1981) 457-501.

Fasciano, D. "Le Numen chez Ovide," *RCCM* 15 (1973), 257-296.

Faur, J.-C. "Caligula et la Maurétanie: La fin de Ptolémée," *Klio* 55 (1973), 249-253.

Fayer, C. "La 'dea Roma' sulle monete greche," *StudRom* 23 (1975), 273-288.

Fayer, C. *Il Culto della Dea Roma. Origine e diffusione nell' Impero*, Pescara, 1976.

Fears, J.R. "The Solar Monarchy of Nero...," *Historia* 25 (1976), 494-496.

Fears, J.R. *Princeps a diis electus: The Divine Election of the Emperor as a Political Concept at Rome* (Papers and Monographs of the American Academy in Rome 26), Rome, 1977.

Fears, J.R. "Ο ΔΗΜΟΣ Ο ΡΩΜΑΙΩΝ GENIUS POPULI ROMANI: A Note on the Origins of Dea Roma," *Mnemosyne* 31 (1978), 274-286.

Fears, J.R. "The Cult of Jupiter and Roman Imperial Ideology," *ANRW* 2, 17, 1 (1981) 3-141.

Fears, J.R. "The Cult of Virtues and Roman Imperial Ideology," *ANRW* 2, 17, 2 (1981) 827-948.

Fears, J.R. "The Theology of Victory at Rome: Approaches and Problems," *ANRW* 2, 17, 2 (1981) 736-826.

Ferchiou, N. "Note sur deux inscriptions du Jebel Mansour (Tunisie)," *CT* 25 (nos. 99-100) (1977), 9-20.

Fink, R.O., Hoey, A.S., and Snyder, W.F. "The Feriale Duranum," *YCS* 7 (1940), 1-222.

Fink, R.O. "Victoria Parthica and Kindred Victoriae," *YCS* 8 (1942), 81-101.

Fink, R.O. *Roman Military Records on Papyrus* (Philological Monographs of the American Philological Association 26), Case Western Reserve University Press, 1971.

Fishwick, D. "The Imperial Cult in Roman Britian," *Phoenix* 15 (1961), 159-173, 213-229.

Fishwick, D. "The Annexation of Mauretania," *Historia* 20 (1971), 467-487.

Fishwick, D. "The Name of the Demigod," *Historia* 24 (1975), 624-628.

Fishwick, D. and Shaw, B.D. "Ptolemy of Mauretania and the Conspiracy of Gaetulicus," *Historia* 25 (1976), 491-494.

Fishwick, D. and Shaw, B.D. "The Formation of Africa Proconsularis," *Hermes* 105 (1977), 369-80.

Fishwick, D. *Studies in Roman Imperial History*, Leiden, 1977.

Fishwick, D. "Augustus Deus and Deus Augustus," in *Hommages à Maarten J. Vermaseren*, Leiden, 1978, 1, 375-380.

Fishwick, D. "Claudius *submersus,*" *AJAH* 3 (1978), 76-77.

Fishwick, D. "The Development of Provincial Ruler Worship in the Western Roman Empire," *ANRW* 2, 16, 2 (1978) 1201-1253.

Fishwick, D. and Shaw, B.D. "The Era of the Cereres," *Historia* 27 (1978), 343-54.

Fishwick, D. "A Gold Bust of Titus at Emerita," *AJAH* 6 (1981), 86-96.

Fishwick, D. "The Altar of Augustus and the Municipal Cult of Tarraco," *MDAI(M)* 23 (1982), 222-233.

Fishwick, D. "An Early Provincial Priest of Lusitania," *Historia* 31 (1982), 249-252.

Fishwick, D. "A Priest of the Three Gauls from Argentomagus," *Historia* 32 (1983), 384.

Fishwick, D. "An Altar Coin at Heidelberg," in W. Heckel and R.A. Sullivan (edd.), *Ancient Coins of the Graeco-Roman World. The Nickle Numismatic Papers*, Waterloo, Ontario, 1984, 159-164.

Fishwick, D. "Coins as Evidence: Some Phantom Temples," *EMC* 28, n.s. 3 (1984), 263-270.

Fishwick, D. "From Flamen to Sacerdos," *BCTH* n.s. 17B (1984), 337-344.

Fishwick, D. "Pliny and the Christians: the Rites *ad imaginem principis,*" *AJAH* 9 (1984), 123-130.

Fishwick, D. "Le culte impérial sous Juba II et Ptolémée de Maurétanie: le témoignage des monnaies," *BCTH* n.s. 19B (1985), 225-233.

Fishwick, D. "Une dédicace à la domus divina à Lambaesis," *110ᵉ Congrès national des Sociétés savantes, Montpellier, 1985; IIIᵉ Colloque sur l'histoire et l'archéologie d'Afrique du Nord,* 367-372.

Fishwick, D. "Les monnaies dites 'à l'autel de Lyon': interpretation des motifs figurés audessus du monument," *Bull. des Musées et Monuments Lyonnais* 7 (1982-86), 131-138.

Fishwick, D. "Une variante des monnaies dites 'à l'autel de Lyon'," *Bull. des Musées et Monuments Lyonnais* 7 (1982-86), 263-268.

Fishwick, D. "Imperial Sceptre-heads in Roman Britain," *Britannia* 19 (1988), 399 f.

Fishwick, D. "A Sacred Edict(?) at Mactar," *ZPE* 73 (1988), 113-115.

Fishwick, D. "Numen Augusti," *Britannia* 20 (1989), 231-234.

Fishwick, D. "L. Munatius Hilarianus and the Inscription of the Artemisii," *ZPE* 76 (1989), 175-183.

Fishwick, D. "Votive Offerings to the Emperor?," *ZPE* 78 (1989), 121-130.

Fishwick, D. "Di Caesarum," *AntAfr* 25 (1989), 111-114.

Fishwick, D. "Statue Taxes in Roman Egypt," *Historia* 38 (1989), 335-347.

Fishwick, D. "Dio and Maecenas: the Emperor and the Ruler Cult," *Phoenix* 44 (1990), 267-275.

Fishwick, D. "Le sanctuaire des Trois Gaules et le culte impérial fédéral" in A. Pelletier, J. Rossiaud (edd.), *Histoire de Lyon, des Origines à nos jours*, Le Cotéau, 1990, 1, 43-65.

Fishwick, D. "Prudentius and the Cult of Divus Augustus," *Historia* 39 (1990), 475-486.

Fishwick, D. "Votive Offerings to the Emperor?," *ZPE* 80 (1990), 121-130.

Fishwick, D. "Ovid and Divus Augustus," *CPh* 86 (1991), 36-41.

Fishwick, D. "Le culte de la *domus divina* à Lambèse" in *L'Armée et les Affaires militaires: 3e Congrès national des sociétés savantes, Strasbourg, 1988, IVe Colloque sur l'histoire et l'archéologie d'Afrique du Nord*, Paris, 2, 329-341.

Fishwick, D. "A Temple of Vesta on the Palatine?," *Hommages à Tadeusz Kotula*, forthcoming.

Fishwick, D. "Prayer and the Living Emperor" in *Mélanges in Honor of Alexander G. McKay*, forthcoming.

Fishwick, D. "Le Numen impérial en Afrique romaine," *115e Congrès national des sociétés savantes, Avignon, 1990, Ve Colloque sur l'histoire et l'archéologie d'Afrique du Nord*, forthcoming.

Fitz, J. "Der Besuch des Septimius Severus in Pannonien im J. 202 u. Z.," *AArchHung* 11 (1959), 237-263.

Fitz, J. "A Concilium Provinciae Pannonia Inferiorban," *Alba Regia* 11 (1970), 152-153.

Fitz, J. "Le iscrizioni del capitolium di Gorsium," *RSA* 1 (1971), 145-155.

Fitz, J. "The Excavations in Gorsium," *AArchHung* 24 (1972), 1-52.

Forni, G. "El culto de Augusto en el compromiso oficial y en el sentimiento oriental," *Bol. del Seminario de Estud. de Arte y Arqueol.* 39 (1973), 105-113.

Francissen, F.P.M. "Numen inest in loco. De Romeinen en het sacrale in de natuur," *Hermeneus* 49 (1977), 247-275.

Fraser, P.N. *Ptolemaic Alexandria*, Oxford, 1972, Vols. 1-3.

Fredricksmeyer, E.A. "Divine Honors for Philip II," *TAPA* 109 (1979), 39-61.

Fredricksmeyer, E.A. "Three Notes on Alexander's Deification," *AJAH* 4 (1979), 1-9.

Fredricksmeyer, E.A. "On the Background of the Ruler Cult" in *Ancient Macedonian Studies in Honor of Charles F. Edson* (Publ. Inst. Balkan Studies 158), Thessaloniki, 1982, 190-201.

Frere, S.S. Britannia: *A History of Roman Britain*, London, 1967.

Frézouls, E. "Les Ocratii de Volubilis d'après deux inscriptions inédites" in *Mélanges d'Archéologie et d'Histoire offerts à A. Piganiol*, Paris, 1966, 1, 233-248.

Fuhrmann, M. "Die Romidee der Spätantike," *HZ* 207 (1968), 529-561.

Fugier, H. *Recherches sur l'Expression du Sacré dans la Langue latine*, Paris, 1963.

Gagé, J. "La Victoria Augusti et les auspices de Tibère," *RA* 32 (1930), 1-35.

Gagé, J. "Divus Augustus. L'idée dynastique chez les empereurs julio-claudiens," *RA* 34 (1931), 11-41.

Gagé, J. "Les sacerdoces d'Auguste et ses réformes religieuses" *MEFR* 48 (1931), 75-108.

Gagé, J. "Un thème de l'art impérial romain: La Victoire d'Auguste," *MEFR* 49 (1932), 61-92.

Gagé, J. "Σταυρὸς νικοποιός. La victoire impériale dans l'empire chrétien," *Rev. d'Hist. et de Phil. rel.* 13 (1933), 370-400.

Gagé, J. "La théologie de la Victoire impériale," *RH* 171 (1933), 1-34.

Gagé, J. "Vespasien et la mémoire de Galba," *REA* 54 (1952), 290-315.

Gagé, J. *Apollon Romain* (BEFAR 182), Paris, 1955.

Gagé, J. "Psychologie du culte impérial romain," *Diogène* 34 (1961), 47-68.

Gagé, J. "Apollon impérial, garant des 'Fata Romana'," *ANRW* 2, 17, 2 (1981) 561-630.

Galsterer, H. *Untersuchungen zum römischen Städtewesen auf der iberischen Halbinsel*, Berlin, 1971.

Galsterer, H. "Zu den römischen Bürgermunicipien in den Provinzen," *EpigStud* 9 (1972), 37-43.

Galsterer-Kröll, B. "Zum *ius Latii* in den Keltischen Provinzen des Imperium Romanum," *Chiron* 3 (1973), 277-306.

Gamer, G. *Kaiserliche Bronzestatuen aus den Kastellen und Legionslagern*

an Rhein- und Donaugrenze des römischen Imperiums (Diss. München), Bonn, 1969.

Gascou, J. *La Politique municipale de l'Empire romain en Afrique proconsulaire de Trajan à Septime-Sévère*, Rome, 1972.

Gascou, J. "P. Iulius Liberalis, sacerdotalis provinciae Africae, et la date du statut colonial de Thysdrus," *AntAfr* 14 (1979), 189-196.

Gascou, J. "La politique municipale de Rome en Afrique du Nord. I. De la mort d'Auguste au début du IIIe siècle," *ANRW* 2, 10, 2 (1982) 136-229.

Gatti, C. "Dione Cassio XLIV, 7; una proposta di interpretazione," *CRDAC* 8 (1976-77), 71-82.

Gayraud, M. "Temple municipal et temple provincial du culte impérial à Narbonne," *RSL* 35 (1969), 304-316.

Gayraud, M. "Narbonne aux trois premiers siècles après Jésus Christ," *ANRW* 2, 3 (1975) 829-859.

Gayraud, M. *Narbonne antique des Origines à la Fin du IIIe siècle* (Rev. Arch. de Narbonnaise, Suppl. 8), Paris, 1981.

Geiger, F. *De sacerdotibus Augustorum municipalibus*, (Diss. Hal.), Halle, 1913.

Gesche, H. *Die Vergottung Caesars* (Frankfurter Althistorische Studien 1), Kallmünz, 1968, 40-53.

Gesche, H. *Caesar* (Erträge der Forschung 51), Darmstadt, 1976.

Gesztelyi, T. "Mercury and Augustus," *ACD* 9 (1973), 77-81.

Gilliam, J.F. "The Roman military feriale," *HThR* 47 (1954), 183-196.

Gilliam, J.F. "On Divi under the Severi" in *Hommages à Marcel Renard* (Collections Latomus 102), Brussels, 1969, 284-289.

Gonzáles, J. "Tabula Siarensis, Fortunales Siarenses et Municipia Civium Romanorum," *ZPE* 55 (1984), 55-100; 60 (1985), 146.

von Gonzenbach, V. "Genius Augusti-Theos Sebastos," *Stockholm St. in Class. Arch.* (Festschrift C. Kerényi) 5 (1968), 81-117.

Granino Cecere, M.G. "Apollo in due iscrizioni di Gabii: (ii) Ancora una dedica a tutte le divinità 'Secundum interpretationem Clarii Apollinis'," *Miscell. Grec. Rom.* 10 (1986), 281-288.

Grant, M. *Aspects of the Principate of Tiberius; Historical Comments on the Colonial Coinage issued outside Spain* (Numismatic Notes and Monographs 116), New York, 1950.

Grant, M. *From Imperium to Auctoritas*, Cambridge, 1969.

Green, W.M. "Notes on the Augustan Deities," *CJ* 23 (1927-28), 86-93.

Grenier, A. "Numen. Observations sur l'un des éléments primordiaux de la religion romaine," *Latomus* 6 (1947), 297-308.

Grenier, A. "Les capitoles romains en Gaule et le capitole de Narbonne," *CRAI* (1956), 316-323.

Grenier, A. "La date du capitole de Narbonne," *Hommages à W. Deonna* (Coll. Latomus 28), Brussels, 1957, 245-248.

Grenier, A. *Manuel d'Archéologie gallo-romaine*, Paris, 1960, Vol. IV.

Grether, G. "Livia and the Roman Imperial Cult," *AJPhil* 67 (1946), 222-252.

Gros, P. *Aurea Templa. Recherches sur l'Architecture religieuse de Rome à l'Epoque d'Auguste* (Bibl. Ecole franç. d'Athènes et de Rome 231), Paris, 1976.

Gros, P. "L'Augusteum de Nîmes," *RAN* 17 (1984), 123-134.

Gros, P. "La fonction symbolique des édifices théâtraux dans le paysage urbain de la Rome augustéenne" in *L'Urbs. Espace urbain et Histoire (1er siècle av. J.C. - IIIᵉ Siècle ap. J.C.)* (Coll. de l'Ecole franç. de Rome 98), Rome 1987, 319-346.

Gros, P. "Remarques sur les fondations urbaines de Narbonnaise et de Cisalpine au début de l'empire," *Quaderni* 10, 11, 12 (Atti del Convegno "Studi Lunensi e prospettive sull' Occidente romano," Lerici, settembre 1985), 1987, 73-95.

Gros, P. and Theodorescu, D. "L'"autel" du forum d'Assise," *MEFRA* 99 (1987), 693-710.

Gros, P. "Un programme augustéen: Le centre monumental de la colonie d'Arles" *JDAI* 102 (1987), 339-363.

Gros, P. and Torelli, M. *Storia dell' Urbanistica. Il mondo romano*, Rome-Bari, 1988.

Gros, P. "Théâtre et culte impérial en Gaule Narbonnaise et dans la Péninsule ibérique" in W. Trillmich and P. Zanker (edd.), *Stadtbild und Ideologie* (Kolloquium in Madrid vom 19. bis 23. Oktober 1987: ABAW phil.-hist. Kl. n. F. 103), Munich, 1990, 381-390.

Gründel, R. "*Anni Carthaginis = anni sacerdotii Cererum?*," *Klio* 46 (1965), 351-54.

Gsell, S. *Histoire Ancienne de l'Afrique du Nord*, Paris, 1928, Vol. 8.

Guarducci, M. "Enea e Vesta," *MDAI(R)* 78 (1971), 73-89.

Guey, J. and Audin, A. "Les guirlandes de l'autel d'Auguste," *Bull. des Musées et Monuments Lyonnais* 5, (1956), 41-46, 55-62.

Guey, J. and Audin, A. "L'amphithéâtre des Trois Gaules," *Gallia* 21 (1963), 125-154; 22 (1964), 37-61.

Guey, J. "Les inscriptions (et à propos des inscriptions) de l'amphithéâtre" in *Les Martyrs de Lyon (1977)* (Colloques internationaux du centre national de la recherche scientifique 575), Paris, 1978, 107-109.

Guiraud, P. *Les Assemblées provinciales dans l'Empire romain*, Paris, 1887.

Gundel, H.G. "Devotus numini maiestatique eius. Zur Devotionsformel in Weihinschriften der römischen Kaiserzeit," *Epigraphica* 15 (1953), 128-150.

Haase, W. "Voraussetzungen und Motive des Herrscherkultes von Kommagene," *Antike Welt: Zeitschrift für Archäologie und Urgeschichte* 6 (1975), Sondernummer Kommagene.

Habicht, Chr. *Gottmenschentum und griechische Städte*² (Zetemata 14), Munich, 1970.

Habicht, Chr. "Die augusteische Zeit und das erste Jahrhundert nach Christi Geburt" in den Boer (ed.), *Le Culte* 41-88.

Hadley, R.A. *Deified Kingship and Propaganda Coinage in the Early Hellenistic Age: 323-280 B.C.*, Ann Arbor, 1965.

Halsberghe, G.H. "Le culte de Dea Caelestis," *ANRW* 2, 17, 4 (1984) 2203-2223.

Hammond, M. "The Transmission of the Powers of the Roman Emperor from the Death of Nero in A.D. 68 to that of Alexander Severus in A.D. 235," *MAAR* 24 (1956), 63-133.

Hammond, M. "Imperial Elements in the Formula of the Roman Emperors during the first two and a half centuries of the Empire," *MAAR* 25 (1957), 17-64.

Hammond, M. *The Antonine Monarchy* (Papers and Monographs of the American Academy in Rome 19), Rome, 1959.

Hammond, M. "The Antonine Monarchy: 1959-1971," *ANRW* 2, 2 (1975) 329-353.

Hanell, K. "Zur Diskussion über die Ara Pacis," *Hum. Vetenskapssamfundet i Lund, Årsberätt.*, Lund, 1935-1936, 191-202.

Hanell, K. "Das Opfer des Augustus an der Ara Pacis. Eine archäologische und historische Untersuchung," *ORom* 2 (1960), 33-123.

Hänlein-Schäfer, H. *Veneratio Augusti. Eine Studie zu den Tempeln des ersten römischen Kaisers* (Archaeologica 39), Rome, 1985.

Hano, M. "A l'origine du culte impérial: les autels des Lares Augusti. Recherches sur les thèmes iconographiques et leur signification," *ANRW* 2, 16, 3 (1986) 2333-2381.

Hauschild, Th. "Römische Konstruktionen auf der oberen Stadtterrasse des antiken Tarraco," *AEA* 45/47 (1972/74), 3-44.

Heinen, H. "Zur Begründung des römischen Kaiserkultes," *Klio* 11 (1911), 129-177.

Helgeland, J. "Roman Army Religion," *ANRW* 2, 16, 2 (1978) 1470-1505.

Henig, M. *Religion in Roman Britain*, New York, 1984.

Henrichs, A. "Vespasian's visit to Alexandria," *ZPE* 3 (1968), 51-80.

Hermann, P. "Antiochus der Grosse und Teos," *Anadolu* 9 (1965), 29-159.

Herz, P. *Untersuchungen zum Festkalender der römischen Kaiserzeit nach datierten Weih- und Ehreninschriften* (Diss. Mainz), Mainz, 1975.

Herz, P. "Kaiserfeste des Prinzipatszeit," *ANRW* 2, 16, 2 (1978) 1135-1200.

Herz, P. "Der Brotstempel von Eisenberg," *Donnersberg-Jahrbuch* (1979), 83-85.

Herz, P. "Kaiserbilder aus Ostia," *BCAR* 87 (1980-81), 145-157.

Herz, P. "Die Arvalakten des Jahres 38n. Chr.," *BJ* 181 (1981), 89-110.

Herz, P. "Diva Drusilla," *Historia* 30 (1981), 324-336.

Herz, P. "Das Kenotaph von Limrya. Kultische und juristische Voraussetzungen," *MDAI(I)* 35 (1984), 178-192.

Herz, P. "Der römische Kaiser und der Kaiserkult. Gott oder primus inter pares?" in D. Zeller (ed.), *Menschwerdung Gottes - Vergöttlichung von Menschen* (Novum Testamentum et Orbis Antiquus 7), Göttingen 1988, 115-140.

von Hesberg, H. "Archäologische Denkmäler zum römischen Kaiserkult," *ANRW* 2, 16, 2 (1978) 911-995.

von Hesberg, H. "Archäologische Denkmäler zu den römischen Göttergestalten," *ANRW* 2, 17, 2 (1981) 1032-1199.

Hill, G.F. *Notes on the Ancient Coinage of Hispania Citerior* (Numismatic Notes and Monographs 50), New York, 1931.

Hiltbrunner, O. "Die Heiligkeit des Kaisers (Zur Geschichte des Begriffs sacer)," *Frühmittelalterliche Studien* 2 (1968), 1-30.

Hirschfeld, O. "I sacerdozi dei municipi romani nell' Africa," *Ann. dell' Ist. di Corrisp. Arch. di Roma* 38 (1866), 28-77.

Hirschfeld, O. "Zur Geschichte des römischen Kaisercultus," *SDAW* (1888), 857-860.

Hirschfeld, O. *Die kaiserlichen Verwaltungsbeamten bis auf Diokletian*[2], Berlin, 1905 (1963).

Hoffman Lewis, M.W. *The Official Priests of Rome under the Julio-Claudians* (Papers and Monographs of the American Academy in Rome 16), Rome, 1955.

Hölscher, T. *Victoria Romana*, Mainz, 1967.

Homo, L. *L'Empereur du bon Sens*, Paris, 1949.

Hopkins, K. *Conquerors and Slaves* (Sociological Studies in Roman History 1), Cambridge, 1978.

Horsfall, N. "The Ides of March: some new Problems," *G & R* 21 (1974), 191-199.

Houston, G.W. "Vespasian's Adlection of Men in senatum," *AJPhil* 98 (1977), 35-63.

Hull, M.R. *Roman Colchester*, London, 1958.

Imhoff, M. "Invictus," *MH* 14 (1957), 197-215.

Inan, J. and Rosenbaum, E. *Roman and Early Byzantine Portrait Sculpture in Asia Minor*, London, 1966.

Inan, J. and Alföldi-Rosenbaum, E. *Römische und Frühbyzantinische Porträtplastik aus der Türkei*, Mainz, 1979.

Instinsky, H.U. "Kaiser und Ewigkeit," *Hermes* 77 (1942), 313-355.

Instinsky, H.U. "Historische Fragen des Mainzer Drususdenkmals," *JRGZ* 6 (1960), 180-196.

Isager, J. "Vespasiano e Augusto," in K. Ascani et al. (edd.) *Studia Romana in honorem P. Krarup septuagenarii*, Odense, 1976, 64-71.

Jacques, F. "Le cens en Gaule au IIe siècle et dans la première moitié du IIIe siècle," *Ktema* 2 (1977), 285-328.

Jones, A.H.M. *Studies in Roman Government and Law*, Oxford, 1960.

Jones, C.P. "Diodorus Pasparos and the Nikephoria of Pergamon," *Chiron* 4 (1974), 183-205.

Jucker, H. "Marc Aurel bleibt Marc Aurel," *Pro Aventico* 26 (1981), 7-36.

Jürgens, H. *Pompa Diaboli* (Tübinger Beiträge zur Altertumswissenschaft 46), Stuttgart, 1972.

Kajanto, I. "Fortuna," *ANRW* 2, 17, 1 (1981) 502-558.

Kalavrezou-Maxeiner, I. "The Imperial Chamber at Luxor," *DOP* 29 (1975), 227-251.

Kaufman, P.T. "Numismatic evidence for the Extension of the Imperial Cult of Roma et Augustus in Tres Galliae," *NCirc* 85 (1977), 210-212.

Kienast, D. "Der heilige Senat. Senatuskult und 'Kaiserlicher' Senat," *Chiron* 15 (1985), 253-283.

Kolbe, H.G. "Lare Aineia?," *MDAI(R)* 77 (1970), 1-9.

Kneissl, P. "Zur Entstehung der Provinz Noricum," *Chiron* 9 (1979), 261-273.

Kneissl, P. "Entstehung und Bedeutung der Augustalität. Zur Inschrift der ara Narbonensis (CIL XII 4333)," *Chiron* 10 (1980), 291-326.

Knoche, U. "Die augusteische Ausprägung der dea Roma," *Gymnasium* 59 (1952), 324-349.

Kolendo, J. "Études sur les inscriptions de Novae," *Archaeologia* (Sofia) 16 (1965), 124-148.

Koonce, K. "ΑΓΑΛΜΑ and ΕΙΚΩΝ," *AJPhil* 109 (1988), 108-110.

Kornemann, E. "Die Zahl der gallischen civitates in der römischen Kaiserzeit," *Klio* 1 (1901), 331-348.

Kornemann, E. "Zur Geschichte der antiken Herrscherkulte," *Klio* 1 (1901), 51-146.

Kornemann, E. "''Αναξ καινὸς 'Αδριανός," *Klio* 7 (1907), 278-288.

Kornemann, E. *Doppelprinzipat und Reichsteilung im Imperium Romanum*, Leipzig and Berlin, 1930.

Kotula, T. "Les origines des assemblées provinciales dans l'Afrique romaine," *Eos* 52 (1962), 147-167.

Kotula, T. "Encore sur la mort de Ptolémée, roi de Maurétanie," *Archeologia* 15 (1964), 76-94.

Kotula, T. "A propos d'une inscription reconstituée de Bulla Regia (Hamman-Darradji)...," *MEFR* 79 (1967), 207-220.

Kotula, T. "Remarques sur les traditions puniques dans la constitution des villes de l'Afrique romaine," *Vestigia* 17 (1972), 73-83.

Kotula, T. "Culte provincial et romanisation. Le cas des deux Maurétanies," *Eos* 63 (1975), 389-407.

Kotula, T. "L'épigraphie latine et le culte impérial au 1er siècle de l'Empire," *Gérion* 1 (1983), 215-218.

Kotula, T. "Les Augustales d'Afrique," *BCTH* 17B (1984), 345-357.

Kraft, K. "Der politische Hintergrund von Seneca's Apocolocyntosis," *Historia* 15 (1966), 96-122.

Krascheninnikoff, M. "Über die Einführung des provinzialen Kaisercultus im römischen Westen," *Philologus* 53, n.F. 7 (1894), 147-189.

Kruse, H. *Studien zur offiziellen Geltung des Kaiserbildes im römischen Reiche* (Studien zur Geschichte und Kultur des Altertums 19, 3), Paderborn, 1934.

Kunderewicz, C. "Quelques remarques sur le rôle des ΚΑΙΣΑΡΕΙΑ dans la vie juridique de l'Egypte romaine," *Journal of Juristic Papyrology* 13 (1961), 123-129.

Kunkel, H. *Der römische Genius*, (MDAI[R] Ergänzungsheft 20),

Heidelberg, 1974.

Künzl, E. "Zwei silberne Tetrarchenporträts im RGZM und die römischen Kaiserbildnisse aus Gold und Silber," *JRGZ* 30 (1983), 381-402.

Ladage, D. *Städtische Priester- und Kultämter im lateinischen Westen des Imperium Romanum zur Kaiserzeit* (Diss. Köln), Cologne, 1971.

Laffi, U. "Le iscrizioni relative all' introduzione nel 9 A.C. del nuovo calendario della provincia d'Asia," *SCO* 16 (1967), 5-98.

Lambrechts, P. "La politique 'apollinienne' d'Auguste et le culte impérial," *La Nouvelle Clio* 5 (1953), 65-82.

Larsen, J.A.O. *Representative Government in Greek and Roman History* (Sather Classical Lectures 28), Berkeley and Los Angeles, 1955.

Lasfargues J. and Le Glay, M. "Découverte d'un sanctuaire municipal du culte impérial à Lyon," *CRAI* (1980), 394-414.

Latte, K. "Augur und Templum in der Varronischen Auguralformel," *Philologus* 97 (1948), 143-159.

Latte, K. *Römische Religionsgeschichte*² (Handb. d. Altertumswiss. 5,4), Munich, 1967 (1976).

Lebek, W.D. "Schwierige Stellen der Tabula Siarensis," *ZPE* 66 (1986), 31-48.

Lebek, W.D. "Die drei Ehrenbogen für Germanicus," *ZPE* 67 (1987), 129-148.

Lebek, W.D. "Die Mainzer Ehrenbogen für Germanicus, den älteren Drusus und Domitian (Tab. Siar. Frg. I, 26-34; Suet., Claud. 1, 3)," *ZPE* 78 (1989), 45-82.

Lebek, W.D. "Die posthumen Ehrenbögen und der Triumph des Drusus Caesar," *ZPE* 78 (1989), 83-91.

Le Glay, M. "Les Flaviens et l'Afrique," *MEFR* 80 (1968), 201-246.

Le Glay, M. *La Religion romaine*, Paris, 1971.

Le Glay, M. "Hadrien et l'Asklépieion de Pergame," *BCH* 100 (1976), 347-372.

Le Glay, M. "Le culte de Rome et de Salus à Pergame..." in S. Şahin et al. (ed.), *Studien zur Religion und Kultur Kleinasiens* (Festschrift Friedrich Karl Dörner), Leiden, 1978.

Le Glay, M. "Le culte impérial à Lyon, au IIᵉ siècle ap. J.-C." in *Les Martyrs de Lyon (177)* (Colloques internationaux du centre national de la recherche scientifique 575), Paris, 1978, 19-31.

Leschi, L. "Inscription de l'arc dit de Crescens à Djemila" in *Études d'Epigraphie, d'Archéologie, et d'Histoire africaines*, Paris, 1957,

165-167.

Leveau, Ph. "Caesarea de Maurétanie," *ANRW* 2, 10, 2 (1982) 683-738.

Levick, B. "Mercy and Moderation on the Coinage of Tiberius" in B. Levick (ed.), *The Ancient Historian and his Materials. Essays in Honour of C.E. Stevens on his seventieth birthday*, Farnborough, 1975, 123-137.

Levi della Vida, G. "Due iscrizioni imperiali neo-puniche di Leptis Magna," *Africa Italiana* 6 (1935), 1-29.

Liebeschuetz, J.H.W.G. *Continuity and Change in Roman Religion*, Oxford, 1979.

Liegle, J. "Pietas," *ZN* 42 (1932), 59-100.

Linderski, J. "The Augural Law," *ANRW* 2, 16, 3 (1986) 2146-2312.

Liou-Gille, B. *Cultes 'héroiques' romains. Les Fondateurs*, Paris, 1980.

L'Orange, H.P. *Apotheosis in Ancient Portraiture*, Oslo, 1947.

L'Orange, H.P. *Studies on the Iconography of Cosmic Kingship in the Ancient World*, Oslo, 1953.

MacCormack, S.G. *Art and Ceremony in Late Antiquity*, Berkeley, 1981.

MacDowall, D.W. "Nero's Altar of Lugdunum Type," *GNS* 15 (1965), 90-93.

MacMullen, R. *Paganism in the Roman Empire*, New Haven and London, 1981.

Mannsperger, D. "Apollon gegen Dionysos. Numismatische Beiträge zu Oktavien's Rolle als Vindex Libertatis," *Gymnasium* 80 (1973), 381-404.

Mannsperger, D. "ROM ET AUG. Die Selbstdarstellung des Kaisertums in der römischen Reichsprägung," *ANRW* 2, 1 (1974) 919-996.

Marghitan, L. and Petolescu, C.C. "*Vota pro salute principis*," *StudClas* 16 (1974), 245-247.

Marghitan, L. and Petolescu, C.C. "*Vota pro salute imperatoris* in an inscription at Ulpia Traiana Sarmizegetusa," *JRS* 66 (1976), 84-86.

Markowski, H. "De quattuor virtutibus Augusti in clupeo aureo ei dato inscriptis," *Eos* 37 (1936), 109-128.

Martin, J.P. *Providentia Deorum. Recherches sur certains aspects religieux du pouvoir impérial romain* (Collection de l'Ecole française de Rome 61), Rome, 1982.

Mastino, A. *Le Titolature di Caracalla e Geta attraverso le Iscrizioni* (Indici) (Studi di Storia Antica 5), Bologna, 1981.

Mattingly, H. "The Roman Virtues," *HThR* 30 (1937), 103-117.

Mattingly, H. "The Imperial Vota," *Proc. Brit. Acad.* 36 (1950), 155-195; 37 (1951), 219-268.

Maxfield, V.A. *The Military Decorations of the Roman Army*, London, 1981.

McCann, A.M. *The Portraits of Septimius Severus* (MAAR 30), Rome, 1968.

McCormick, H. *Eternal Victory. Triumphant Rulership in late Antiquity, Byzantium, and the early medieval West*, Cambridge, 1986.

McElderry, R.K. "Vespasian's Reconstruction of Spain," *JRS* 8 (1918), 53-102.

Mellor, R.J. *Dea Roma: The Development of the Idea of the Goddess Roma* (Diss. Princeton), Princeton, 1967.

Mellor, R.J. ΘΕΑ ΡΩΜΗ *The Worship of the Goddess Roma in the Greek World* (Hypomnemata 42), Göttingen, 1975.

Mellor, R.J. "The Goddess Roma," *ANRW* 2, 17, 2 (1981) 950-1030.

Merkelbach, R. *Die Quellen des griechischen Alexander-romans*, Munich, 1954.

Merkelbach, R. "Der Rangstreit der Städte Asiens und die Rede des Aelius Aristides über die Eintracht," *ZPE* 32 (1978), 287-296.

Merten, E.W. *Zwei Herrscherfeste in der Historia Augusta* (Antiquitas 5), Bonn, 1968.

Meyer, E. "Alexander der Grosse und die absolute Monarchie," *Kleine Schriften*[2], Halle and Saale, 1924, 1, 265-314.

Meyer, E. "Zur Geschichte des Wallis in römischer Zeit," *BZG* 42 (1943), 59-78 at 60-69.

Meyer, E. "Augusti," *MH* 16 (1959), 273-274.

Meyer, E. "Augusti Ein Nachtrag," *MH* 17 (1960), 118.

Meyer, E. "Nochmals Augusti," *Klio* 52 (1970), 283-5.

Meyer, E. "Augusti," *Chiron* 5 (1975), 393-402.

Millar, F. "The Fiscus in the first two Centuries," *JRS* 53 (1963), 29-42.

Millar, F. *The Emperor in the Roman World* (31 BC-AD 337), London, 1977.

Millar, F.G.B. "The Imperial Cult and the Persecutions" in den Boer (ed.), *Le Culte* 145-165.

Millar, F. "The Imperial Cult and the Persecutions" in den Boer (ed.), *Le Culte*, 145-165.

Mócsy, A. *Pannonia and Upper Moesia*, London, 1974.

Momigliano, A. "The Peace of the Ara Pacis," *JWI* 5 (1942), 228-231.

Mowat, R. "La *Domus Divina* et les *Divi*," *Bull. Epig.* 5 (1885), 221-240, 308-316; 6 (1886), 31-36.

Mrozek, S. "'*Primus omnium*' sur les inscriptions des municipes italiens," *Epigraphica* 33 (1971), 60-69.

Müller, F. "Augustus," *Meded. Koninkl. Acad. Wetenschap., Afdel. Letterk.* A 11 (1927), 245-347.

Mundle, I. "Dea Caelestis in der Religionspolitik des Septimius Severus und der Julia Domna," *Historia* 10 (1961), 228-237.

Musurillo, H. *The Acts of the Christian Martyrs*, Oxford, 1972.

Nicolet, C. "L'inscription de l'autel de Narbonne et la 'Commendatio' des Chevaliers," *Latomus* 22 (1963), 721-732.

Niebling, G. "Laribus Augustis Magistri Primi," *Historia* 5 (1956), 303-331.

Niemeyer, H.G. *Studien zur statuarischen Darstellung der römischen Kaiser* (Monumenta Artis Romanae 7), Berlin, 1968.

Nilsson, M.P. "Pagan Divine Service in Late Antiquity," *HThR* 38 (1945), 63-69.

Nilsson, M.P. "Lampen und Kerzen im Kult der Antike" in *Opuscula Selecta*, Lund, 1960, 189-214.

Nilsson, M.P. *Geschichte der griechischen Religion* (Handb. d. Altertumswiss. 5,2), Munich, 1974.

Nock, A.D. "Studies in the Graeco-Roman Beliefs of the Empire," *JHS* 45 (1925), 84-101.

Nock, A.D. "Notes on Ruler Cult, I-IV," *JHS* 48 (1928), 21-43.

Nock, A.D. "Religious Development from Vespasian to Trajan," *Theology* 16 (1928), 152-160.

Nock, A.D. "Σύνναος Θεός," *HSCP* 41 (1930), 1-62.

Nock, A.D. "The Vocabulary of the New Testament," *JBL* 52 (1933), 131-9.

Nock, A.D. "*Seviri* and *Augustales*," *Annuaire de l'Institut de Philol. et d'Hist. orientales* (Mélanges Bidez) 2 (1933-34), 627-638.

Nock, A.D. "The Cult of Heroes," *HThR* 37 (1944), 141-173.

Nock, A.D. "The Emperor's Divine Comes," *JRS* 37 (1947), 102-116.

Nock, A.D. "*Soter* and *Euergetes*" in S.L. Johnson (ed.), *The Joy of Study, Papers on New Testament and related subjects presented to honor F.C. Grant*, New York, 1951, 127-148.

Nock, A.D. "The Roman Army and the Religious Year," *HThR* 45 (1952), 186-252.

Nock, A.D. "Neotera, Queen or Goddess?," *Aegyptus* 33 (1953), 283-296.

Nock, A.D. "Deification and Julian," *JRS* 47 (1957), 115-123.

Nock, A.D., [ed. Z. Stewart], *Essays on Religion and the Ancient World*, Oxford, 1972, Vols. 1-2.

Norden, E. *Aus altrömischen Priesterbüchern* (Skrift. utg. av hum. Vetensskapssamfundet i Lund 29), Lund, 1939, 16-40.

North, J.A. "Praesens Divus," *JRS* 65 (1975), 171-177.

Oliver, J.H. *The Sacred Gerusia* (Hesperia Suppl. 6), Baltimore, 1941.

Oliver, J.H. "The *Divi* of the Hadranic period," *HThR* 42 (1949), 35-40.

Opperman, H. (ed.), *Römische Wertbegriffe*, Darmstadt, 1974.

Orr, D.G. "Roman Domestic Religion: The Evidence of the Household Shrines," *ANRW* 2, 16, 2 (1978) 1557-1591.

Otto, W.F. "Römische 'Sondergötter'," *RhM* 64 (1909), 449-468.

Palladini, M.L. "L'aspetto dell' imperatore-dio presso i Romani," *Contributi dell' Istituto di Filologia Classica* (Pubbl. dell' Univ. Catt. del Sacro Cuore) 1 (1963), 1-65.

Pallu de Lessert, A.C. "Les assemblées provinciales et le culte provincial dans l'Afrique romaine. Nouvelles observations," *Bull. Trim. de la Soc. de Géog. et d'Arch. de la Province d'Oran* 11 (1891), 1-53.

Palmer, R.E.A. "Severan Ruler Cult and the Moon in the City of Rome," *ANRW* 2, 16, 2 (1978) 1085-1120.

Pasoli, A. *Acta Fratrum Arvalium*, Bologna, 1950.

Pasquinucci, M.M. "L'"altare" del Tempio del Divo Giulio," *Athenaeum* 52 (1974), 144-155.

Pastor Muñoz, M. "El culto imperial en el 'Conventus Asturum'," *Hispania Antiqua* 4 (1974), 203-223.

Pekáry, T. "Goldene Statuen der Kaiserzeit," *MDAI(R)* 75 (1968), 144-148.

Pekáry, T. *Das römische Kaiserbildnis in Staat, Kult und Gesellschaft* (Das römische Herrscherbild: Abt. 3; Bd. 5), Berlin, 1985.

Pekáry, T. "Das Opfer vor dem Kaiserbild," *BJ* 186 (1986), 91-103.

Perret, V. "Le capitole de Narbonne," *Gallia* 14 (1956), 1-22.

Petersen, L. *Zur Geschichte der Personification in griechischer Dichtung und bildender Kunst*, Würzburg, 1939.

Pflaum, H.-G. *Le Marbre de Thorigny* (Bibl. de l'Ecole des Hautes Etudes 292), Paris, 1948.

Pflaum, H.-G. *Essai sur les Procurateurs équestres sous le Haut-Empire romain*, Paris, 1950.

Pflaum, H.-G. *Les Carrières procuratoriennes équestres sous le Haut-*

Empire romain, Paris, 1960.

Pflaum, H.-G. "La part prise par les chevaliers romains originaires d'Espagne à l'administration impériale" in *Les Empereurs romains d'Espagne* (Actes du Colloque International du Centre National de la Recherche Scientifique, Madrid-Italica, 31 mars-6 avril), Paris, 1965, 87-121.

Pflaum, H.-G. "Les juges des cinq décuries originaires d'Afrique romaine," *AntAfr* 2 (1968), 153-195.

Pflaum, H.-G. "Les flamines de l'Afrique romaine," *Athenaeum* 54 (1976), 152-163.

Piccottini, G. "Die Stadt auf dem Magdalensberg—ein spätkeltisches und frührömisches Zentrum im südlichen Noricum," *ANRW* 2, 6 (1977), 263-301.

Pietrusinski, D. "Eléments astraux dans l'apothéose d'Octavien Auguste chez Virgile et Horace," *Eos* 68 (1980), 267-283.

Pietrusinski, D. "L'apothéose d'Octavien Auguste par le parallèle avec Jupiter dans la poésie d'Horace," *Eos* 68 (1980), 103-122.

Piganiol, A. "La couronne de Julien César," *Byzantion* 13 (1938), 243-248.

Pippidi, D.M. "Le 'Numen Augusti'," *REL* 9 (1931), 83-112.

Pippidi, M. "Dominus Noster Caesar..." in *id.*, *Recherches sur le Culte impérial*, Paris, 1939, 121-148.

Platner, S.B. and Ashby, T. *A Topographical Dictionary of Ancient Rome*, London, 1929.

Pleket, H.W "An Aspect of the Emperor Cult: Imperial Mysteries," *HThR* 58 (1965), 331-347.

Pleket, H.W. "Nine inscriptions from the Cayster-Valley in Lydia: A re-publication," *Talanta* 2 (1970), 55-88.

Poinssot, Cl. "M. Licinius Rufus, patronus pagi et civitatis Thuggensis," *BCTH* n.s. 5 (1969), 215-258.

Pollini, J. *Studies in Augustan "Historical" Reliefs* (Diss. California), Berkeley, 1978.

Poncet E. and Morel, L.-B. "Le revers des monnaies dites à l'autel de Lyon," *RN* 4th ser., 8 (1904), 46-63.

Pötscher, W. "Numen," *Gymnasium* 66 (1959), 353-374.

Pötscher, W. "'Numen' und 'numen Augusti'," *ANRW* 2, 16, 1 (1978) 355-392.

Prayon, F. "Projektierte Bauten auf römischen Münzen" in B. von Freytag gen. Löringhoff et. al. (edd.), *Praestant Interna* (Festschrift U. Hausmann), Tübingen, 1982, 319-330.

Price, S.R.F. "Between Man and God: Sacrifice in the Roman Imperial Cult," *JRS* 70 (1980), 28-43.

Price, S.R.F. "Gods and Emperors: The Greek Language of the Roman Imperial Cult," *JHS* 104 (1984), 79-95.

Price, S.R.F. *Rituals and Power. The Roman Imperial Cult in Asia Minor*, Cambridge, 1984.

Quoniam, P. "Hadricn et le théâtre de Lugdunum," *Bull. des Musées et Monuments Lyonnais* 1 (1959), 67-76.

Quoniam, P. "Deux notables deBullaRegia,"*Karthago* 11 (1961-62), 3-8.

Radke, G. "Augustus und das Göttliche" in *Antike und Universalgeschichte* (Festschrift H.E. Stier), Münster, 1972, 257-279.

Radke, G. *Die Götter Altitaliens*² (Fontes et Commentationes. Schriftenreihe des Instituts für Epigraphik an der Universität Münster 3), Münster, 1979.

Raepsaet-Charlier, M.-T. "La datation des inscriptions latines dans les provinces occidentales de l'empire romain d'après les formules "IN H(ONOREM) D(OMUS) D(IVINAE)" et "DEO, DEAE"," *ANRW* 2, 3 (1975) 232-282.

Rainer, A. *Das Bild des Augustus auf den frühen Reichsprägungen. Studien zur Vergöttlichung des ersten Prinzeps* (Schriftenreihe der Numismatischen Gesellschaft Speyer 21), Speyer am Rhein, 1981

Ramage, E.S. "Denigration of Predecessor under Claudius, Galba and Vespasian," *Historia* 32 (1938), 201-214.

Rawson, E. "Caesar's Heritage: Hellenistic Kings and their Roman Equals," *JRS* 65 (1975), 148-159.

Reynolds, J.M. "Vota pro salute principis," *PBSR* 30, n.s. 17 (1962), 33-36; 33, n.s. 20 (1965), 52-54.

Reynolds, J.M. "The Origins and Beginning of Imperial Cult at Aphrodisias," *PCPS*, 206, n.s. 26 (1980), 70-84.

Reynolds, J.M. *Aphrodisias and Rome* (JRS Monograph 1), London, 1982.

Rice, E.E. *The Grand Procession of Ptolemy Philadelphus*, Oxford, 1983.

Richard, J.C. "Recherches sur certains aspects du culte impérial: Les funérailles des empereurs Romains aux deux premiers siècles de notre ére," *ANRW* 2, 16, 2 (1978) 1121-1134.

Richmond, I.A. and Wright, R.P. "Stones from a Hadrianic War Memorial on Tyneside," *Arch. Ael.* 4th ser. 21 (1943), 93-106.

Richmond, I.A. "The Four Coloniae of Roman Britain," *AJ* 103 (1946), 57-60.

Ritter, H.W. "Livias Erhebung zur Augusta," *Chiron* 2 (1972), 313-338.

Robert, L. "Notes et Discussions," *RPh* 17 (1943), 184-185.

Robert, L. "Le Culte de Caligula à Milet et la Province d'Asie" in *Hellenica* VII, Paris, 1949, 206-238.

Robert, L. "Inscription d'Athènes," *REA* 62 (1960), 316-324.

Robert, L. "Recherches épigraphiques: Inscription d'Athènes," *REA* 62 (1960), 316-324.

Robert, L. "La titulature de Nicée et de Nicomédie: La gloire et la haine," *HSCP* 81 (1977), 1-39.

Rocca-Serra, G. "Une formule cultuelle chez Suétone (Divus Augustus 98, 2)" in *Mélanges de Philosophie, de Littérature et d'Histoire Ancienne offerts à Pierre Boyancé* (Coll. École franç. de Rome 22), Rome, 1974, 671-680.

Romanelli, P. *Storia delle Province romane dell' Africa*, Rome, 1959.

Rose, H.J. "Numen inest: Animism in Greek and Roman Religion," *HThR* 28 (1935), 237-257.

Rose, H.J. "Numen and Mana," *HThR* 44 (1951), 109-120.

Rostovtzeff, M. "L'Empereur Tibère et le culte impérial," *RH* 163 (1930), 1-26.

Rougé, J. "'Ο ΘΕΙΟΤΑΤΟΣ ΑΥΓΟΥΣΤΟΣ," *RPhil* 43 (1969), 83-92.

Rouse, W.H.D. *Greek Votive Offerings*, Cambridge, 1902.

Russu, I.I. "Domus Divina în Dacia," *Studii Classice* 9 (1967), 211-218.

Salzmann, D. "Zur Münzprägung der mauretanischen Könige Juba II und Ptolemaios," *MDAI(M)* 15 (1974), 174-183.

Santero, J.M. "The 'Cultores Augusti' and the Private Worship of the Roman Emperor," *Athenaeum* 61 (1983), 111-125.

Sasel, J. "Huldigung norischer Stämme am Magdalensberg in Kärnten," *Historia* 16 (1967), 70-74.

Saumagne, Ch. "Volubilis, municipe latin," in *Nouv. Rev. Hist. de Droit français* (1952), 388-401.

Sayas Abengochea, J.J. "El culto al emperador" in R. Menéndez Pidal *et al.*, *Historia de España*, Madrid, 1982, 2, 399-413.

Schäfer, T. "Flaminat und hasta. Bemerkungen zur Selbstdarstellung eines munizipalen Magistraten," *Scritti in Ricordo di Graziella Massari Gaballo e di Umberto Tocchetti Pollini*, Milan, 1986, 123-130.

Scheid, J. "Les prêtres officiels sous les empereurs julio-claudiens," *ANRW* 2, 16, 1 (1978) 610-654.

Scheid, J. and Broise, H. "Deux nouveaux fragments des actes des Frères Arvales de l'année 38 ap. J.C.," *MEFRA* 92 (1980), 215-248.

Schilling, R. "Le culte de l'Indiges à Lavinium," *REL* 57 (1979), 49-68.

Schilling, R. "Les découvertes de Lavinium," *PP* 36 (1981), 84-86.

Schilling, R. "La déification à Rome. Tradition latine et interférence grecque" in *Studi pubblicati in memoria di Angelo Brelich: R & C* 3 (1982), 559-575.

Schmitz, H. *Stadt und Imperium. Köln in römischen Zeit*, Cologne, 1948, Vol. 1.

Schumacher, L. "Die vier hohen römischen Priesterkollegien unter den Flaviern, den Antoninen und den Severern (69-235 n. Chr.)," *ANRW* 2, 16, 1 (1978) 655-819.

Schwarz, J. "Dies Augustus," *REA* 46 (1944), 266-279.

Scott, K. "The Deification of Demetrius Poliorcetes," *AJPhil* 49 (1928), 137-166, 217-239.

Scott, K. "Emperor Worship in Ovid," *TAPA* 61 (1930), 43-69.

Scott, K. "Greek and Roman honorific months," *YCS* 2 (1931), 199-278.

Scott, K. "The Significance of Statues in Precious Metals," *TAPA* 62 (1931), 101-123.

Scott, K. *The Imperial Cult under the Flavians*, Stuttgart and Berlin, 1936.

Scott, R.T. "Providentia Aug.," *Historia* 31 (1982), 436-459.

Scott Ryberg, I. *Rites of the State Religion in Roman Art* (MAAR 22), Rome, 1955.

Scott Ryberg, I. "Clupeus Virtutis" in *The Classical Tradition* (Studies in Honor of H. Caplan), Ithaca, 1966, 232-238.

Seston, W. "Les donateurs de l'amphithéâtre des Trois Gaules" in *Hommages A. Grenier* (Coll. Latomus 58), Brussels, 1962, 1407-1417.

Sherwin-White, A.N. *The Roman Citizenship*², Oxford, 1973.

Sigal, L. "Les 'Fabri Subaediani' d'après une inscription du Musée de Narbonne," *Bull. Commis. Arch. Narbonne* 16, 1 (1924), 141-156; 18, 3 (1933-35), 324-327.

Simon, E. *Ara Pacis Augustae* (Monumenta artis antiquae 1), Tübingen, 1967.

Skrabar, V. "Denkmäler des Larenkultes aus Poetovio," *JOEAI* 20 (1919), Beiblatt 279-294.

Smadja, E. "L'inscription du culte impérial dans la cité: l'exemple de

Lepcis Magna au début de l'empire," *Dialogues d'Histoire Ancienne* 4 (1978), 171-186.

Smith, M. "The Image of God. Notes on the Hellenization of Judaism ...," *Bull. John Rylands Library* 40 (1957-58), 473-512.

Smith, R.R.R. "The Imperial Reliefs from the Sebasteion at Aphrodisias," *JRS* 77 (1987), 88-138.

Snyder, W.F. "'Ἡμέραι Σεβασταί," *Aegyptus* 18 (1938), 197-233.

Snyder, W.F. "Public Anniversaries in the Roman Empire," *YCS* 7 (1940), 225-317.

Snyder, W.F. "Progress Report on the Ἡμέραι Σεβασταί," *Aegyptus* 44 (1964), 145-169.

Sokolowski, F. "Divine Honors for Antiochus and Laodike at Teos and Iasos," *GRBS* 13 (1972), 171-176.

Speidel, M.P. and Dimitrova-Milceva, A. "The Cult of the Genii in the Roman Army and a New Military Deity," *ANRW* 2, 17, 2 (1978) 1542-1555.

Squarciapino, M.F. *Leptis Magna*, Basel, 1966.

Stambaugh, J.E. "The Functions of Roman Temples," *ANRW* 2, 16, 1 (1978) 554-608.

Stead, M. "The High Priest of Alexandria and All Egypt" in *Proceedings of the 16. International Congress of Papyrology*, New York 1980, Chicago, 1981, 411-418.

Stein, E. *Die kaiserlichen Beamten und Truppenkörper im römischen Deutschland unter dem Prinzipat*, Vienna, 1932.

Strack, P.L. *Untersuchungen zur römischen Reichsprägung des zweiten Jahrhunderts*, Stuttgart, 1931, Vol. 1.

van Straten, F.T. "Gifts for the Gods" in H.S. Versnel (ed.), *Faith, Hope and Worship. Aspects of Religious Mentality in the Ancient World* (Studies in Greek and Roman Religion 2), Leiden, 1981, 65-151.

Sutherland, C.H.V. "Aspects of Imperialism in Roman Spain," *JRS* 24 (1934), 31-42.

Swift, E.H. "*Imagines* in Imperial Portraiture," *AJA* 27 (1923), 286-301.

Syme, R. *Tacitus*, Oxford, 1958, Vols. 1-2.

Syme, R. "Tacitus' Sources of Information," *JRS* 72 (1982), 68-82.

Taeger, F. *Charisma. Studien zur Geschichte des antiken Herrscherkultes*, Stuttgart, 1957, Vol. 1; 1960, Vol. 2.

Taylor, L.R. "Augustales, Seviri Augustales and Seviri: a Chronological Study," *TAPA* 45 (1914), 231-253.

Taylor, L.R. "Livy and the Name Augustus," *CR* 32 (1918), 158-161.

Taylor, L.R. "The Worship of Augustus in Italy during his lifetime," *TAPA* 51 (1920), 116-133.

Taylor, L.R. "*Seviri Equitum Romanorum* and Municipal *Seviri*: a Study in Pre-Military Training among the Romans," *JRS* 14 (1924), 158-171.

Taylor, L.R. "Tiberius' Refusals of Divine Honors," *TAPA* 60 (1929), 87-101.

Taylor, L.R. *The Divinity of the Roman Emperor,* Middletown, Connecticut, 1931; reprinted 1981.

Taylor, L.R. "The 'Sellisternium' and the Theatrical 'Pompa'," *CPh* 30 (1935), 122-130.

Taylor, L.R. "Tiberius' *Ovatio* and the *Ara Numinis Augusti*," *AJPhil* 58 (1937), 185-193.

Thomasson, B.E. "Zum Gebrauch von Augustorum, Augg. und Aug. als Bezeichnung der Samtherrschaft zweier Herrscher," *ZPE* 52 (1983), 125-35.

Thompson, D.B. *Ptolemaic Oinochoai and Portraits in Faience,* Oxford, 1973.

Thraede, K. "Die Poesie und der Kaiserkult" in den Boer (ed.), *Le Culte* 273-303.

Tondriau, J. "Le point culminant du culte des souverains," *LEC* 15 (1947), 101-113.

Tondriau, J. "Comparisons and Identifications of Rulers with Deities in the Hellenistic Period," *Rev. of Rel.* 13 (1948), 24-47.

Tondriau, J. "Alexandre le Grand assimilé à différentes divinités," *RPh* 23 (1949), 41-52.

Torelli, M. *Typology and Structure of Roman Historical Reliefs* (Jerome Lectures 14), Ann Arbor, 1982.

Torelli, M. "Culto imperiale e spazi urbani in età flavia dai rilievi Hartwig all'arco di Tito" in *L'Urbs. Espace urbain et Histoire (1er siècle av. J.C.-IIIe siècle ap. J.C.)* (Coll. de l'Ecole franç. de Rome 98), Rome 1987, 563-582.

Toutain, J. *Les Cultes païens dans l'Empire romain,* Paris, 1905-07 (1967), Vol. 1.

Toutain, J. "Inscription relative à la création du municipium Volubilitanum," *BCTH* (1943), pp. XII-XVI.

Toutain, J. "Notes sur la création du municipium Volubilitanum en Maurétanie Tingitane (44 après J.-C.)" in *Mélanges Félix Grat,* Paris, 1946, 1, 39-52.

Toynbee, J.M.C. "Nero Artifex: The Apocolocyntosis reconsidered," *CQ*

36 (1942), 83-93.

Toynbee, J.M.C. "The 'Ara Pacis Augustae'," *JRS* 51 (1961), 153-156.

Tuchelt, K. *Frühe Denkmäler Roms in Kleinasien I:Roma und Promagistrate* (MDAI[I] Beiheft 23), Tübingen, 1979.

Tuchelt, K. "Zum Problem 'Kaisareion-Sebasteion'. Eine Frage zu den Anfängen des römischen Kaiserkultes," *MDAI (I)* 31 (1981), 167-186.

Turcan, R. "La 'fondation' du temple de Vénus et de Rome," *Latomus* 23 (1964), 42-55.

Turcan, R. "Le culte impérial au IIIᵉ siècle," *ANRW* 2, 16, 2 (1978), 996-1084.

Turcan, R. "L'autel de Rome et d'Auguste 'Ad Confluentem'," *ANRW* 2, 12, 1 (1982) 607-644.

Vermeule, C.C. *The Goddess Roma in the Art of the Roman Empire*[2], Cambridge, Mass., 1974.

Versnel, H.S. "Heersercultus in Griekenland," *Lampas* 7 (1974), 129-163.

Versnel, H.S. "Religious Mentality in Ancient Prayer" in H.S. Versnel (ed.), *Faith, Hope and Worship. Aspects of Religious Mentality in the Ancient World* (Studies in Greek and Roman Religion 2), Leiden, 1981, 1-64.

Vetters, H. "Eine Standarte aus Ephesos," *MDAI(I)* 25 (1975), 393-397.

Vetters, H. "Virunum," *ANRW* 2, 6 (1977) 302-354.

Veyne, P. "Ordo et Populus, génies et chefs de file," *MEFR* 73 (1961), 229-274.

Veyne, P. "Augustal de l'an 1 - premier pontarche," *BCH* 90 (1966), 144-155.

Veyne, P. "Les honneurs posthumes de Flavia Domitilla et les dédicaces grecques et latines," *Latomus* 21 (1962), 49-98.

Veyne, P. *Le Pain et le Cirque*, Paris, 1976.

Vitucci, G. "Alle origini del culto della dea Roma," *C & S* 65 (1978), 71-74.

Vogt, J. "Zum Herrscherkult bei Julius Caesar" in G.E. Mylonas (ed.), *Studies presented to David Moore Robinson on his Seventieth Birthday*, St. Louis, Missouri, 1953, 2, 1138-1146.

Wagenvoort, H. "Wesenszüge altrömischer Religion," *ANRW* 1, 2 (1972) 348-376.

Wagenvoort, H. "Felicitas Imperatoria," *Mnemosyne* 4 (1954), 300-322.

Waldmann, H. *Die kommagenischen Kult-reformen unter König*

Mithradates I Kallinikos und seinem Sohne Antiochus, Leiden, 1973.

Wallace-Hadrill, A. "The Emperor and his Virtues," *Historia* 30 (1981), 298-323.

Walton, F.R. "Religious Thought in the Age of Hadrian," *Numen* 4 (1957), 165-170.

Ward, M.M. "The Association of Augustus with Jupiter," *SMSR* 9 (1933), 203-224.

Wardman, A. *Religion and Statecraft among the Romans*, Baltimore, 1982.

Weaver, P.R.C. *Familia Caesaris*, Cambridge, 1972.

Webster, T.B.L. "Personification as a mode of Greek thought," *JWI* 17 (1954), 10-21.

Weinstock, S. "The Image and Chair of Germanicus," *JRS* 47 (1957), 144-154.

Weinstock, S. "Victor and Invictus," *HThR* 50 (1957), 211-247.

Weinstock, S. "Pax and the 'Ara Pacis'," *JRS* 50 (1960), 44-58.

Weinstock, S. "Two Archaic Inscriptions from Latium," *JRS* 50 (1960), 112-118.

Weinstock, S. "Treueid und Kaiserkult," *MDAI(A)* 77 (1962), 306-327.

Weinstock, S. "The Posthumous Honours of Germanicus" in *Mélanges d'Archéologie et d'Histoire offerts à A. Piganiol*, Paris, 1966, 891-898.

Weinstock, S. *Divus Julius*, Oxford, 1971.

Welin, E. "Die beiden Festtage der Ara Pacis Augustae," *Dragma M.P. Nilsson dedicatum*, Lund, 1939, 500-513.

Welles, C.B., Fink, R.O., Gilliam, J.F. *The Excavations at Dura-Europus, Final Report V, 1: The Parchments and Papyri*, New Haven, 1959.

Wilcken, U. "Arsinoitische Tempelrechnungen aus dem J.215 n.Chr.," *Hermes* 20 (1885), 430-476.

Wilcken, U. "Zur Entstehung des hellenistischen Königskultes," *SPAW* 28 (1938), 298-321.

Wilcken, U. *Grundzüge und Chrestomathie der Papyruskunde*, Leipzig, 1912(1963), Vols. I-II.

Williamson, C.H. "A Roman Law from Narbonne," *Athenaeum* 65 (1987), 173-189.

Wilkes, J.J. *Dalmatia*, London, 1969.

Winter, E. "Der Herrscherkult in den Ägyptischen Ptolemäertempeln" in H. Maehler and V.M. Strocka (edd.), *Das ptolemäische Ägypten* (Akten des internationalen Symposions 27-29 September 1976 in Berlin), Mainz, 1978, 147-160.

Wiseman, T.P. "The Temple of Victory on the Palatine," *Antiquaries Journal* 61 (1981), 35-52.

Wissowa, G. "*Constitutio Arae*," *Hermes* 39 (1904), 156-160.

Wissowa, G. *Religion und Kultus der Römer* ² (Handb. d. Altertumswiss. 4,5) Munich, 1912.

Wlosok, A. (ed.), Römischer Kaiserkult (WdF Vol. 372), Darmstadt, 1978.

Wlosok, A. "Einführung" in *eadem* (ed.), *Römischer Kaiserkult*, (WdF Vol. 372), Darmstadt, 1-52.

Wolff, H. "*Civitas* und *Colonia Treverorum*," *Historia* 26 (1977), 204-242.

Woods, D.E. "The Temple of Augustus-Tarragona," in *Classica et Iberica* (Festschrift J. M.-F. Marique, S.J.), Worchester, Mass., 1975, 345-354.

Wörrle, M. *Stadt und Fest im kaiserzeitlichen Kleinasien: Studien zu einer agonistischen Stiftung aus Oenoanda* (Vestigia 39), Munich, 1988.

Wrede, H. *Consecratio in Formam Deorum. Vergöttlichte Privatpersonen in der römischen Kaiserzeit*, Mainz, 1981.

Wuilleumier, P. *Lyon, Métropole des Gaules*, Paris, 1953.

Wuilleumier, P. "Le municipe de Volubilis," *REA* 28 (1926), 323-334.

Zanker, P. "Über die Werkstätten augusteischer Larenaltäre und damit zusammenhängende Probleme der Interpretation," *BCAR* 82 (1970/71), 147-155.

Zanker, P. "Prinzipat und Herrscherbild," *Gnomon* 86 (1979), 353-368.

Zanker, P. *Provinzielle Kaiserporträts* (ABAW 90), Munich, 1983.

Ziolkowski, M. "Il culto dell'imperatore nella religione degli eserciti romani in Britannia (I-III sec. d.C.)," *Atti dell'Istituto Veneto di Scienze, Lettere ed Arti* 142 (1983-84), 267-278.

III. INDICES

1. NAMES AND SUBJECTS

abbreviations, conventions for in Britain: 412 f.
abstractions,
    cult of: 85 f., 85[14 f.]
    origin of: 455
    historical development of: 455 ff.
    personalization of: 456 ff.
    in ideology of principate: 457 f.
    place in state religion: 460 f.
    as independent god-heads: 460 ff.
    place in private cult: 461 f.
    applied to emperor: 462 ff.
    conceived as *comes*: 465 ff.
    immanent in emperor: 469 ff.
    as specializations of *numen*: 470
    imagined in different ways: 470
    place within imperial cult: 472
    contribution to imperial mystique: 473
    later development of: 473
    place in imperial propaganda: 473[126]
Abundantia: 460
Acceptius Maior: 606
accessions,
    celebration of: 515[256], 530, 530[331]
acclamations: 375[1-2], 532
    in ruler cult: 569 f., 570[577], 570[578]
    rhythmic: 570
Achaeans, assembly of: 425
Achilles: 42
Acionna: 449
Actium: 81
Acts of Arval Brethren: 482 ff., 482[46], 505 f., 514
    under Flavians: 485
    see also Arval Brethren
Acutianus: 604

Q. Adginnius Martinus: 310, 363[12]
Adventus: 460
Aedemon: 285, 287, 287[34], 289
aedes gentis Flaviae: 576
L. Aelius Caesar, birthday of: 493, 582
P. Aelius Antipater: 302[9]
P. Aelius Damocratidas: 269[3]
P. Aelius Martinus: 598
P. Aelius Maximus: 302[9]
Aelius Servandus: 607
Aelius Verus, statue of: 523[293]
Aeneas: 51, 51[35], 52, 52[36], 53, 54[50]
Aeneas Indiges: 52
Aequitas: 460
Aesculapius: 449, 451[37], 568
    cult image of: 546
    temple of at Lambaesis: 604
Aesculapius and Salus, temple of at Lambaesis: 541
Aeternitas: 460
Aeternitas Augusta: 154, 463[64]
Aeternitas Imperii: 461
Africa, cult of *numen* in: 388[7], 395
Africa Proconsularis,
    provincial cult of: 257 ff.
    era of provincial cult of: 258 ff., 268
    change in title of provincial priest: 263 ff.
Agnin: 343[156]
agonothete, costume and functions of: 617
Agrippa: 78[41], 83[4], 524[299]
    subjugates Spanish tribes: 142
    presents Emerita with theatre: 180
    statue of at Pantheon: 547
Agrippa II of Judaea: 181
Agrippina: 137, 202, 297, 486[66]
    gilded bronze bust of: 543[406]
    image of carried in procession: 556
Agrippina Maior, image carried in procession: 556
Ainay, Church of St. Martin at: 105
ala Longiniana: 244 ff.
ala Sulpicia: 318, 354, 359

ala Vocontiorum: 599
Alexander: 7, 59, 60, 60³⁴, 113, 338, 456
  visits Siwa: 8 f.
  career of: 8 ff.
  city cults of: 9
  divine honours of: 9 f.
  relationship to Greek cities: 9 f.
  as Pharaoh: 9²⁵
  desire to be deified: 10
  state cult of: 13 f.
  priest of: 14
  image of: 22
  priesthoods of: 23
  Indian triumph of: 24¹⁹
  ambassadors to: 25²²
  compared with gods: 29
  costumed as Hermes: 30
  receives sacrifice: 34
  gives aid after death: 39
  as master of world: 57, 57¹⁰
  as monarch: 67
  link with Victory: 114
  portraits of: 343
Alexander Helios: 111⁹⁷
Alexander Severus: 325, 333, 349, 365, 366, 416, 419, 429⁴¹, 488, 489, 571⁵⁸⁷
  statue of: 589
  celebration of birthday: 589 f.
Alexandreia: 577
Alexandria, priesthood at: 24
Alexandrians: 104, 198, 495¹²⁷, 544
Allectus: 467
allectus arcae Galliarum: 136
Alpine provinces, provincial cult of: 298 f.
altar, as divine honour: 21 f.
Altar of Augustus at Tarraco: 121¹⁶⁷, 144³¹⁵, 146, 171 ff., 180 f., 503
  situated in lower forum: 173 f.
  religious status of: 176 f., 177⁴⁶
Altar of Three Gauls: 102 ff., 200, 200³² f.
  portrayed on coins: 104 ff.

legend on: 105, 110, 125 ff.
relics of: 105 f., 106[62]
imagery of: 106 f.
inner reliefs of: 107 ff.
link with Victories: 117 f.
date of dedication: 118
outer reliefs of: 118 ff.
objects upon: 120 ff.
form of: 122 ff.
purpose of busts on: 123 f.
baldaquins on: 124 f., 125[197]
dedication of: 97 ff., 125 f.
Amatius: 73
Amatorius Peregrinus: 604
Amicitia: 460
Ammon: 10
oracle of: 8
Amphiaraus: 4[7]
Amphictyonians, *koinon* of: 271
amphitheatres, location of: 580 ff.
Amun Re: 38
son of: 9
Anavus: 441
Anaximbrotus: 16
Andronikos: 577[627]
Aniketos: 114
M. Annius: 47
anniversaries, imperial marked by sacrifice: 505 ff.
anniversaries of emperor,
epigraphical evidence for in Italy: 491 f.
celebrated by rites: 517
marked by banquets: 586
anniversaries, of imperial house: 482 ff.
Annona: 460
Annona Augusti Ceres: 464
Anteros Asiaticus: 512
Anthony: 61[43], 62, 69, 70, 71[112], 73, 74, 75, 76, 80, 108[71], 109, 111[97], 117, 484
costumed as Dionysus: 30
cult of: 48

implements earlier legislation: 74 f.
Antigonids, honours to at Athens: 25
Antigonus the one-eyed: 24[19], 25[22], 34
    honours to: 12, 21
Antinous, deification and birthday of: 493, 493[121]
Antiochus I: 17, 26, 33, 36
Antiochus I of Commagene: 18, 21, 24[20], 26, 39
    inscription at Nemrud Dağ: 18 f.
    horoscope of: 19
Antiochus III: 16, 17, 23, 37, 49, 186, 477
Antiochus IV: 17, 28
Antiochus VI of Syria: 15[65]
[Q.] Antistius Adventus: 422, 422[80]
Tib. Antistius Faustus: 333
Tib. Antistius Marcianus: 318
Antonaia: 48
Antoneia: 577
Antoneia Geteia: 577
Antonia, birthday of: 484
Antonia Minor,
    niece of Augustus: 145
    as *sacerdos* of Divus Augustus: 563
Antoninus: 489
Antoninus Pius: 183, 220[3], 283, 327[49], 330, 410, 419[76], 451[34], 520, 531,
    538
    restores Narbo: 252
    restores provincial centre at Narbo: 255
    statue of at Cuicul: 264
    as *dominus noster*: 334[86]
    and Fortuna: 466
    birthday of: 487[77], 491[104], 492, 496[133, 134], 538, 605
    adoption of: 488[77], 492, 496[136], 498, 539[381]
    dies imperii of: 488[78]
    image of: 538[378]
    likeness of: 539
    statue of: 541, 542[395-396]
    statue of at temple of Fortuna Primigenia?: 547
    bronze head of: 560
    accession of: 602
C. Antonius Rufus: 476

Antonius Musa: 79[44]
Aphaia, temple of on Aegina: 122[181]
Aphrodisias, Sebasteion at: 551[462]
Aphrodite: 38, 42
   temple of at Mytilene: 548
Aphrodite Stratonikis: 447[11]
Apocolocyntosis, interpretation of: 201
Apollinopolis Heptakomia, folk festival at: 583
Apollo: 46, 80, 80[58], 81, 81[70], 82, 87 f., 87[32], 88, 105[53], 109[80], 117, 342,
   382, 444, 451[34], 451[37], 454[51], 505, 617, 618
   temple of at Miletus: 23
   temple of on Palatine: 82, 590[698]
   temple of at Rome: 88, 484
   association with palm: 176[34]
   temple of at Cyprus: 548
Apollo Actius, prominent on coins: 88[35]
Apollo of Claros, oracle of: 596, 596[17]
Apollo of Didyma: 17
Apollon Pasparios: 447[11]
Apollonius: 527
apotheosis, in Rome: 53 f.
Appius Claudius Pulcher: 47
L. Apronius Caesianus: 546
Apuleius, provincial priesthood of: 580
Aquileia: 346[180]
   rites at: 511
Q. Aquius Antonianus: 312[24]
Ti. Aquius Apollinaris: 310, 311, 311[24], 316[52], 325[34], 363[14]
Manius Aquilius: 47
Ara Fortunae Reducis: 203 ff., 209
Ara Numinis Augusti, at Rome:
   dedication of: 177[46], 378, 387, 388
   dedication represented on Grimani relief?: 378[13]
Ara Numinis Augusti, at Narbo: 174, 246, 252, 379, 424, 497, 531, 610f.
   records anniversaries: 482
   regulates cult acts: 482
   sacrifice at: 483[48]
   prescribes sacrifices: 502
   offerings to: 507, 509[219], 516, 517, 518
   illuminates religious activities of *Augustales*: 610 f.

Ara Pacis: 98, 103, 117, 122, 122[177], 128, 154[28], 173, 175, 182, 203 ff., 205[47], 476, 554
Ara Pietatis Augustae: 161[74]
Ara Ubiorum: 103[39], 137 ff., 143, 145, 475
    cult at: 138 f.
ara Vespasiani, at Chusira: 268[64]
Arabica: 357
Arae Cereris Matris et Opis Augustae: 204, 208[64]
Arae Flaviae: 311, 330
    cult centre at: 298, 311
Arae Sestianae: 139, 141 ff., 141[301]
    cult at: 143 f.
Arch of Beneventum: 502[170]
Arch of Titus: 468
Argentarii, arch of: 336, 338, 340, 343, 347
Argives: 40 f.
Aristogeiton: 3
Aristotle: 60[34]
Armilustrium: 606
Arminius: 139
Arsinoe,
    financial records at temple of Jupiter Capitolinus: 494, 567
    festivities at in honour of Caracalla: 583
Arsinoe II: 14, 29, 32, 35, 36, 39
    altars to at Alexandria: 39[50]
Arsinoe III: 39
Arsinoe Philadelphus, priesthood of: 15[64]
Arsinoe-Zephyritis: 39
Arsinoeia: 36
Artabanus: 535[361]
Artemis Azzanathkona: 593
Artemis: 39, 492, 618
    temple of at Ephesus: 23, 549[444], 551
    temple of at Termessus: 548[440]
    cult of at Ephesus: 564[541]
    choristers of at Ephesus: 568
    eulogized: 571
Artemis Soteira, shrine of at Megara: 548[438]
Artemisium, at Naples: 546[430]
Arval Brethren: 297

offer sacrifices: 483 ff., 518
see also Acts of Arval Brethren
Arverni: 581
Asclepius: 43, 342
    temple of at Pergamum: 23
    temple of at Messene: 122[181]
    eulogized: 571
Asia,
    provincial festival of: 551[463], 577, 577[627]
    imperial choir of: 569, 586
    provincial cult of: 572
    provincial council of: 586
Asians: 126 f.
Asiarch: 577
Asklepios and Hygieia, temple of at Gytheum: 552, 564[541]
assimilation: 28 f., 341
Atespatus: 535, 535[363]
Athene: 6, 17, 34, 40
Athene Polias: 341, 522[285]
Athens: 25
Atia: 80
Atlas: 538
atrium Vestae: 89[44]
Attalids, civic cults of: 18
Attalistai: 18
Attalus III: 22, 23
attributes, of a god given to a ruler: 29 f.
Aufidia Antiochis: 125[197]
Aufidius Coresnius Marcellus: 601
C. Aufidius Victorinus: 396[38]
Aug. sacr.,
    significance of: 438 f., 442 ff.
    as stereotype: 444 f.
Augurius: 281, 578
Augusta,
    implication of: 425, 465
Augusta Minerva: 450
Augustales: 110, 118[148], 379[16], 476[9], 576, 579, 585, 586, 609-616
    origins of: 609
    cult of emperor: 610 ff.

association with *cultores domus divinae*: 612
  performance of rites: 613 f., 614[21,] 616
  shrines of: 613[18]
  dedications by: 613[20]
  superintend cult of Lares Augusti: 615 f., 616
  social functions of: 616
Augustales Mercuriales: 609
Augustalia: 162
Augustan Concordia: 461
Augustan days, in Egyptian documents: 494 f.
Augustan Fides: 461
Augustan Fortune: 461
Augustan Gods,
  use of genitive: 446, 446[2], 448
  use of adjective: 446 ff., 446[6]
Augustan insignia: 117, 154, 154[27]
Augustan Pax: 461
Augustan Pietas: 461
Augustan Providentia: 461
Augustan Salus: 461
Augustan Victory: 461
Augustan Virtus: 461
Augusteum: 327[49], 512, 519, 524 f., 524[298, 299], 560[509], 572, 584, 618, 619
Augusti,
  applied to divinity: 462 ff.
  implication of: 463 ff.
Augustus: 79[44], 82-92, 104, 105[53], 233[61-3], 238[83], 240, 270, 270[6], 271,
    271[13], 273, 285, 299, 330, 362 , 380, 380[23], 384, 387, 388, 401[22],
    424[10], 439, 443, 449, 451, 453, 453[48], 454[51], 458, 460, 463, 468, 472,
    484, 487, 490[92], 491[94], 517, 520[275], 521[280, 281, 283], 569, 586, 611, 614,
    616
  called *theos*: 28[49]
  transforms Dea Roma: 52
  moderation of: 55
  statue of at Pantheon: 78[41], 83[4], 547
  statue of in guise of Apollo: 82
  needs sacralization in cult: 83
  statue of as Apollo: 83, 90[50]
  religious policy of in Rome: 83 ff.
  objects to statues in precious metal: 83[4]

given title *Augustus*: 84, 84[8-9], 87, 90

attribution of *numen* to: 86

accepts title *pater patriae*: 87, 108[75]

associated with state deities: 87

promotes Mars: 87

emphasizes Apollo: 87 f., 87[32], 88[36]

emphasizes Jupiter: 88, 88[38]

link with Mercury: 88, 88[39]

house of on Palatine: 88[37], 89[44], 90[50]

link with Jupiter: 88[38], 128

identified with Mercury: 88[40]

as Pontifex Maximus: 89, 99, 117

proximity to gods: 89

as focal point of state religion: 89 f.

ascription of divinity to in lifetime: 90 f.

overall policy of: 90 f.

unofficial policy of: 90 f., 91[55 f.]

myth of special nature of: 90[50], 91[52]

possessed of special power: 90[50]

cult of *genius* of: 91[55]

policy in Western provinces: 92 f.

private cult of: 92[56]

visits Gaul: 97 f., 98 f.

inspires Lugdunum altar: 103

granted civic crown: 108

compared with Jupiter: 108[75]

receives shield of virtues: 109, 111

virtues of: 109

insignia of on monuments: 110, 111 f.

link with Victory: 111 ff.

statuette of: 124, 532, 545

cult of without Roma: 130

oath to at Gangra: 130[233]

birthday of: 132[244], 406, 483, 484, 484[53], 484[57], 485, 488[78], 489, 490, 491, 491[103], 492, 495, 569, 605,

given *torques* by Three Gauls: 137

inscription to at Noricum: 140

visits Spain: 142, 143, 172

stays at Tarraco: 146

installs ruler cult in newly pacified territories: 148

consecrated *divus*: 150 f.
Eternity of: 151, 152[13], 154
represented as Jupiter: 153, 153[19]
as *divus*: 159 f.
reply to Tarraconians: 171, 503
divinity of: 171[5]
visits Tarraco: 172, 500
adopts Tiberius as successor: 182, 184
reconstructs temples: 197
regulates imperial cult: 198, 390
enters Rome overnight: 205
never visited Africa: 265
worshipped without Roma: 273[21]
as Zeus: 274[27]
founds colonies in Mauretania: 285
municipal cult of in Asia: 297[21]
purpose of in installing provincial cults: 299
never visited Sardinia: 299[33]
municipal cult of without Roma: 363[14]
libations to: 375[2]
birthday celebrated at Narbo: 379
birthday celebrated at Forum Clodii: 380
genius of at Forum Clodii: 381[29]
acts of cult to: 385[49]
"divinity" of: 387
linked with deity: 436 ff.
dedication to: 445
coins show victories belong to emperor: 467[88]
between gods and men: 472
paid cult through deified Abstractions: 472
anniversaries observed at Narbo: 482
festivals of: 483 f., 496[136]
municipal temple of at Cumae: 490
occasions of: 490 f.
marries Livia: 495
receives sacrifice on anniversaries: 505 f.
birthday celebrated by sacrifice: 509, 510, 516
supplication to?: 509[219]
sacred contest to, at Naples: 510[221]
image of: 514

statue of: 523
temple of at Puteoli?: 524[299]
image of as boy: 533
bust of: 535, 535[363], 540[385], 545
statue of at Forum Clodii: 537
image placed in temples: 548
temple of at Sardis: 548
statue of at Delos: 549
tensa of: 555[490]
image of at Gytheum: 564, 566
triple invocation to by seafarers: 532, 569, 569[573]
name of included in Carmen Saliare: 570
birthday of marked by games: 576
birthday of marked by banquets: 585
standardizes military practice: 593 f.
see also Octavian

Augustus, Augusti:
title of emperor(s) in general: 132, 231, 231[49], 234, 234[68], 237[77], 270, 274[31], 275, 275[36-37], 304, 310, 318, 321, 322, 326, 327, 331, 332, 333, 334, 335, 355, 364, 365, 380[23], 388-396, 397-422, 436-445, 446, 448, 457, 462-465, 471, 473, 508

Augustus/a:
means 'of Augustus': 425 f.
applied to gods: 446 ff., 450 f., 453[44], 462
as conventional epithet: 448 f., 449
used to appropriate god's power for emperor: 448 ff., 454, 457
implies identification with god?: 449 f., 449[19,23]
implication of: 462 ff., 462[55]

Augustus Acionna: 450
Augustus and Livia, temple of at Vienne: 167[117], 308[1]
Augustus Apollo: 450
Augustus *deus*: 452 f.
Augustus Mars Britovius: 504, 526
Augustus Mars Mullo: 450
Augustus Mercurius: 450
Augustus Rudiobus: 450
Augustus: see also Octavian
Aur(elius) Si[---]us: 605
Aurelian: 433[45], 449
Aurelius Italicus: 551

Aurelius Leontes: 589
Aurelius Victorinus: 606
L. Aurelius Verus: 233[61], 264[35], 275[36], 310, 320, 321, 327[49], 424[9], 587
    birthday of: 487[77], 491[104], 495, 538, 582
    adoption of: 488[77], 498
    dies imperii of: 496[135]
    statue of: 523[293], 542, 542[395]
    silver-plate bust of: 536, 543
    likeness of: 538, 539
    likeness of in Egypt: 548
Marcus Aurelius: 183, 233[61], 264[35], 275[36], 301, 305, 310, 312[27], 313[32], 320, 321, 325, 327, 327[49], 366, 424[9], 445, 493, 494, 495, 498[150], 546, 555
    natalis: 132[244]
    as Caesar: 330
    as heir apparent: 330[68]
    associated as Caesar with Antoninus Pius: 331[73]
    portraits of: 337
    and Fortuna: 466
    birthday of: 487[77], 491[104], 496[134], 497, 578, 601
    adoption of: 488[77], 498
    victories of: 493 f.
    receives *trib. pot.*: 493[119]
    dies imperii of: 495, 496[135]
    gold statue of: 522[289]
    statuettes of in households: 533
    gold bust of: 535 f., 543
    bust of: 536, 538
    likeness of: 539, 548
    statue of: 541, 542[396]
    and Commodus, letter of to Athenian *gerousia*: 545, 552
    and Commodus, policy of on imperial images: 545
    eikon of: 546
    image placed in temple: 548
    and L. Aurelius Verus, letter of to Ephesian *gerousia*: 552
    returns to Rome?: 569[567]
    reduces expense of gladiatorial games: 580
    birthday of marked by banquet: 587
T. Aurelius Decimus: 600
C. Aur(elius) Sigillius: 600

Avidius Cassius: 492[109]
accession of: 492
[A]trectius At[ili]a[nus]: 601

Bacchus: 337 ff., 338[112], 340
Baetica,
    provincial council of: 219 f., 220[3]
    provincial cult of: 219 ff., 227, 238 f., 279 f.
    titles of provincial priests: 269, 279, 279[55], 355
Balbinus: 595
    statue of: 562[525]
banquets: 584 ff.
    associated with imperial anniversaries: 585 ff.
    in imperial cult of provinces: 586 f.
Basilica Julia: 161
M. Bassaeus Rufus, statue of: 546
Batavi: 354, 358, 360, 360[40]
bell, employed in ceremonies at Tarraco: 504 f., 526
Bellum Cantabricum: 172, 174
benefactors,
    cult of: 3
    divine honours to: 11 f., 27
Beneventum, arch at: 529
Berenice: 14, 15
Berenice II: 15, 39
birthday of emperor,
    observed in west: 497 f.
    celebrated by panegyrics: 572[593]
Bithynians: 126 f.
Bituriges Cubi: 535, 581
Blandina: 578
Blessings and Virtues, see Abstractions: 455 ff.
Bocchus: 112
Boii: 135, 579
Bonus Eventus: 460
Bostar: 291[56]
Boudicca: 196, 216
    revolt of: 202 f.
bowing, as cult act: 528, 534
Brasidas: 3

Brescia, relief at: 512
Britain,
   provincial cult of: 217 f.
   provincial cult of under Claudius: 288
   provincial council of: 410, 410[47]
   provincial patrons of: 410
Britannia: 231[50]
Britannicus, image carried in procession: 556
Brixia, Capitoline temple at: 546
Bructeri: 354, 359, 359[34]
Brutus: 534
Marcus Bucc[onius?]: 324
L. Burbuleius Optatus Ligarianus: 253
busts: 535 f.
busts, on altar of Three Gauls: 121 ff., 124[192]
busts, transportation of: 123 f., 243[20]
   in cult of Gallia Narbonensis: 242 f.

C. Caecilius Gallus: 263, 267
C. Caesar: 330[65], 439, 505, 614
   birthday of: 483, 491[101]
C. Calpurnius Flaccus: 247
C. Catullius Deciminus: 322 f.
C. Claudius Diaphenes: 177
C. Clodius Crescens: 539
C. Clodius Magnus: 539
C. Cornelius Egrilianus: 499
C. Cornelius Gallus: 130[231], 198, 199[23]
Caecilia Nigellina: 268
L. Caecilius Urbanus: 434
Q. Caecilius Metellus Pius: 55
Caeculus: 448
Caelius Vibianus: 418
Caere, altar of C. Manlius at: 510 f.
Caesar: 54, 55, 87[27], 90[48], 108[71-72], 424[10], 451, 473, 483, 491[94]
   cult of: 47 f.
   cult of at Mytilene: 51
   link with Romulus: 53
   as god: 56
   divine ancestry of: 56, 87[28]

priesthoods of: 56
divine honours of: 56 ff.
identified with Romulus: 57, 59 f.
monuments of on Capitol: 57
statue carried in procession: 58, 73², 555, 562⁵³¹
shares temple with Quirinus: 58 f.
statues of: 59, 59²⁴ ᶠᶠ·, 60, 61
divine honours of in 44 B.C.: 60 f.
chair carried to theatre: 61 f., 61⁴⁹
symbols carried in procession to circus: 62
and his Clementia, temple to: 62 f., 76, 152¹⁷
Anthony as priest of: 62 f., 65⁷²
as Iuppiter Iulius: 62 ff.
identified with Jupiter: 63
cult image of: 63 f.
deification in lifetime: 63 f.
as Divus Iulius: 64
deification effected after death: 64 f.
relationship with Jupiter: 66 f.
as king: 67 f.
kingly trappings of: 68 f.
acclaimed as king: 69
as de facto monarch: 70 f.
final position of: 71 f.
significance of career: 72
cult of slain dictator: 73
funeral rites of: 73
monument of on site of cremation: 73³
star of: 74, 74¹¹
statue in temple of Venus Genetrix: 74, 76
completion of apotheosis: 75
not first of divi: 83
granted civic crown: 108
begins Curia Iulia: 111
re-erects Victories on Capitol: 112
link with Victory: 114, 115¹²⁹
"unconquered": 115
link with Venus Genetrix: 115¹²⁸
divine honours of in East: 127
enrolled among Gods of Rome: 159⁶³

at Munda: 175
as title: 329 ff.
military cult of: 330
significance of term: 333 ff.
use of term: 334[82]
gives special meaning to *divus*: 426[22]
qualities celebrated on coins: 457
birthday of: 489
deposits *eikon* of Cleopatra: 545
golden chair of: 555
clothed ivory statue of: 562[531]
L. Caesar: 330[65], 381, 614
birthday of: 491[101]
Caesar, significance of: 333 f.
Caesar(s), cult of at Altar of Three Gauls: 326 ff., 348, 365 f.
Caesarea, temple of Roma and Augustus at: 129, 147, 521
Caesarea, festival of: 514, 528, 617
at Gytheum: 552
Isthmian: 569
Caesares,
living members of imperial house: 223, 224, 231, 232, 233, 233[60-63], 234, 234[65], 237, 238[80], 239[86], 318, 319, 321, 326, 328, 328[53], 331, 332, 335, 614, 614[25]
Caesares imperatores, interpretation of: 231 ff.
Caesareum: 56, 187, 439, 519, 524[299], 556, 569, 589 f., 589[693], 590, 595
at Alexandria: 569
Caesars, altar of at Lugdunum: 317
calendar: 132, 499
of imperial cult: 482 ff.
of Roman state: 482 ff.
of Roman state, later development of: 486[66]
local: 487
on papyri: 488 f.
preserved in manuscript: 489
anniversaries of Roman observed in East: 495 f.
in western provinces: 499 f.
in western imperial cult: 500 f.
regulated by provincial governor: 500[159]
anniversaries of Roman observed in West: 517 f.
Caligula: see Gaius

Callicrates: 39
Calpurnia: 60[38]
L. Calpurnius Augustalis: 228[35]
Camée de Vienne: 471
Camillus: 456, 536
Campus Agrippae: 86[16]
Campus Martius: 84[7], 205[47], 206
Camulodunum: 195 ff., 218
    temple at: 103[39], 195 ff., 282, 308[3]
    development of ruler cult at: 199 ff.
    see further Temple of Divus Claudius at Camulodunum
Camuni: 328
Cancellaria Reliefs: 468
Candidus: 444
candles, ritual use of: 567 f.
Cantabri: 176
Capitol: 88, 112, 456, 484
    sacrifices on: 484 f., 506
    vows made and paid: 507
Capitolia: 522
Capitoline games: 478
Capitoline gods: 529
Capitoline temple: 141[298]
Capitoline Triad: 340, 441, 461, 478, 506, 507, 554
Capitolium,
    of Narbo: 196, 249 ff.
    of Rome: 252
Captiline Games: 572
Caracalla: 258, 305, 306 f., 318, 319, 320[18], 321, 321[21], 322, 325, 327,
    330, 333, 338, 342, 342[149], 343, 343[156], 344, 345, 347, 348, 348[195],
    365, 366, 403, 407, 419[76], 428[38], 434, 441, 451[34], 453[50], 473[131], 478[16],
    488, 600, 603
    visits Gorsium: 306
    becomes Augustus: 329, 331, 332, 333, 599
    becomes Caesar: 329, 331, 332, 333, 494
    becomes princeps iuventutis: 329[60]
    Alexander mania of: 342[141]
    at Alexandria: 339[120]
    born at Lugdunum: 347
    birthday of: 487[77], 491[104], 494, 496[134], 551, 583

bust of: 537, 538, 542[396]
statue of: 539
likeness of in temples of at Oxyrhynchus: 549
statue of at Arsinoe: 583
Caratacus: 197
Carausius: 467, 468
P. Carisius: 142
Carmen Saliare: 84[7]
carmen saeculare: 88, 570, 570[575]
Carnutes: 101
Cassander: 12
Cassius: 71, 534
M. Cassius Caecilianus: 368
Castor and Pollux, temple of: 141[298], 378
Castulo, equestrian cursus at: 221 ff.
Catulus: 57
celebrations of imperial cult,
    onlookers: 528 f.
    participation in: 528 ff.
    distributions of wine and incense for: 530 f., 530[333], 531
    private offerings: 531
P. Celer: 284[18]
census, of Three Gauls: 332 f., 332[76]
P. Cere Saturninus: 536
ceremonial, of imperial cult: 475 ff.
Cereres: 227[33]
    priests of: 258 f., 260, 266, 268
Ceres: 451[37], 462[55]
Ceres Augusta: 464
Ceres Mater, altar of: 102
Ceres-Demeter: 342
Cerialis Anicius: 212, 215
Cherusci: 139
Christ, cult of: 521[278]
Christians: 281, 527 f., 530, 533, 533 f., 543, 565, 573, 577
    opposed to ruler cult: 40
    persecuted at Lyon: 135, 136, 578 f., 579[636], 580, 580[640]
Cicero: 47
Cimbri: 54
circus, associated with imperial cult: 581 f., 582[653]

city-States, cults of: 11 f.
civic crown: 86²⁰, 107 f.
civitas Coriosolitum: 364
civitas Taunensium: 498¹⁴⁸
Claudius: 199, 233, 240, 240³, 270, 270⁴, 270⁶, 270⁷, 271, 272¹⁸, 290,
    292, 293, 316⁵¹, 409, 410, 424¹⁰, 458, 464, 497, 506, 508
    date born at Lugdunum: 98 f., 500¹⁶³
    fiftieth birthday of: 104
    sanctions groves: 104
    ducked in river: 134²⁵⁹, 573, 573⁵⁹⁶
    tablet at Lugdunum: 137²⁷⁵
    and Noricum: 139, 141
    deification of: 158
    place in provincial cults of Tarraconensis and Lusitania: 158
    temple of at Camulodunum: 195
    letter to Thasians: 198
    policy on ruler cult: 198 f.
    consecration of: 202
    letter to hymnodes: 271
    as Zeus: 274²⁷
    divides Mauretania: 282, 286, 292
    establishes colonies and municipalities in the Mauretaniae: 287
    divus title of: 297¹⁶
    equestrian statue of ?: 318¹⁰
    altar cult of at Camulodunum: 390
    birthday of: 484, 487, 487⁷⁵, 488⁷⁸, 491, 497¹⁴³, 603
    accepts honours from Alexandrians: 495¹²⁷
    statue of: 523
    bust of: 542
    refuses gold statue of Pax Augusta Claudiana: 544
    letter to Alexandrians: 550
    cult of his *eikones*: 564
Cl(audius) Piso: 602
M. Claudius Germanus: 289
Q. Claudius Saturninus: 289
Tiberius Claudius Claudianus: 598
Ti. Claudius Cogidubnus: 423
Tiberius Claudius Secundus: 538
Clementia: 86¹⁶, 458, 459, 460, 461
    sacrifice to: 507

Clementia Augusti: 470
Clementia Caesaris: 457
Clementia Nostra: 474
Cleopatra: 15, 67, 109, 111[97]
  eikon beside cult statue of Venus Genetrix: 79, 545
Cleopatra Selene: 111[97], 285, 286
client states: 146 ff.
Clodius Albinus: 327, 328[52], 332, 348[195]
  named Caesar: 329
  given Caesar title: 330[69]
  defeated at Lugdunum: 332, 365, 501
  at Lugdunum: 347
Cogidubnus: 217, 410[45], 427
coh(ors) I Sept(imia) Belg(arum) Aldxandrian(a): 603
cohors I Septimia Belgarum Gordiana: 607
cohors II Breucorum Gordiana: 607
cohors II Maurorum: 603
cohors II Tungrorum Gordiana: 598
cohors III Britannorum: 441
cohors IV Vigilum: 546
cohors VI Asturum: 354, 358, 358[30], 359, 359[34], 360, 360[40]
cohors VI Praetoria: 498
cohors XX Palmyrenorum: 419, 593 f.
coins, choice of types: 458, 458[25]
Colonia Claudia Ara Agrippinensis: 137
comet, appearance of: 64[63]
Commagene, state cult of: 18 ff., 21, 24
Commodus: 258, 311, 312[24], 320, 326, 328, 329, 330, 338, 453, 458, 473,
  496[133], 546, 580
  post mortem: 328[51]
  consecration of: 337, 348, 348[193]
  festival of: 488[77]
  birthday of: 488[78], 495, 498[147], 604
  takes *toga virilis*: 498
  likeness of?: 538
  statue of: 542[396]
  golden chair of: 555
  identified with Hercules: 579[635]
  birthday marked by festivities: 586
Commodus Hercules: 520[274]

compita: 53, 55, 120, 376[4], 509[217], 511, 525
    ministri of cult at: 154[27]
    cult at: 616
concilium III Daciarum: 498[150]
Concordia: 116, 455, 458, 459, 460, 461, 468, 469, 507
    temple of at Rome: 484[57], 544[409]
    statuette of?: 539
Concordia Augusta: 86, 464
    image of: 539
Concordia Nova,
    temple of: 86[18]
Constantia: 458, 460
Constantia Augusti: 464
Constantine,
    removes statues of self: 546
    statue of: 562, 564[538], 567 f.
    statue accompanied by torches: 564
    builds *aedes gentis Flaviae* at Hispellum: 576, 576[621]
Constantius II, occasions of: 489
constitution,
    of altars: 203 ff.
    of temples: 210 ff.
conventus,
    cult of in Northwest Spain: 298, 356[19]
    priests of: 356, 328[53]
conventus Asturum, priesthood of: 356
conventus Noricorum, assembly room of?: 140
Core: 571
Cornelia, mother of Gracchi: 53
P. Cornelius Dolabella: 145
P. Cornelius Scipio: 514, 528
Cotta Maximus: 532, 532[341]
councils, of provinces: 93
Counts Zichy: 303
cow, as sacrificial victim: 506 f.
L. Crescentius Gratinus: 603
Crispina: 560[511]
crown, radiate: 153[20]
crowns: 477 f., 477[12], 477[15], 478[16]
cult image: 22

carried in procession at Rome: 557
cult names, applied to rulers: 26
cult places, in western ruler cult: 518 ff.
cult statue: 520 ff.
    colossal: 521
    clothing of: 566
cult title, attached to a ruler's name: 29
cultores,
    of imperial image and Lares: 434, 490[92], 537 f., 538[375], 612[16], 615[34]
    of *domus divina*: 434, 512[238], 612, 613
    of *domus Augusta*: 540, 541, 613[17]
Cumae,
    calendar at: 490
    municipal temple of Augustus at: 490
    rites at: 509 f., 517
cuneus Frisionum Aballavensium Philipp(ianorum): 607
curator: 248[53]
    at Tarraco: 247, 247[50]
    at Narbo: 247 f., 254, 254[93]
Curia Iulia: 111, 111[97]
Cybele: 342
    sanctuary of at Lugdunum: 312[24], 314[42]
Cyrene: 36

Dacia,
    provincial cult of: 301 f.
    provincial council of: 302, 302[8]
    personification of: 600
Dalmatia, regional cults in: 302
daimon, libation to: 376[2]
Damona: 443
Daphnis: 80[58]
Darius: 8, 534
dated inscriptions: 593 ff.
    use of as evidence: 486 f.
dative,
    of dedication: 437[8]
    of honour: 440 ff., 440[24]
    votive: 437 f., 440, 440[24]
day, named after a ruler: 26

Dea Caelestis: 342, 342[146], 453[50]
Dea Dia: 531, 531[339]
Dea Iuno: 342
Dea Roma: 48 ff., 72, 295, 594, 596
    included in cult of Hither Spain: 273, 276
Dea Vagdavercustis: 505[190]
Decius, accession of: 492
dedications: 34 f., 436 ff.
    of altars: 203 ff.
deification: 40
    private: 77 f.
    ritual of: 328[50]
    expresses gratitude: 387[64]
deified concepts, theology of: 459 ff.
deified females, priesthood of: 166
Delphi, authority of: 6
Demeter: 566, 571
    mysteries of at Ephesus: 574[604]
Demeter Thesmophoros, mysteries of: 571
Demetrius of Phalerum: 12
Demetrius Poliorcetes: 6[4], 20, 22, 23, 25[22], 28, 30, 34, 36, 37, 38, 41, 42,
    44, 57, 113, 375[2]
    honours to: 12, 21
    associates of: 12[49]
    dismounts from chariot: 27
democracy, effect of: 6
Demos: 583
    cult of: 50[26f.]
    of the Athenians: 52
Deus Albius: 443
Deus Borvo: 444
Deus Hercules: 444
Deus Mars Augustus: 450
Deus Mercurius: 444
Di Augusti: 451, 451[34], 451[37], 523, 613[20]
Di Comites: 469
Di Conservatores: 451
Di Iuvantes: 451
Di Manes: 51
Di Mauri: 451

Di Militares: 451
Di Penates: 533, 610
Diadochi: 113, 456
    cults of: 12
Diana: 117, 305, 531
Diana Aug(usta): 613[17]
Dikaios: 457
Dike: 456
Diocletian: 320[18], 356[24], 400[20], 474
    persecution of: 578
Diocletian and Maximian, Jovian-Herculian ideology of: 338
Diodorus Pasporus: 12[43]
Dion of Syracuse: 4, 4[9], 38
Dionysiac Mysteries: 573
Dionysus: 38, 48, 80
    temple of at Teos: 23
    statue of: 125[197]
    temple of near Piraeus: 549
Dionysus and Tiberius, combined cult of: 567, 569
Dioscuri: 342
Disciplina: 390, 459, 460
    Diva Augusta: 242, 278, 312[26], 485, 520
    in cult of Lusitania: 157, 158
    omitted at Camulodunum temple: 216, 217
    birthday of: 496[134]
    sacrifice to: 506, 507
    statue of carried in procession: 555
Diva Claudia: 485
Diva Domitilla Augusta: 465[76]
Diva Drusilla: 520[274]
    image of carried in procession: 556
Diva Faustina,
    silver bust of: 539
    eikon of: 546
    gold statue of taken in procession: 555
Diva Matidia, birthday of: 496[134]
Diva Poppaea: 485
Diva Sabina: 520[277]
Divi,
    retain place in *fasti*: 297

included in cult of Three Gauls: 309 f., 311
importance of under Antonines: 311 f., 311²², 326
political importance of under Severi: 327
cult of: 419
priests of: 486
temples of in Rome: 486
birthdays of under Antonines: 501
divina,
    implication of: 424 ff.
divine birth, legends of: 8²⁰, 80, 80⁵²
divine honours: 11, 12, 21 ff., 32 ff., 39 f.
    'qua' king: 13
    attitude to: 41
    refusal of: 127²⁰⁶
divinity,
    as honour earned by benefactions: 40
    opposition to: 40 f.
divinus,
    shifts in meaning: 429
    applied to living emperor: 430 f., 431⁵¹
Divus Antoninus Pius,
    birthday of: 498
    dies imperii of: 498¹⁴⁸
    temple of at Rome: 546
Divus Augustus: 138²⁸², 242, 274, 278, 296, 296⁸, 312²⁶, 427, 461, 483⁵¹,
    485, 489⁸⁸, 517, 524, 618
    temple of at Tarraco: 150 ff., 163, 198, 213⁸⁹, 328⁵¹, 346¹⁷⁶, 427
    provincial cult of in Tarraconensis: 155
    in cult of Lusitania: 157, 157⁴⁸, 158
    worship of at Rome: 158 ff., 506¹⁹⁷
    statue accompanies likenesses of gods: 160⁶⁴
    eikon of in temple of Mars Ultor: 161, 161⁷²
    temple of at Rome: 161, 182 f., 197, 296¹⁵, 427, 484, 484⁵⁷, 485⁵⁹,
    506, 520, 546
    official cult of: 161 ff.
    image of at Bovillae: 162⁷⁸
    cult of at Tarraco: 163
    statue of by theatre of Marcellus: 163⁸⁴
    priesthood of: 165 f.
    omitted at Camulodunum temple: 216, 217

municipal temple of at Narbo: 245 f., 246[40], 254
linked with temple at Tarraco: 316
begins list of *divi*: 451
festivals of: 484 ff.
birthday of: 495, 496[134], 497, 505[191], 506
sacrifice to: 506, 508, 507, 512
rites before statue of: 520[274]
pulvinar of: 527
mausoleum of: 539
image of at Ephesus: 551
eikon of at Gytheum: 552
statue of carried in procession: 555
mysteries of: 567
image of at Pergamum: 573
dedication of temple of at Rome: 576, 585
games in honor of: 576
Divus Augustus and Diva Augusta, temple of at Vienne: 167[117], 308[1]
Divus Augustus Pater: 151[9]
Divus Claudius: 274, 278, 485, 486[66]
temple of at Camulodunum: 197, 200, 202, 213 ff., 216[96], 218
temple of in Rome: 202
temple of on Mons Caelius: 217, 202, 296 f.
not in cult of Narbonensis: 245[32]
cult of: 297[19]
birthday of: 497[141]
sacrifice to: 507, 508
Divus Claudius II: 469
Divus Hadrianus: 520[277]
dies imperii of: 496[135]
vicennalia of: 569[567]
divus, in Tacitean usage: 214 f.
Divus Iulius: 76, 427
temple of at Rome: 73, 75 f., 76[18], 87, 152[17], 546
cult of at Ephesus: 76 f.
celebrated in Eclogues: 78
statue in Pantheon: 83[4]
priest of at Rusicade: 267[61]
flamen of: 476
birthday of: 489[85], 490, 529
Divus Marcus, temple of at Gorsium: 305

Divus Nerva, birthday of: 496[134], 498[147]
Divus Severus, birthday of: 551
Divus Verus,
    gold statues of at Tarraco: 179[58], 559
    birthday of: 493, 493[121]
    golden clothes of?: 563
Doclea: 329
Dolabella: 73
Domita: 525
Domitia Europes: 525[302]
Domitian: 219, 223, 224, 230, 231, 234, 234[68], 235[70], 237, 238, 238[80], 238[83], 261, 267, 297, 297[20], 298[28], 298[29], 302, 311, 328[53], 334, 341, 427[24], 429[43], 430, 442, 478, 480, 486[66], 547
    divides Moesia: 146
    building programme of: 486[68]
    gold likeness of: 546
    golden chair of: 555
    institutes Capitoline games: 572
Domitilla: 297[20]
L. Domitius Ahenobarbus: 122, 145
Cn. Domitius Polycarpus: 525[302]
domus, definition of: 423 f.
domus Augusta: 151, 299, 424 f., 425[18], 426, 433, 611[13]
domus divina: 160, 217, 345, 346, 391, 393, 416, 417, 423-435, 541, 605
    attested in Britain: 417
    honoured on continent: 417, 417[69]
    in literary sources: 423
    in inscriptions: 423 f.
    refers to living members of imperial house: 427 ff.
    on par with emperor himself: 433 ff.
    direct dedications to: 434 f.
domus imperatoria: 132, 145, 217, 424, 430, 485, 492[113], 494, 507, 516, 548, 612
Drimacus: 3
Druids: 101
Drusilla: 377, 485[60]
    birthday of: 485
Drusus, stepson of Augustus: 138, 468
    at Lugdunum: 97, 98, 99, 100, 142
    cenotaph of: 138, 500[162]

dedicates temple among Lingones: 144
dedicates altar at Lugdunum: 308, 328
birthday of: 491[101]
supplicatio at cenotaph of: 502, 502[173]
Drusus, son of Tiberius: 133, 162[75], 362[12], 487[74], 532[344]
   birthday celebrated by supplication to Vesta: 516
   statue of: 521[283]
   image carried in procession: 556
dynastic cults: 13 ff.

Edusa: 448
Egnatius Victor: 602
C. Egrilius Fuscianus: 600
Egypt,
   divine power of ruler in: 38 f., 199
   ruler cult in: 492 ff., 493[116]
Eirene: 456
Elagabalus: 258, 325, 333, 342[146], 349, 365, 366, 541
   restores amphitheatre at Tarraco: 280
   picture of in senate house: 534
Elder Cato: 545
Elder Scipio: 545, 555
Eleusis, sanctuary of: 548
Embassy, of Mytileneans: 172, 177
Embassy, of Spaniards: 150, 155, 158, 163, 173, 213[89], 284
Emerita,
   local ruler cult at: 183
   provincial temple at: 156, 178
   municipal temple at: 174[21], 183, 183[25]
   circus at: 281[69], 582[655]
   sacrifice at: 503
   imperial image at: 558
Empedocles: 42
emperor,
   cult of in Celtic World: 389 ff.
   associated with divinity in a dedication: 436 f.
   dedications to *ut deus*: 437 ff., 443[36]
   dedications to in isolation: 438 ff.
   associated with deity other than Roma: 439 ff.
   on par with gods: 445

birthday celebrated by sacrifice in western provinces: 516
ambiguous status of: 518
shown as god: 520 f., 520[273]
Ennius: 53
L. Ennius: 532
ephebes: 569[570]
Ephesus,
 temple of Roma and Divus Iulius at: 77, 188
 imperial temple associated with *vota*: 496, 496[138]
ephithets: 26 ff.
Epicurus: 7
Epidaurus, liturgy at: 568[563]
Epigoni: 12
Epimenides: 42
epiphany, of a ruler: 28
Epona: 444
epulum Iovis: 585
Etnosus: 441
Euangelia: 24[19]
Euhemerism: 54
Euhemerus: 7
eulogies, in ruler cult: 571 ff., 572[591]
Eulogius: 281, 578
Eumenes II: 18
Eumenistai: 18
Eunomia: 456
Eusebes: 457
ex-voto's: 38 f., 43, 43[80]

Fabia Bira: 292, 293
Fabius, martyred at Caesarea: 288[41], 578
Fabius Maximus: 457
Paullus Fabius Maximus: 47, 495
fabri Narbonenses: 249 ff.
Sextus Fadius Secundus Musa: 249, 249[63], 250, 252, 253, 254, 254[93]
Fasti Ostienses: 487
Faustina the Elder,
 birthday of: 489
 silver bust of: 542[395]
Faustina the Younger: 346, 347, 424[9]

Faustus: 537
Fecunditas: 458, 460
Felicitas: 86, 457, 460, 461, 466, 470, 507
Felicitas Augusti/Augusta: 463, 466
Felicitas Tiberi: 86[22], 466
Felix: 539
    medallion of: 308, 316, 316[53]
Feriale Campanum: 490
Feriale Cumanum: 116, 493, 509 f., 513
Feriale Duranum: 418 f., 488 f., 493, 501, 517, 562, 565[545], 593 ff.
    follows conventions of Roman religion: 501
    prescribes sacrifices/supplications: 507 f., 595 f.
    as standard calendar: 593 f.
    attested by dated inscriptions: 597 ff.
    list of festivals: 598 ff.
festivals: 24 f.
    bear name of ruler: 24
    imperial celebrated in Rome: 483 ff.
    imperial celebrated in Italy: 490 ff.
    imperial celebrated in eastern provinces: 492 ff.
    imperial celebrated in western provinces: 497 ff., 515 ff.
    of imperial cult, celebration forbidden: 530[330]
    processions at provincial in east: 557
    in honour of emperor, celebrated by games: 577
    martyrdom of Christians at imperial: 577
festive clothing: 529
festive dress, of common people: 481, 481[38], 481[41]
Festus: 605
Fides: 455, 456, 460, 468, 469
fillets: 475, 475[3], 476[5]
flamen Dialis: 56[3], 62, 66, 89[43], 426, 476, 478, 479
flamen Martialis: 426
flamen Quirinalis: 63, 63[60]
Flamines Maiores, head-gear of: 476
Flavia Germanilla: 289, 292
Flavian family, gentilitial cult of: 430[51]
Flavius Aelianus: 606
Flavius Flavialis: 443
Flavius Lunaris: 443
[T.] Fl(avius) Aper Commodianus: 601

T. Flavius Constans: 505[190]
T. Flavius Felix: 441
Titus Fla(vius) Rufinus: 498
T. Flavius Postuminus, statues of at temple of Mars Mullo: 547
Titus Flavius Praxias: 513[243]
T. Flavius Xenion: 495
T. Flaviu[s. .]arin[us]: 600
Fortuna: 86, 296, 390, 448, 455, 456, 458, 460, 461, 465[79], 466
statue of at Cuicul: 263
Fortuna Augusti: 86[21], 465, 466, 466[82]
Fortuna Caesaris: 86[21]
Fortuna Muliebris: 211
    temple of: 212
Fortuna Primigenia, temple of at Praeneste: 103, 547
Fortuna Redux: 86[21], 207, 459, 460, 461
    altar of: 102, 122, 122[180], 183
    sacrifice to: 507
Forum, as cult centre: 522, 523, 523[293]
Forum Boarium: 336
Forum Clodii,
    festivals at: 490
    rites at: 510
Forum Iulium: 87
founders of cities: 3
Fructuosus: 281, 578
[C.?] Fulvius Maximus: 445

Gaetuli: 285
Gaius: 35, 207, 233, 259, 265, 423, 430, 439, 441, 458, 464, 483[51], 484[57], 485[59], 528[318], 547, 547[435], 572
    plays role of a god: 30[67]
    gives games at Lugdunum: 134, 572, 580, 583
    entertained by Three Gauls: 137
    develops cult of Divus Augustus: 162, 485
    dedicates temple of Divus Augustus: 197, 484
    aware of human status: 199[27]
    institutes province of Mauretania Caesariensis: 259
    executes Ptolemy of Mauretania: 285
    as dominus noster: 334[84]
    swears by numen of sister: 377

Clementia of: 483[48]
birthday of: 484, 604
sacrifices to: 502
sacrifice for: 514
golden shield of: 555
transports image of Drusilla: 556
golden statue of: 562, 563
honoured by hymns: 570
celebrates dedication of temple of Divus Augustus: 576
Gaius Caesar: see C. Caesar
Galba: 86[21], 299, 333, 464, 485
and Fortuna: 465
image of carried in procession: 556
Gallia Narbonensis,
provincial council of: 248[56]
provincial charter of: see Lex Narbonensis
provincial cult of: 240 ff.
statue of provincial priest of: 223, 223[19]
Gallienus: 421, 507[206]
decennalia of: 554
procession of: 564
Gallus: 320[18]
games: 574 ff.
political significance of: 575 f., 575[612], 576[619]
relation to imperial cult: 575 f., 577, 581[652]
associated with emperor: 576
as liturgy of provincial priest: 577, 579
M. Gavius Firmus: 605
M. Gavius [?Appalius Maximus]: 396[38]
Gemma Augustea: 91, 128
genitive, replaced by corresponding derivative adjective: 426
genius,
libations to: 375, 375[2]
chief festival of: 375[2]
distinguished from *numen*: 377 ff., 377[11]
identified with *numen*: 377[10], 386
characteristics of: 382 f., 382[33]
representations of: 383, 383[36-37]
associated with candles, lamps: 567
Genius Augusti: 85[13], 376 ff., 461, 465, 506, 511, 537[375]

no state cult of under Augustus: 52
cult of: 84 f., 419
cups for libations to: 84[10]
libations to: 375, 375[2]
oath by: 377, 377[6]
sacrifice to: 507, 508 f.
cult of in western provinces: 516
altar of at Arles?: 519[268]
public cult of: 611
genius of Caesar, oath by: 377
Genius Populi Romani: 338[117], 461, 462, 464[69]
cult of: 50[26], 52
representation of: 382[35]
sacrifice to: 507
Genius Publicus: 456, 462
state cult of: 50[26], 52
sacrifices to: 382[35]
Gens Augusta: 128
altar of at Carthage: 128, 128[214]
shrine of at Carthage: 503
Gens Flavia: 273
cult of on Quirinal: 297[20]
Gens Iulia: 80, 162[78], 285
Gens Septimia: 520[273]
Germanicus: 133, 362[12], 487[74], 508[208], 532[344]
at Ara Ubiorum: 138
appointed *flamen Augustalis*: 110, 161 f., 162[75-76]
posthumous honours of: 161[69]
birthday of: 488[78], 490, 491[104], 508
triumphal arch of on Rhine: 500[162], 502[173]
birthday celebrated by supplication to Vesta: 517
statue of: 521[283]
ivory image of carried in procession: 556
acclaimed in Egypt: 570
Germanicus the Christian: 577[627]
Germany,
divided into Upper and Lower: 230, 230[47], 249
public *fiscus* of: 235
Gesacus: 449
Geta: 320[18], 322, 338, 342, 343, 365, 428[38], 434, 441, 473[131], 478[16], 603

given Augustus title: 318[11]
name erased in inscriptions: 322[26]
given Caesar title: 329, 331, 332, 599
claim to Augustus title: 330
included in cult of Three Gauls: 349
accession of: 492
gladiatorial contests,
    origins of: 574
    expense of: 580
god,
    appropriated by gentile adjective: 447 f.
    powers defined by epithet: 447 f., 447[11]
godhead, achieved through merit: 39 f.
gods, statues of Roman carried in procession: 554, 554[485]
Gordian: 445, 595
Gordian Caesar: 562[525]
Gorsium,
    seat of provincial worship of Lower Pannonia: 303 ff.
    becomes *municipium*: 306
Gottmensch: 34, 43, 44, 47
Gracchi: 457, 533
    cult of: 53
    statues of: 565
Grand Camée de France: 471
grass crown: 108[71]
groves: 103, 103[47]
gymnasia: 499
Gytheates, letter of Tiberius to: 159
Gytheum,
    imperial festival at: 514, 618
    thymelic contest at: 582

Hades: 43
Hadrian: 271, 274[31], 276, 279, 305[34], 308, 313, 313[31], 327, 328, 350, 355, 356, 362, 381, 410, 493, 515[256], 517, 520[278], 547[432], 569, 617
    emphasizes cult of Urbs Roma Aeterna: 128, 132, 266
    natalis: 132[244]
    visits Spain: 150
    builds new Capitolium at Narbo: 196, 252 ff.
    builds temple of Roma and Venus: 197

builds provincial temple of Three Gauls: 200, 217, 306, 316, 558
reforms British provincial cult?: 217
visits Tarraco: 247[50]
visits Gaul: 252 f., 314, 314[39]
enlarges cult of Three Gauls: 266[49], 314 f., 350, 364, 390
partitions Dacia: 302
restores temple of Divus Augustus at Tarraco: 305[34], 316, 358
builds and restores temples: 306, 314, 314[37]
builds temple at Nemausus: 306, 315, 315[47]
constructs provincial temple at Gorsium: 306, 316
journeys of: 306
visits Britain: 306
visits Lugdunum: 306
visits Pannonia: 306
attachment to Roma: 313
emphasizes *divi*: 313
linked with Jupiter: 337
establishes festival of Natalis Urbis: 356
founds priesthood of Urbs Roma: 356 f.
visits Egypt: 358[28], 493[119], 494
birthday of: 487[77], 488[78], 496[134], 497, 497[144]
dies imperii of: 491
adoption of: 495
visits western provinces: 500
accession celebrated by rites: 515[256]
given image of Augustus: 533
dedication to: 537
silver busts of: 542
eikones of at temple of Zeus Olympios: 548
likeness of in Egypt: 548
head of: 560
supposed temple of at Aegeae: 582[656]
accession of celebrated by festivities: 586
Hadrianeia: 577
Haos: 449
Harmodius: 3
hat,
    of provincial priest: 475 f., 476
    of municipal priest: 476, 476[6]
Haterii, relief of: 125[197]

Hector: 38, 42
Hekate, image of: 568
Hera: 6
    statue of at Argos: 521
Heracles: 4[7], 8
Heraion of Samos: 547[437], 548
Heraia: 25
Herculanei Augustales: 609,
Hercules: 46, 185, 337 ff., 338[112], 340, 342, 382, 448, 453, 469, 469[103], 605
    cult statue of: 341
Hercules Augustus: 449, 601
Hercules Magnus: 579[635]
Hercules Saxanus: 442
Herennius, accession of: 492
M. Herennius Albanus: 541
Heres Martea: 462
Herod the Great: 129, 147
Herodes: 577
heroes,
    cult of: 3-5, 185
    Roman cult of: 51
Hestiaia Boulaia: 22
Hilaritas: 460
M. Hirrius Fronto Neratius Pansa: 310
Aulus Hirtius: 90[48]
Hither Spain,
    council of: 150, 150[7], 155, 163
    dedication of provincial temple: 151 f., 152[13], 153, 154
    architectural features of provincial temple: 152 f., 152[17]
    remains of provincial temple: 153 f., 154[25]
    provincial cult of: 154 ff., 163 f., 242 f., 273 ff., 316
    location of provincial temple: 155[31], 519[270]
    provincial priests of: 156, 164, 223, 269, 275 f.
    statues of out-going high priests: 223, 277, 277[43-44], 277[46]
Hither Spain: see also Tarraco
Marcus Holconius Celer: 310[14]
Homonoia: 456
honorific statues, of emperor and family: 521 f.
Honos: 460, 461, 468

Hoplon: 564, 565
Sextus Hortensius Clarus: 524
Hygia: 449
hymn-singing,
    in imperial cult: 569 f.
    in western ruler cult: 571
hymnnodes of Pergamum, celebrations of: 495 f., 514
hymns: 24²⁰
    cult use of: 568 ff., 569⁵⁷²
    sung at Rome: 570

Q.[...]ius Ianuarius: 542³⁹⁵
Ianus Curiatius: 447
Ianus Quirini/Quirinus: 447, 462
Iddibal Caphada Aemilius: 378
identification: 28 ff., 341
    of emperor with god in inscriptions: 453 f.
Ignatius: 469
Ilion: 33
illumination, in pagan divine service: 566 f.
image,
    honorific: 23
    purpose of in temple: 549 f.
image: see also likeness
image of emperor: 477, 539
    rites before: 533 f., 533³⁵², 535, 538, 564 ff.
    in military context: 534³⁶¹
    military cult of: 534³⁶¹
    cult of in western provinces: 535 ff.
    attested in inscriptions: 536 ff.
    as offering in temple: 540 ff., 540³⁸⁷
    placed in temples of Greek east: 547 ff.
    arrival of: 552 f.
    distribution of: 553⁴⁷²
    introduced into processions at Rome: 555
    accompanied by lights and musicians: 563 f.
images,
    cult of imperial: 532 ff.
    cult of imperial by colleges: 538 ff.
    material of imperial: 543 ff.

where placed in temple: 547
of emperors, special tax for in Egypt: 548
of deity placed in temple: 550, 550[451]
of emperor, multiple placed in temple: 550
transported in Egypt: 550 f.
in Asia Minor: 551 f.
carried by bearers: 551 ff.
in Greece: 552
transported in Latin West: 556 ff.
care of imperial: 561, 561[517, 522]
clothing of imperial: 562
garlanding of imperial: 562, 562[524]
imago: 532 ff.
definition of: 542 f., 542[399]
imperator, usage of: 235 ff.
imperial family, sacred basis of: 430 f.
imperial festivals, marked by rites in west: 501 ff.
imperial mysteries, marked by feasting: 586 f.
imperial standards: 560 f.
imperial symbols,
distributed in western provinces: 110
on altar at Tarraco: 172 f., 172[10], 174 f., 174[25]
imperial temples, design of: 519[270]
incense: 133[246], 513, 513[241], 526[305]
at Lugdunum: 504
Indiges: 52[37]
Indiges Pater: 52
G. Indutius Felix: 396
individualism: 6
Indulgentia: 460
M. Ingenuius Ingenuinus: 604
inquisitor Galliarum: 136
insignia, of provincial priest: 475 ff.
Iol Caesarea,
altar of Augustus at: 147 f., 286
Iseum at: 285
temple of Augustus at: 147 f., 147[336], 286
Isis: 35, 38, 286, 286[28], 599
Isotheoi Timai: 21 ff., 46
Ithyphallikos: 6[4], 20[88], 37, 42, 187

iudex arcae ferrariarum: 361[5]
iudex arcae Galliarum: 136
Iullus, *praetor*: 585
Iulius Capito: 244[26]
Iulius Terentius: 595
C. Iulius Barbarus: 498
C. Iulius Celsus: 134, 315, 581
C. Iulius Crescens: 264, 264[35], 267
C. Iulius Crescens Didius Crescentianus: 263, 264[35]
C. Iulius Demosthenes: 617
C. Iulius Eurycles: 582
C. Iulius Lacon: 582
C. Iulius Nymphius: 546
C. Iulius Paulinus: 604
C. Iulius Rufus: 133, 315, 362[12], 581, 581[651]
C. Iulius Spartiaticus: 270, 423, 425
C. Iulius Vercondaridubnus: 98[9], 101, 188
G. Iul(ius) Dig[nus]: 606
G. Iul(ius) Roga[tianus]: 607
L. Iulius Cerealis: 264 f.
P. Iulius Liberalis: 263[31]
Q. Iulius Crescens: 264[35]
Sex(tus) Iul(ius) Epictetus: 613[17]
Iunia Theodora: 283
L. Iunius Paulinus: 582[656]
M. Iunius Silanus: 47
Iuppiter: see Jupiter
ius Latii: 290, 299, 299[30]
Iustitia: 459, 460
Iuventas: 455
Iuventus: 456

Jews: 527
Juba II: 92[59], 147, 285, 286,
    establishes altar for cult of Augustus: 104
Jugurtha: 112
Julia, daughter of Augustus: 140
Julia, the younger: 140
Julia Augusta, cult of: 166[105]
Julia Domna: 341, 342, 342[143], 346, 347, 428[38], 441, 451[34], 529, 603

associated with Juno: 338[116]
on Arch of Argentarii: 343
birthday of?: 488[77]
called *mater castrorum*: 494
statue of: 539
Julia Mamaea: 602
statue of: 589
birthday of: 604
Julian: 478, 536
Juno: 506
attendant spirit of a woman: 386[58]
Juno Regina: 603
Jupiter: 87, 88, 90[47], 151, 153[19], 340, 343, 455, 468, 473, 473[129], 506, 509, 512[235], 517, 520[273], 523, 567
Ammon: 153[23]
temple of at Tarraco: 154[29]
altar of on Capitol: 175
flaminate of: 476
Jupiter Capitolinus,
temple of in Rome: 57, 57[7], 67, 197, 545, 585
temple of at Arsinoe: 488, 548, 550 f., 568
statue transported at Arsinoe: 551
temple accounts of at Arsinoe: 562
statue of at Arsinoe: 583
Jupiter Feretrius, Capitoline temple of: 211
Jupiter Indiges: 52
Jupiter Julius, interpretation of: 66, 66[83]
Jupiter Optimus Maximus: 362[12], 385, 418, 507, 598, 600, 602, 605, 606, 614[21]
altars to: 595 f.
Jupiter Optimus Maximus Conservator: 601
Jupiter Optimus Maximus Dolichenus: 304, 600
priests of in Lower Pannonia: 305
Jupiter Pantheus Augustus: 449
Jupiter Tonans: 505[188]
temple of: 183
Jupiter Victor: 455

Kaisareia: 492, 577
Kaisareion: 548

Kallinikos: 114
Kensorinea: 48
kissing of hand: 534
Krascheninnikoff: 148

Laetitia: 460
Lagides: 286
lamb, as sacrificial offering: 531, 531[339]
lamps, ritual use of: 566 f.
Laodice: 16, 23, 186, 477
Lar Aineias: 52
lararium: 533, 533[347]
   of Ovid: 565
Lares: 84[11], 85[13], 380, 382, 511, 531, 538, 554, 567, 610
   on altar at Lugdunum: 119 f.
   domestic cult of: 376, 376[3-4], 385, 615[34]
   sacrifice to: 508, 509
Lares Augusti: 85, 85[13], 120, 502[171], 517, 537, 537[372], 615
   cult of: 54 f., 376[4], 504, 508
   ministri of: 110
Lares Compitales: 84 f., 85[13], 385, 610
Lares Hostilii: 447
Latin festival: 69
laurel tree, as ensign of imperial priest: 476[9]
laurel trees, at Augustus' door: 108 f.
League of Asia: 172
lectisternium: 62, 81, 584
   at Gytheum: 566
   as honours of kings: 566[548]
legio I Adiutrix: 606
legio I Adiutrix Pia Fidelis Antoniniana: 602
legio I M(inervia?): 602, 605
legio I Minervia [Alexandriana] Pia Fidelis: 601
legio II Adiutrix: 606
legio II Adiutrix Pia Fidelis: 603
legio II Augusta: 605
legio II Italica Pia: 605
legio III Augusta: 546
legio IV Macedonica: 143
legio VI Victrix: 143, 354, 360

legio VII Gemina Felix: 600
legio VIII Augusta: 222, 224, 237
legio X Gemina: 143, 442, 606
legio XIII Gemina Antoniniana: 600
legio XIIII Gemina Gordiana: 604
legio XXII Antoniniana Primigenia: 453[50]
legio XXX Ulpia Victrix Severiana Alexandriana: 601
Lepcis Magna: 339[118]
    temple of Roma and Augustus at: 167, 265, 450 f., 521 f., 523, 541
    arch at: 338, 339[118], 340, 341, 343, 468, 529
Lepidus: 117, 260, 490
Lex Narbonensis: 102, 123 f., 220 f., 240 ff., 245, 255, 262, 277, 478 f.,
    478 ff., 482, 501, 502, 526, 528, 540, 579 f.
libations: 36 f., 37[40]
    jugs for: 36 f.
    cups associated with: 375[1]
    to Augustus: 375[2]
    bowls for: 514
Liberalitas: 460
Libertas Publica Populi Romani: 463[56]
Libertas: 456, 458, 460
Licinian-Sextian laws: 455
C. Licinius Marinus Voconius Romanus: 224[22]
Q. Licinius Silvanus Granianus: 272[19], 272[20], 355
lighting, in cult practice: 121[168]
likeness: see image
likenesses, of imperial family: 539
Lingones, temple among: 144 f.
Liturgy of imperial cult: 475 ff.
    at Alexandria: 532
    poetic version of Western: 590[698]
    in Latin West: 588 f.
Livia: 140, 162, 197, 270, 270[6], 271, 271[13], 276, 283, 451, 465, 465[75], 495,
    500, 517, 520[275], 586, 618
    place of in cult of Tarraconensis: 158
    proposed temple to in Baetica: 160
    consecration of: 160[69]
    divine honours of under Tiberius: 160[69]
    synnaos with Divus Augustus: 160[69], 485
    made priestess of Augustus: 162 f., 163[83]

priest of at Emerita: 183
temple to in Asia: 198[18]
birthday of: 205[47], 206[55], 484, 490, 491[103], 495, 496[134], 506, 516, 569, 613[19]
Juno of: 381[29]
cult to: 385[49]
image of at Gytheum: 514, 564, 566
statue of: 521[283], 522, 523, 532[341]
statuette of: 532
bust of: 535, 535[363], 541, 545
statue of at Forum Clodii: 537
image placed in temples: 548
eikon of: 552
birthday marked by games: 576
institutes Palatine games: 576, 583
birthday marked by games and banquet: 585
see also Diva Augusta
living man, cult of: 4 f.
M. Livius Drusus: 90[48]
Lower Moesia, provincial cult of: 302
Lucilla: 424[9]
birthday of: 495
Lucius Caesar: see L. Caesar
Luculleia 47
Lucullus: 47
ludi Apollinares: 75
ludi Augustales: 162, 556, 576
ludi Ceriales: 74
ludi circenses: 160[64], 576
ludi Martiales: 118[148], 162
ludi Megalenses: 585
ludi Palatini: 163[83], 576, 583
ludi plebei: 584
ludi Romani: 61, 75, 556, 584
ludi Saeculares: 117
see also Secular Games
ludi Veneris Genetricis: 115[128]
ludi Victoriae Caesaris: 60[33], 61[43], 74, 114[120], 115, 115[128]
ludi Sarmatici: 493[119]
ludi Victoriae Sullanae: 114[120]

ludi Victoriae: 114[120]
ludi votivi: 162[78]
Lug: 99 f., 99[18], 112, 118, 132, 500
Lugdunum,
    federal cult at: 99, 131 ff., 232, 362 ff., 390
    Gauls meet at: 100 f.
    mint of: 104, 117, 176
    circus at: 134[255], 281[69], 582
    amphitheatre at: 167, 315, 315[45]
    municipal temple at: 167[118], 245[39]
    municipal cult at: 251[69], 312[25]
    medallion shows provincial monuments at?: 308, 316
    fragments of provincial temple at: 308[1]
    altar of Caesars at: 317 ff.
    dating by letter-forms at: 323[28]
    sides with Clodius Albinus: 347
    captured by Septimius Severus: 347 f.
    processions in municipal cult at: 559
    oratory at: 572
    August festival at: 578, 578[632]
    martyrdoms of Christians at: 578 f.
    odeon at: 584
Luna: 342
Lunus-Mên: 342
Lupercalia: 69 f.
luperci Iulii: 61
Lusitania,
    provincial cult of: 156 ff., 163, 164, 242, 278 f., 278[48]
    provincial council of: 163[89]
    titles of provincial priests of: 269, 278 f.
    provincial temple of: 278[52]
Lycia, provincial cult of: 283
Lysander: 7, 25
Lysandreia: 25
Lysimachus of Thrace: 21[2], 27
    statue of at Priene: 23[10]

Macedonians, *koinon* of: 271
Mactar, temple of Roma and Augustus at: 566
Maecenas: 79, 539[382]

Magdalensberg, double temple on: 167
magic, practice of: 7
magistri Augustales: 609, 612, 613[19], 616
magistri Herculanei: 609
magistri Mercuriales: 609
magistri vicorum: 504, 610, 615, 615[29,] 616
Magna Mater: 366[28]
Maiestas: 460
Maison Carrée: 252, 308[1], 330[65]
Mandulis: 603
Manes: 382
C. Manlius, altar of: 510, 511[226]
Marcellia: 46
Marcellus,
    birthday of?: 491[103]
    theatre of: 525[299], 583[665]
    golden statue of carried in procession: 555
Marcellus, son of M. [Sabini]us Nepotianus: 605
C. Marcellus: 46
M. Marcellus: 53
Marciana: 301[5], 313[30], 313[31]
    birthday of: 604
C. Marcius Censorinus: 48
P. Marcius Sextianus: 602
Q. Marcius Barea: 451
Marcomanni: 305, 488[82]
Marcus Holconius Celer: 310[14]
Marcus, likeness of in Egypt: 548
Maricc: 92 f., 135, 579
Marius: 112, 114
C. Marius: 54
Marius Gratidianus: 53, 54, 85[12], 533, 567
    statues of: 565
Mars: 87, 87[30], 455, 461, 469, 505, 509, 511, 511[232], 554
    statue of at Cuicul: 263
Mars Augustus: 600
Mars Campester: 600
Mars Militaris, temple of: 605
Mars Mullo, temple of at Rennes: 547
Mars Pater Victor: 600

Mars Segomo: 363[12]
Mars Ultor, temple of: 59[24], 64[63], 87, 87[30], 89[43], 112, 161, 161[72], 167[118], 182 f., 330[66], 483[51], 484, 545, 546
    festival of: 118[148]
    aedicula of: 183, 183[22]
[Mars] Propugnator: 602
Martiales: 609
Sextus Mart(ius?) Cocillus: 443
martyrdoms: 527
    at Lugdunum: 135, 135[264]
    at Tarraco: 281
    associated with imperial games: 577 ff.
Matidia: 313[31]
    Augusta: 465[77]
Mauretania,
    division of: 282, 282[1]
    religious climate of : 285 f.
Mauretania Caesariensis: 259
    council of: 282, 288[41]
    provincial cult of: 282 ff.
    provincial patrons of: 288
Mauretania Tingitana,
    provincial cult of: 282 ff.
    provincial patrons of: 288
    council of: 289[47]
Mauretaniae, Romanization of: 284 f.
Mauretanian kings, posthumous cult of: 92[59]
Maxentius: 553[475]
Maximian: 320[18], 400[20]
Maximinus: 590
Maximus: 590
    statue of: 562[525]
Maximus, son of Maximinus Thrax: 492[109]
Mediannus: 444
Mediusacer: 444
Megalesia: 485[60]
C. Memmius Fidus Iul(ius) Albius: 605
Menecrates: 44
Menoeceus: 469
Mens: 456, 457, 460, 468, 469

Mercator: 244, 246, 247, 248, 249
Mercuriales: 615
Mercurius: 443, 453
Mercurius Augustus: 449, 450
Mercury: 444, 531, 568, 604
    temple of at Furnos Maius: 257
Messalina,
    statue of: 523
    gold statue of?: 544
M. Messius Gallus: 251
Metellus Pius: 457
Metroon at Olympia: 274[27]
Miletus, Severan calendar at: 495[131]
military cult of emperor, public rites: 594 f.
military decorations: 359 f.
military standards, care of: 561
militiae equestres: 135[265], 224, 354, 358 f.
Miltiades: 3
Minerva: 423, 449, 451[37], 469, 506
    temple of on Aventine: 210[76]
Minerva Augusta: 449
C. Minicius Italus: 359
ministri: 85[13], 110, 154[27], 173[11], 610, 615
Minos: 467
Minucius, the god: 53
L. Minucius Augurinus: 53
Mithras: 474
Moderatio: 458, 460
Moles Martis: 462
Mommsen: 148
Mons Caelius: 158, 202, 217, 296
Mons Claudianus: 315[43]
months, named after a ruler: 26
Moukieia: 47
Q. Mucius Scaevola: 47
P. Mummius Saturninus: 257, 258, 259, 261, 262
L. Munatius Hilarianus: 539[382], 546[430]
L. Munatius Plancus: 47, 100, 107[69]
municipal cults, Augustan in Latin West: 146
municipal priests, Greek titles of: 269 f.

municipal priests, Latin titles of: 166[109]
municipalities, celebrate imperial festivals in Italy: 490 ff., 509 ff.
Munificentia: 460
mysteries, in ruler cult: 562[529], 573 f.
Mytilene, decree of: 171 f., 177, 189, 497, 503, 513
Mytilene, temple to Roma and Augustus at: 177

N. AVG.: 405 ff.
Namgiddo: 536
Naples,
 games at: 133[250]
 sacrifice to Augustus at: 510
 Romaia Sebasta at: 556, 572[592], 575
Narbo,
 altar of Numen Augusti at: see Ara Numinis Augusti
 cult of Numen Augusti at: 146
 Capitolium of: 196, 249 ff., 251 ff., 252[81], 522, 522[287]
 municipal temple at: 243 ff., 246[40], 252[80]
 provincial temple at: 254 ff.
 local board at: 379, 379[16]
 imperial images at: 558
 circus at: 582[655]
 theatre at: 583[665]
Narbonensis,
 municipal cult in: 250 f.
 provincial centre of: 255 f.
Narcissus: 533
 Natalis Urbis: 313
 festival of: 356
Nea Hera: 342
Nebuchadnezzar: 534
Νειλαῖα: 494
Nemausus,
 temple to Plotina at: 306, 315[47]
 libations at: 504
 Dionysiac artists at: 584
 thymelic contest at: 584
Nemesis, temple of at Rhamnonte: 548
nemus Caesarum: 103[46]
Neoi Helioi: 342

Neos, as title: 30 f.
Nepotianus: 605
Neptunalia: 603
Neptune: 80, 423, 461, 469, 505
Nerio Martis: 462
Nero: 158, 233, 258, 261, 269, 270[4], 270[6], 270[7], 282, 283, 296 f., 409,
    410, 430, 464, 484, 486[66], 492[109], 506, 507, 546, 570, 611
    receives radiate crown: 15[65]
    emphasizes Apollo: 88[36]
    congratulated by Three Gauls: 137
    inscription on Parthenon: 137[275]
    cult of deified daughter: 166[105]
    early reign of: 213
    temple to as *divus*: 214
    contemplates evacuation of Britain: 217
    courts divine honours: 295
    adopts radiate crown: 296
    receives submission of Tiridates: 481
    accession of: 492
    dies imperii of: 495
    statue of in *curia*: 522[289]
    bust of: 537
    statues of in temple of Mars Ultor: 545 f.
    image carried in procession: 556
    images of: 563
Neronia: 202
Nerva: 264[36], 301, 312, 333, 472, 473, 569
    accession of: 605
Nervi: 323
Nescania, sacrifice to emperor at: 502 f.
Nicopolis: 81
Nikator: 114, 457
Nikatoreion: 17
Niké: 113
Nike-Victoria: 456
Nikephoros: 114
Nisus: 467
Nobilitas: 458, 460
M. Nonius Balbus: 161[69], 733
    honoured by games at Herculaneum: 576

Noricum,
    'house of representatives' on Magdalensberg: 139 f.
    provincial cult centre at: 139 f.
Numa: 469
numen,
    cult of under Severi: 345 f.
    oath by: 377
    characteristics of: 383 f.
    different senses of: 384 f.
    used of emperor in singular: 397 ff., 398[6,9]
    in Africa: 399, 411, 455
    used in singular of emperors in plural: 399 f.
    of singular reigning emperor in Britain: 400 f.
    abbreviations for: 401 ff.
    cult of imperial in Britain: 217 f., 413 ff., 594
    of emperor, transcriptions of abbreviations: 419 ff.
    of Augustan gods: 452
    of Abstractions: 462
    of Victoria Augusti: 466
Numen Augusti: 378 ff.
    significance of concept of: 386 f., 388
    popularity of cult of: 388, 390 f.
    altar of at Tarraco: 504, 526
    see also Ara Numinis Augusti
Numen Augustum,
    altar of at Forum Clodii: 380, 510, 537, 576, 585
    as collective divinity: 380[23]
    sacrifice to at Forum Clodii: 516
numen/numina of emperor/s, abbreviations for in Britain: 412 f.
Numerius Atticus: 159[62]
Numicius: 51
numina,
    as class of spirits: 383[38]
    used of one emperor in poetry: 398, 398[7]
Numina Augustorum, interpretation of: 388 ff.
Numisius Martius: 462
Cn. Numisius Modestus: 280, 541
NVM. AVG.: 407 ff.
Nysa, statue of: 125[197]

oak wreath: 107 f., 162[76]
oath of allegiance, to emperor: 130[233]
    by soldiers: 418, 418[72], 596
oaths, by imperial *numina*: 395 f.
Ocratina: 288, 289, 292
Ocratius: 288
Octavia: 48, 171
    portico of: 525[299]
    images of carried in procession: 556
Octavian: 51, 73, 89, 152[17], 384, 490[93]
    costumed as Apollo: 30
    adoption as Caesar: 73, 75
    early aims of: 73 f.
    attempts to display Caesar's golden throne: 74
    as imperator: 74[7]
    seizure of consulate: 75
    early attitude to divine honours: 77 f.
    accepts inviolability of a tribune: 78
    accepts laurel crown: 78
    statue in temples of Italian municipalities: 78 f., 545
    cautious attitude to divine honours: 78 ff.
    divine birth of: 80
    in costume of Apollo: 80 f.
    relationship with Apollo: 80 ff.
    conceived under Capricorn: 80[52]
    as Apollo on coins: 81
    moderation of: 83
    divine honours of: 84, 84[7 ff.]
    granted name Augustus: 84, 107[69], 517
    returns from East: 87[29]
    granted grass crown: 108[71]
    final victory of: 109
    regulates cult of emperor: 126
    transforms Roma: 127 f.
    loyalty of provinces to: 148
    returns from Actium: 375
    libations decreed by senate: 375[2]
    victory of at Alexandria: 497[141]
    called god: 531
    bust of: 535, 541
    see also Augustus

P. Octavius Flavus: 227[31]
odeon, at Lugdunum: 311[24], 314[42]
Odrysian dynasty: 283
Odysseus: 38, 42
Oenoanda,
    festival at: 617
    ritual at: 618
official language, inflation of: 430
Olympia, Metroon at: 367
Olympias: 8, 342[143]
Olympic games: 3, 25
Onesimus: 537
Ops: 468
Ops Augusta, altar of: 102
Optatus: 541, 542
oratory, in western imperial cult: 572 f.
Ordo: 529
Sextus Orgius Suavis: 444
L. Osidius: 323
Osiris: 30
Ostia,
    temple of Roma and Augustus at: 141, 167
    cult of *imagines* at: 346[181]
    mosaic in Augusteum at: 512
Ostorius Scapula: 197[14], 199
Otho: 262, 299, 485
C. Otidius Iovinus: 264, 266
Ovid, performs morning rites: 532
ox, as sacrificial victim: 506 f.
Oxyrhynchus, calendar at: 493 f.

pagus Condate,
    sanctuary at: 101[26], 104, 364
    patronate of: 325
Palatinae laurus: 109
Palatine: 81, 88, 161, 576, 590[698]
    emperor's household shrine on: 483[51]
    games: see *ludi*
Pallas: 533
palm: 175 f.

Palmyrene Gods, temple of: 595
Palmyrenes, 20th cohort of: 488
Pamphylia: 283
Panathenaia: 48
panegyrics, of emperor: 571 f., 571[587]
Pannonia Inferior, provincial cult of: 302 f.
Pannonia Superior, provincial cult of: 302 f.
Pantheon: 87[30], 161[72], 253, 314, 524[299]
L. Papirius: 164
M. Papirius Celer: 599
Parentalia: 51
Parilia: 73[2], 313, 555
    games at: 57 f., 58[15]
Parthenon: 341
Parthians: 112
participation, in celebrations of imperial cult: 528 ff.
Patientia: 460
Pax: 86[18], 116, 459, 460
    temple of in Forum of Vespasian: 295 f.
Pax Augusta: 86, 460
Pax Augusta Claudiana, gold statue of: 544, 544[417]
Pax Augusti/Augusta: 463, 464
Penates: 382, 535[361], 567
Pergamum,
    temple of Roma and Augustus at: 495, 495[132], 495 f.
    imperial choir at: 562, 569
    mysteries at: 573 f.
Perpetuitas: 460
Perseus: 8, 175
Pertinax: 327
    consecration of: 337
    accession of: 492
    gold *eikon* of taken in procession: 555
    birthday of: 603
Perusine War: 76
Pescennius Niger: 337
Petronius, governor of Syria: 546[435]
Petrucorii: 366[28]
Pharaoh, son of Amun Re: 15
Philadelphus: 14

Philip II of Macedon: 23, 40, 41, 42, 44, 58
 enthroned with Twelve Gods: 19[85]
 image of carried in procession: 555[486]
Philippi (emperors): 406, 408, 419
Philotera: 14
Phoebus: 80, 583
Pietas: 86[16], 456, 457, 459, 460, 461, 469, 485[59]
 altar of: 508
Pietas Augusta: 464, 465, 465[75], 465[76], 465[77]
Pionius: 37[40], 534
Pistis: 46
Plato: 41, 42
Plautianus: 428[38]
Plautilla: 338, 342, 428[38], 560[511]
Pliny, *procurator* in Tarraconensis: 142
Plotina: 306, 313[31], 313[33], 315, 315[47]
 image of: 551
Pluto: 451[37]
poetry, as vehicle of state policy: 91[53]
Pola, municipal temple at: 167, 308[1]
Polycarp: 527, 577[627]
pompa circensis: 58, 58[16], 59[24], 123, 161[69], 540, 553, 555, 555[490], 556, 564[541]
Pompeiastai: 47
C. Pompeius Sanctus: 363[12]
[L(?)] Pomp[eius] Faventinus: 353 ff.
M. Pompeius Libo: 363[12]
Sextus Pompeius: 79, 80, 87[27], 117
Pompey: 54, 90[48], 114
 cult of: 47
 qualities of: 457
 theatre of: 522
L.(?) Pomponius Capito: 157
L. Pomponius Paternus: 366[28]
Sextus Pomponius Paternus: 366[28]
T. Pomponius Victor: 231
Pontius Pilate: 619
Poppaea: 458
Populus: 529
M. Porcius Cato: 118[146]

M. Porcius Narbonensis: 272[18]
Porta Collina: 114[120]
Porta Trigemina: 53
porticoes, as cult places: 524, 524[297]
Poseidon: 10, 42
Postumus: 467
Potamon: 51[30], 172, 177
Pothinus: 578
Potina: 448
prayer,
    to and for: 37 f.
    on behalf of emperor and his house: 90[48]
prayers, in imperial cult: 189, 532, 532[342]
precinct: 22
precious metal,
    use of in cult: 536
    connotation of: 544
    attitude of emperors to: 544 f.
Priam: 42
priest, eponymous: 23
priest imperial,
    crown of: 477 f.
    insignia of in Greek east: 477[10]
    presides at games: 478
    paraphernalia of: 504
    at Lyon: 526
    consumes victim: 527
priest of province,
    in Britain: 201, 201[34]
    Greek titles of: 270 f.
    second tenure of office: 364, 364[22]
    Latin titles of: 392, 394 f.
    regalia and costume of: 477 ff., 579 f.
    privileges of: 478 f.
    attendants of: 479[23]
    wife of: 480
priest municipal,
    robes of: 480 f.
    wife of: 480 f., 480[33]
Priesthoods,

variations in titles: 276, 324[33]
tenure of provincial: 355, 355[14]
at age 50 or older: 358[32]
priestly colleges, at Rome: 483, 483[47-48]
priests: 23 f.
in Ptolemaic Egypt: 24
in Seleucid empire: 24
primus, uses of: 225 ff., 289[47]
Probus, the martyr: 577[627]
processions: 24 f., 133, 133[250], 179[58], 243[20], 278, 278[52], 539 f.
linking theatre and temple: 523
in Greek East: 550 ff.
in Rome: 553 ff.
in Latin west: 556 ff.
in municipal cult at Tarraco: 558 f.
at provincial centres of western provinces: 558 ff.
at Amiens: 559
at Lugdunum: 559
at Cigognier: 559 f.
at Conimbriga: 559[507]
at Gytheum: 564, 564[541]
accompanied with singing: 571[582]
at Oenoanda: 617 f.
Procopius: 37[40]
Proskynesis, before images of gods: 527 f., 527[313], 534[355], 534[361]
prostration,
in ruler cult: 527 f.
at supplications: 534
Providentia: 86[16], 458, 459, 459[30], 460, 461, 472[121], 473
altar of at Emerita?: 146[332], 180 ff.
altar of in Rome: 181 f., 184, 484[57], 508
of Tiberius: 463[56]
as *comes*: 468
sacrifice to: 507, 507[204]
Providentia Augusta: 460, 463
cult of: 182
Providentia Augusti: 470, 472
Providentia Tua: 474
Provincial Councils, charges against Roman administrators: 283 f.
provincial patrons: 288

provincial priests: see individual provinces
Ptolemaic rulers, cult of deceased: 15[66]
Ptolemaieia: 14, 25
Ptolemy I Soter: 13, 14, 15, 17, 23, 28
Ptolemy II Philadelphus: 14, 15, 17, 32
Ptolemy III Euergetes: 15[65]
Ptolemy IV Philopator: 15, 17, 30[70], 39
Ptolemy V: 28
Ptolemy XIII: 30
Ptolemy, of Mauretania: 285 f., 286[28]
Ptolemy Philadelphus: 15, 26[33], 160
procession of: 125[197]
Ptolemy Soter and Berenice, votive to: 38, 38[49]
Ptuj, reliefs at: 503 f.
C. Publicius Fortunatus: 394
C. Publicius Priscilianus: 601
Pudicitia: 460
Pupienus: 481, 595

Querolus: 584
Quies: 460
T. Quinctius Flamininus: 582
    cult of: 46 f., 48
    coin of: 47[5]
    with Roma at Chalcis: 51[28]
Quintia: 527
Quintia Flaccina: 166
Quintilian, anecdote of: 171 f., 175 f., 178
Quintus: 47
Quirinus: 53, 58, 58[16], 59, 59[28], 67
    temple of at Rome: 59, 60[34], 61, 64[63], 114, 545

radiate crown: 15[65]
Raecius Gallus: 224[22]
Raphia: 39
Ravenna, frieze at: 512
re-incarnation: 30
Re: 199[24]
Reburrus: 541, 542
refusals of divine honours: 198, 330

religion, definition of: 44 f.
religious psychology: 41 f.
res publica Romana: 50
res Romana: 127
Rhodos, cult of: 50
rites of ruler cult,
    in western provinces: 505, 515 ff.
    at Rome: 505 ff.
    in early imperial art: 508 ff.
    in Italy: 509 ff.
    in pre-Roman period: 512 f.
    in eastern provinces: 512 ff.
    performed by ordinary man: 530 ff.
rites of imperial festivals,
    based on Roman model in Latin provinces: 515 ff.
ritual,
    Roman: 525 ff.
    military: 528
Roma: 46, 127 f., 131 f., 273[21], 274, 350, 355 f., 451, 468[93], 500, 521[280, 281, 283], 544[417]
    cult of under Republic: 49, 187
    temple of at Smyrna: 49
    legend of: 49 f., 49[24]
    Greek conception of: 50
    portraits on coins: 50[25]
    cult of at Ephesus: 77
    cult of in Western provinces: 93, 131[238]
    statuette of: 124
    metamorphosis of: 127 f.
    link with Victory: 128
    link with Augustus: 128 f., 128[212]
    place of in provincial cult of Tarraconensis: 155
    in municipal cult at Tarraco: 177
    not attested at Camulodunum: 201, 390
    evidence for in Africa Proconsularis: 265
    not attested in cult of Lusitania: 278 f., 279[58]
    not attested in cult of Baetica: 279 f., 279[58]
    cult of in Lycia: 283
    not included in cult of Dacia: 302
    in cult of Three Gauls: 309

emphasized by Hadrian: 313

in cult at temple of Three Gauls: 309, 321 ff.

significance of under Severi: 328

omitted from cult at Altar of Three Gauls: 309, 335

without Urbs: 357[26]

in titles of provincial priests: 358

associated with living emperor: 355 f., 391, 392

combined with name of emperor: 438

birthday of: 494

image of: 563

Roma Aeterna: 328[52], 357[26], 358, 359, 594, 596

cult of: 132

birthday of: 601

Roma and Augustus: 218

cult of regulated by Octavian: 126

early cult of: 129 f.

temple of at Caesarea: 129, 147, 521

priesthood of at Lugdunum: 131 f., 135 ff.

cult of at Ara Ubiorum: 138

cult of at Arae Sestianae?: 144

cult of in north-west Spain: 144, 144[316]

altar to at Tarraco: 144[315]

altar of on Elbe: 145

altar to among Lingones?: 145

emphasized in provincial cult: 148

priesthood of: 165

temple of at Ostia: 167

temple of at Vienne: 167[117]

provincial temples to: 199 f.

altar to at Camulodunum: 200 f., 218

temple to at Pergamum: 215

temple of at Lepcis Magna: 265, 450 f., 541, 547

temple of at Mactar: 265

early cult of in East: 297

cult of by Three Gauls: 131, 362 ff.

municipal cult of: 363, 363[14]

in dedications: 436

altar of at Nîmes?: 519

cult statue of in temple at Lepcis Magna: 521

temple of at Mactar: 563

representations of: 557
Roma and Divus Augustus: 310[14]
Roma and Divus Claudius: 310[14]
Roma and Divus Iulius,
    cult of: 126 f., 130, 130[234]
    temple of at Ephesus: 188
Roma and Salus, cult of at Pergamum: 126[203]
Roma and the Augusti, cult of by Three Gauls: 364
Roma and Venus, temple of: 197, 356, 313 f.
Romaia: 49, 49[20]
Romaia Sebasta, procession of at Naples: 556
Romans, cult of in East: 46 ff.
Romulus: 51, 53, 54[50], 57, 59, 67, 68[88], 211
    house of: 90[50]
Romulus-Quirinus: 54, 58
Rosalia: 496, 513[243]
Rosaliae Signorum: 562, 595, 601
ruler, as pseudo-god: 34
ruler cult,
    genuine religion or social exercise?: 42 f.
    observed at Rome: 482 ff.
rulers,
    benefactions of: 6
    divine honours to: 12
Rusicade, sacrifice at: 503
'Ρώμη: 34[12], 46, 48
'Ρώμη Νικηφόρος: 51
M. Rutilius Lupus: 599

M. [Sabini]us Nepotianus: 605
sacerdotes Albani: 132[240]
sacerdos Veneria: 426
Sacra Via: 60
sacrifices: 21, 35 ff.
    in cult of Three Gauls: 132 f.
    in western imperial cult: 501 ff.
    prescribed in Ara Numinis Augusti at Narbo: 502
    on imperial occasions at Rome: 505 f.
    in Greek sacrificial system: 512 f.
    to emperor in Greek practice: 513 f.

for emperor in Greek practice: 514, 514[246]
follow Roman practice in West: 525 ff.
personnel of: 526
participants consume victim: 527
feasting at: 530[328]
by private individuals spontaneously: 531 f.
sacrificial implements: 504 f., 525-527
sacrum, significance of: 439
Saepta: 84[7]
Salus: 86, 456, 458, 460, 468, 506, 507, 602
temple of: 545, 58[21]
Salus Augusta: 86[20], 463[56], 465, 465[75]
Salus Augusti/Augusta: 464
Salus Caesaris: 86[20]
Salus Publica: 86[20], 461, 506, 507
[C. Salvius] Fusc[us]: 542
Samos,
festival at: 25
Heraion at: 25[25]
Sanctus: 578
Santa Maria Maggiore, church of: 488[82]
Sardinia,
change in title of provincial priest: 267[57]
provincial cult of: 299
L. Sariolenus Naevius Fastus Consularis: 547
Sarmatians: 488[82]
Sars: 143
Saturn: 451[37]
altar of: 567
Saturninus: 534
saviour: 27 f.
scenic games,
associated with imperial cult: 582 f., 584[666]
in western empire: 583 f., 583[663-4]
Scipio Africanus: 54, 54[55], 114, 118[146], 457
Sebasteia: 492, 577
Sebasteion: 445, 519, 551[462]
Sebastophoroi: 618
Second Triumvirate: 75
Secular Games: 88, 530[333], 560

see also *ludi Saeculares*
secular honours: 32 f.
Securitas: 458, 460
    sacrifice to: 507
Securitas Populi Romani: 464[69]
Segimundus: 139, 475
Segusiavi: 100, 318 f.
Sejanus: 182, 423, 463[56]
    birthday of: 484
    execution of: 496[136]
    statues of: 522
    golden likenesses of: 544[411]
    golden chair of: 555
Seleucids,
    state cult of: 16 f.
    priests of: 17
Seleucus I: 17, 21, 25
sellisternium: 61, 574, 584
Sema, of Alexander: 14[55], 15
C. Sempronius Speratus: 219 f., 220[3]
Senate,
    authorizes provincial temples: 150[3]
    authorizes temple in Britain: 202, 213 f.
senatus populusque Romanus: 129
T. Sennius Sollemnis: 134 f., 333[79], 361, 365, 366, 580
    provincial priesthood of: 361 ff.
Senones: 325
Sentinus: 448
Sextus Sentius Caecilianus: 294
Septimius Heraclitus: 550 f.
Septimius Severus: 305, 306 f., 317[6], 318, 320[18], 321, 322, 323[29], 327,
    327[49], 330, 331, 332, 334, 342, 345, 348[195], 365, 403, 407, 428[38], 434,
    478[16], 520[273], 529, 555, 603
    associated with Serapis: 87[27], 339 f.
    dreams of temple at Tarraco: 150
    visits Gorsium: 304, 306
    fictitious adoption into Antonine family: 313[32]
    portrait types of: 327[49]
    restores temple at Tarraco?: 328[51]
    portrayed on coins: 337

relationship to Jupiter: 337
assimilated to Hercules: 338
visits Lepcis Magna: 339[118]
associated with Jupiter and Serapis: 340 f.
on Arch of Argentarii: 343
interest in astrology: 343 f.
palace of on Palatine: 344
arch of: 345
marries Julia: 347
modifies cult of Three Gauls: 348 f.
victory at Lugdunum: 365, 501
and Fortuna: 466
Victories of: 468
dies imperii of: 487[77], 492[108]
birthday of: 488[78], 491[104], 494, 499, 496[134], 600
recognized by senate: 492
gold bust of: 536[368]
bust of: 537, 538, 542[395-6]
image placed in temple: 548
hymns at funeral of: 570
captures Ktesiphon: 599
Septizodium: 341, 343 f.
Serapis: 35, 340, 469
hair-style of: 339 f.
in Severan period: 339[120]
temple of at Lepcis Magna: 541
Servilius Ahala: 534
P. Servilius Isauricus: 47[6], 50, 77, 127
Sestius: 141
L. Sestius Quirinalis Albinianus: 142
Severeia: 577
Severi,
cult of at Altar of Three Gauls: 333 ff.
religious developments under: 335 ff.
associated with deities: 336 ff., 341 f., 343, 343[150]
linked with Hercules and Bacchus: 337 f.
addressed with sanctifying language: 342, 344
attitude of to ruler cult: 344 ff.
military cult of: 346, 346[181]
at Lugdunum: 347 ff.

Severus Alexander: 302[8], 468, 541, 593, 602
    named Caesar: 488[77], 602
    birthday of: 495[128], 606
    dies imperii of: 498, 498[148]
    anniversaries of: 508
sevir Claudialis: 609
sevir Flavialis: 609
sevir Neroniensis: 609
sevir Nervialis: 609
sevir Tiberianus: 609
seviri, 452, 479[23], 554[479], 609, 609[2]
    sacrifice by: 512[235], 614[21]
    provide games and banquet: 585
seviri Augustales: 110, 178, 183, 379[16], 434, 452, 531[335], 609-612, 613[19], 615f.
shield of virtues, copy of at Arles: 109, 109[82]
Sibylline books: 81, 88[35]
Sicily, past provincial priests of: 244
sidus Iulium: 74
Marcus Silanus: 259
Silius: 531
P. Silius Nerva: 142
Silures: 197
Silvanus: 448, 537, 605
    temple of: 546
Silvanus Augustus: 604
Similis: 498
simulacrum, definition of: 542 f.
Siwa, priest at: 8
Sminthia Paulleia: 47
Sodales Augustales: 162, 162[77 f.], 483, 485
sodales Titii: 162[77]
sodalities, in imperial cult: 486, 486[67]
Sol: 341, 342, 469
Sol Invictus: 343
Sophistic period: 7
Soriano del Cimino, altar at: 511
Soter: 457
Soteria: 47
Spaniards, embassy of to Rome: 150, 150[6], 153, 163

Spes: 456, 460, 461, 468
Spes Augusta: 86²¹, 463⁵⁶
Spes Perpetua Augusta: 463⁵⁶
Speusippus: 42
St. Agape: 527
St. Chione: 527
St. Crispina: 528
St. Irene: 527
St. Omobono, relief at: 112
St. Perpetua: 578
standards, carried in processions: 552
Statilinus: 448
T. Statilius Taurus: 188
statua, definition of: 542, 542³⁹⁹
statues, of benefactor placed in temple: 79
        to be carried in procession: 179⁵⁸, 243²⁰
        in cult of Gallia Narbonensis: 242 f.
        erected to relatives of honoree: 430⁴⁶
        dedicated at Forum Clodii: 490, 500, 518²⁶⁴
        location of imperial: 520 ff.
        dedication of: 528³¹⁹
        rites before: 532 ff.
        placing of in temple: 545 ff.
        of the gods, clothing of: 562 f., 562⁵³¹
statuettes, of imperial family: 385⁴⁹
Gaius Stertinius Xenophon: 270⁶ᶠ·
Subatianus Proculus: 600, 604
Suchos: 494
Suetonius Paulinus: 203, 213
Sulla: 55, 87²⁷, 112, 114, 457
        cult of: 47
supplications: 89, 89⁴⁶, 481, 505¹⁹⁰, 525 f.
        issuance of wine and incense for: 89⁴⁵
        prescribed on Ara Numinis Augusti at Narbo: 508
        prescribed in Feriale Duranum: 507 f., 595 f.

Tabula Hebana: 543
tabularius Galliarum: 136
Tacitus, emperor: 489⁸⁸
        plans *templum divorum*: 573

Q. Talotius Allius Silonianus: 498
Tarachos: 577[627]
Tarentia Marcella: 251
Tarraco: 242
    upper city of: 173
    lower forum of: 173 f., 174[19]
    municipal cult at: 177, 179[58]
    temple of Divus Augustus at: 178, 328[51], 476, 524[297]
    municipal temple at: 178 f.
    circus at: 256[97], 281, 281[69], 581 f.
    amphitheatre at: 280 f., 578
    building programme at provincial centre: 280 f.
    sacrifice at: 503
    imperial images at: 558
    processions at: 558
    municipal altar at: see Altar of Augustus at Tarraco
    see also Hither Spain
Tarraconensis: see Hither Spain
Taurus: 321
Tebessa, epigraphical calendar at: 499
Tebtunis, local religious calendar at: 493
Tempestates: 462
temple: 22
    sharing: 22 f.
    partnership of a ruler with a god: 37
    imperial with divided *cella*: 521
Temple of Divus Claudius at Camulodunum,
    ritual purification of: 195
    construction of: 196 f., 200
    religious status of: 196 ff., 201 ff.
    altar before: 200, 200[33], 218
    see also Camulodunum
temples, construction of: 197
templum divorum, rites at under emperor Tacitus: 489[88]
Templum gentis Flaviae: 431[51]
Templum Pacis: 197[12]
Tertinius Vitalis: 601
Tetricus I, II: 467
Thasians: 198
Θεὰ ʹΡώμη: 46, 48

Theagenes: 3, 185
theatre,
    as cult centre: 522 f.
    imperial shrine at: 523
    place of in cult: 575
    in western provinces: 583 f.
Thecla: 477, 577[627]
Theocritus: 15
Theodosius: 480
Theodosius II, birthday of: 489
Θεοὶ Ἀδελφοί: 14
Θεὸς Σωτήρ: 14
Θεοὶ Σωτῆρες: 14, 15, 38
theologies: 571 f.
Theopompus: 60[34]
Theseus: 7[5]
Thrace, annexation of: 283
Three Gauls,
    altar of: see Altar of Three Gauls
    council of: 101 f., 134, 136 f.
    temple of: 103, 105[58], 308 ff.
    annual synod of: 132
    ritual at federal sanctuary: 132 f.
    amphitheatre of: 133 f., 134[256], 167, 581
    games at sanctuary: 134 f., 134[260], 573, 575
    statues of priests of: 135 f., 136[267]
    secular side of provincial priesthood: 135 ff.
    assembly building of council: 136[272]
    bronze tablet in sanctuary: 137[275]
    modification of provincial cult: 309 ff.
    amphitheatre enlarged under Hadrian: 315, 315[44]
    provincial cult of: 317 ff., 362 ff.
    cult of Caesar(s): 326 ff.
    provincial cult of under Severi: 333 ff.
    titles of priests inlude topographical phrase: 363 ff.
    erect inscriptions to priests: 364
    cult statues at provincial temple of: 521
    imperial images at sanctuary of: 557
    processions at sanctuary of: 557
Thurinus: 545

Tiberieum: 619
Tiberius: 76, 104, 123, 133, 138, 143³¹¹, 152¹⁷, 167, 171, 173, 180, 197,
    222, 225²⁶, 233, 233⁶¹⁻³, 240, 240³, 248, 263³³, 277, 280, 283, 284,
    285, 316, 345, 362¹², 380, 380²³, 387, 401²², 423, 427, 458, 460, 463,
    468, 472, 491⁹⁴, 496¹³⁶, 544⁴⁰⁹, 552, 586, 611, 614, 618
    dedicates Ara Numinis Augusti: 86 f., 146, 388, 388¹
    refused title Invictus: 116
    oath to by Cypriots: 130²³³
    emphasizes worship of Divus Augustus: 149
    refuses temple in Baetica: 158, 160
    policy on divine honours to self: 158 f., 159⁵⁹, 198
    regulation on statues: 159, 159⁵⁶, 543
    attitude to consecration of Augustus: 159 f.
    escapes from Sejanus: 182, 184
    dedicates temples: 197
    temple to in Asia: 198¹⁸
    founds provincial cult at Tarraco: 273
    refuses oath by his *genius*: 377
    dedicates temple of Castor and Pollux: 378
    genius of: 381²⁹
    cult to: 385⁴⁹
    swordsheath of: 464⁷⁰, 466, 471
    birthday of: 484, 485, 487, 487⁷⁵, 490, 491, 496¹³⁴, 506
    adoption of: 491, 491¹⁰³
    made Pontifex Maximus: 491
    birthday celebrated by sacrifice: 510
    birthday celebrated by supplication to Vesta: 516
    statue of: 521²⁸³, 522, 532
    refuses to prosecute L. Ennius: 532
    bust of: 533³⁴⁵, 535³⁶⁵, 540³⁸⁵
    statue of at Forum Clodii: 537
    statues of family of: 541
    image of in temple of Venus Erycina: 546
    refuses statue beside cult idol: 547
    eikon of: 552
    golden chair of: 555
    image of at Gytheum: 564, 566
    birthday marked by festivities: 586
Tiridates: 481
Titius Rufinus: 602

titulature, unofficial of emperor: 473

Titus: 223, 224, 228³⁶, 230, 231, 233⁶², 235, 235⁷⁰, 236, 237, 238, 238⁸⁰, 275³²,297, 298²⁸, 298²⁹, 328⁵³, 427²⁴, 430, 442, 465⁷⁶, 486⁶⁶
   holds properties in Baetica: 222, 230
   gold bust of at Emerita: 278, 528, 558
   dies imperii of: 487⁷⁶
   birthday of: 491¹⁰⁴, 582, 607
   gold likeness of: 546
   golden chair of: 555

Traianus *pater*: 301⁴, 312²⁸

Trajan: 238⁸³, 265, 266, 274³¹, 302, 305, 312, 313, 313³¹, 333, 359, 469, 473, 474, 488⁷⁸, 520²⁷³, 525, 525³⁰³, 544, 569, 584
   associated with Zeus and Heracles: 87²⁷
   divides Pannonia: 146, 302 f.
   founds colony of Cuicul: 264
   attitude to divine honours: 301
   overruns Dacia: 301
   as "Jovian" emperor: 301³
   emphasizes cult of Heracles: 301³
   makes Oescus a colony: 302
   develops Gorsium: 303
   founds provincial cults of Pannoniae: 303, 311²²
   installs provincial cult in Lower Pannonia: 304, 306
   dies imperii of: 329⁶², 487⁷⁷, 496¹³⁵, 497¹³⁹, 517²⁶², 528
   addressed as *Caesar noster*: 334⁸⁶
   linked with Jupiter: 337
   vice-regent of Jupiter: 473¹²⁹
   birthday of: 491¹⁰⁴, 605
   granted title of Parthicus: 496¹³⁶
   bust of: 536, 539
   statues of in provincial temple at Tarraco: 541
   corresponds with Pliny: 543
   silver bust of: 546
   statues of at Capitoline temple of Jupiter: 546, 547
   refuses statue beside cult idol: 547
   likeness of in Egypt: 548
   image of: 551
   accession of: 599
   τύχη of: 599

Tranquillitas: 460

Q. Trebellius Rufus: 224[22], 226, 240, 241, 241[4], 241[9]
Tres Galliae: see Three Gauls
Treveri: 138
tribes, named after living individuals: 25
tribus Iulia: 61
Tricasses: 581
Trinovantes: 197
Tullia, apotheosis of by Cicero: 54
Tutela, image of: 567
Twelfth Urban Cohort: 536
Tyche: 456
    of Antioch: 52
    of Augustus, oath by: 377[8]

Ubii: 138, 139
Ulattia Metrodora: 319[17]
C. Ulattius: 318, 319, 319[14, 17], 320
C. Ulattius Aper: 319[17]
C. Ulattius Meleager: 319[17]
C. Ulpius Bonus: 302[9]
Ulpius Eurycles: 552
M. Ulpius Aeglus: 538
Upper Moesia, provincial assembly of: 302[11]
Urb Roma Aeterna: 266
Urbs Roma: 353 ff.
    priesthood of: 355, 356 f., 356[22], 360
    cult of in provinces: 357[25]
    birthday of: 495
Ursus: 605
    metrical inscription of: 565

Valens: 467
Valentinian: 467
Valentinian III, birthday of: 489
Valeria Myggyne: 289
Valeria Paetina: 166[108]
Valerian: 281[68], 416, 421, 578
Valerian, son of Gallienus: 553
Val(erius) Valens: 601
L. Valerius Flaccus: 47

L. Val(erius) Optatus: 603
L. Valerius Propinquus: 276
M. Valerius Sassius Pudens: 289
M. Valerius Severus: 289 ff., 289[48], 290[53]
Vanacini: 328
Varus: 138
P. Veidius Pollio: 439
Vellavi: 581
L. Venuleius Apronianus: 531
Venus: 74, 87[30]
Venus and Roma, temple of: 141[298], 546
Venus Erycina, temple of: 546
Venus Genetrix,
    temple of: 59[24f.], 59[30], 64[63], 65[73], 67, 71, 74, 87[28], 115[128]
    cult statue of: 79, 545
Venus Pompeiana, procession of: 554
Vercelli, altar at: 511 f.
Vercingetorix: 100
Vergil: 77 ff.
    birthday of: 531
M. Verrius Flaccus: 499[154]
Verus: see L. Aurelius Verus
Vespasian: 197, 230, 233[62], 235, 235[70], 236, 237, 238, 238[80], 238[81], 239,
    240, 242, 245, 266, 268, 270[5], 275[32], 276, 277, 278[48], 279[58], 282[2],
    295, 296[13], 297[21], 297, 298[28], 310, 316, 333, 356, 360, 410[45], 427[24],
    441, 442, 463[56], 472, 485, 546, 558
    miracles of at Alexandria: 39[54], 296
    temple of at Pompeii: 91[55], 110, 175[27], 479[23], 503, 508[213], 511
    institutes or reforms provincial cults in West: 149, 298 ff.
    introduces Roma in Hither Spain: 201
    attitude to British provincial cult: 217
    rebuilds temple of Divus Claudius in Rome: 217, 296 f., 486[66]
    installs provincial cult in Baetica: 221, 224, 261 f., 273, 277[46],
    286, 389
    institutes provincial cult in senatorial provinces: 221, 238 f.
    installs provincial cult of Narbonensis: 241, 245, 273, 277[46], 261 f.,
    286, 389,
    founds provincial cult of Africa Proconsularis: 258, 263 f., 265, 268,
    273, 277[46], 286, 293, 389
    reorganizes Africa Proconsularis: 260, 268

unpopular in Africa Proconsularis: 262
creates cult of *conventus* of north-west Spain: 273
respects Divus Augustus and Divus Claudius: 274
modifies cult of Hither Spain: 276, 277⁴⁶, 279, 311, 391, 392
enlarges provincial centre at Tarraco: 280 f.
incorporates Lycia in Empire: 283
develops Spain: 287
installs provincial cult in Mauretaniae: 293 f.
stresses abstractions: 295 f.
with radiate crown: 296
cult of as healer: 297 f., 298²³
dedicates temple of Divus Claudius in Britain?: 297¹⁷
establishes cult centre at Arae Flaviae: 298, 311, 330
installs cult of *conventus* in north-west Spain: 298, 311
character of: 300
deified by senate: 300³⁹
and Fortuna: 466
adopts Victoria Augusti: 471
birthday of: 487⁷⁶, 613¹⁹
arrives at Rome: 530³³³
gold likeness of: 546
enters Rome: 585
Vesta: 461, 493, 509, 517
cult of on Palatine: 88³⁷, 90⁵⁰
temple of at Rome: 506¹⁹⁷
associated with cult of Divus Augustus: 506¹⁹⁷
Vestalia: 602
Vestals, procession of: 554
Vestra Pietas: 474
Vestra Tranquillitas: 474
M. Vettius Latro: 359
Vibia Modesta: 478, 481
G. Vibius Salutaris: 492, 548⁴⁴⁰, 552⁴⁶⁶, 561
L. Vibius Secundus: 282
M. Vibius Martialis: 442
vicomagistri: 85¹³, 110, 118¹⁴⁸, 119, 173¹¹, 175, 509, 511
vicorum magistri: 610, 615
Victoria: 60³³, 84⁹, 86¹⁷, 296, 390, 455, 457, 459, 460, 461, 467, 468, 468⁹³,⁹⁵, 469, 470, 507, 602
altar of: 111

dedication of statue of: 111[97]
temple on Palatine: 113, 118
in imperial ideology: 113 f.
personalization of: 114 f.
link with Augustus: 115
role of in Augustan ideology: 115 f.
cult of on Palatine: 116
of successive emperors: 116
of Octavian: 296[8]
statue of: 539
Victoria Augusta: 601
supplication to: 517
Victoria Augusta/Augusti: 463, 473[126]
Victoria Augusti: 86, 296[8], 466, 466 ff., 467[90], 472
as personal victory of Octavian: 471 f.
Victoria Caesaris: 457, 471
Victoria Caesaris Augusti: 464
Victoria Claudii: 464, 471
Victoria Galbae: 464, 471
Victoria Imperi Romani: 464[69]
Victoria Mariana: 114[119]
Victoria Othonis: 464, 471
Victoria Populi Romani: 464[69]
Victoria Sullae: 471
Victoria Vespasiani: 464, 471
Victoria Virgo, shrine of: 118[146]
Victories,
    at Lugdunum: 104 f., 112 ff., 176, 314, 314[43], 315
    origin of twin: 112[109]
    significance of at Lugdunum: 117 f.
    at Camulodunum: 200
    on architrave of temple at Pola: 437[9]
Victorinus: 467
Victoriolae: 468
Victory: 554
    statue of in Curia Iulia: 111, 111[97, 101]
    importance of for Augustus: 111 f.
    statue of commemorated in iconography: 111 f.
    theology of: 113 ff.
    of Curia: 115

association with dedication of altar at Lugdunum: 118
association with palm: 175 f.
Viducasses: 361
Vienna cameo: 163[83]
Vienne, temple of Augustus and Livia at: 167[117], 308[1]
L. Vipstanus Poplicola: 157
Aulus Virgius Marsus: 540[385]
virgo Vestalis: 426
virtues, cult of Republican magistrate's: 47[7], 457[14], 472, 472[123]
Virtus: 390, 406, 459, 460, 468, 469
Visidianus: 448
Vitalis: 445
Aulus Vitellius: 157
L. Vitellius: 134, 299, 468[93], 485, 528[318], 533
attends games at Lyon: 580
Volubilis: 285, 285[25]
becomes *municipium*: 289 f.
Volusianus: 320[18]
L. Volusius Saturninus: 546
vota: 507, 514 f., 515, 515[255], 528
of 3rd January: 496 f., 497[138 f.]
votive dative: see dative, votive
votives, see ex-voto's
vows: 89 f., 90[47]

weather, control of: 39
worship,
definition of: 43 f.
nature of: 43 f.
wreaths: 529 f.

Younger Drusus, birthday of: 490
Younger Scipio: 90[48]

Zeus: 8, 10, 17, 34, 40, 41, 43, 44, 46, 513, 520[273], 569
statue of at Olympia: 521
stoa of at Athens: 521[282]
Zeus Boulaios: 22
Zeus Eleutherios, libation to: 376[2]
Zeus Meilichios: 186

Zeus Olympios, temple of at Athens: 548
Zeus Oromasdes: 19
Zeus Panamaros, image of: 568
Zeus Philippios: 447[11]
Zeus Seleukeios: 447[11]
Zeus Soter, altar of at Pergamum: 22, 23, 36

2. PLACES AND LOCALITIES

Abdera: 524
Abusina: 441
Abydos: 496[134], 496[136]
Acci: 227[31]
Achaia: 233
Acmonia: 513[243]
Actium: 48, 79[45], 79[50], 81, 82, 83, 88, 115, 116, 117, 126, 127, 172, 176, 375, 484, 496[136]
Adadae: 423, 564
Adana: 477[15]
Aegeae: 582[656]
Aegina: 122[181]
Aequum: 287
Aflû: 452
Africa: 93, 110, 148[340], 178, 226, 312[24], 388[7], 395, 399, 400[18], 478, 531[337], 546, 587
    see also Proconsularis
Agedincum: 325
Ager Arvernorum: 442, 444
Ager Haeduorum: 444
Ager Senonum: 444
Agnin: 343[156]
Agri Decumates: 298, 311, 519
Ainay: 105, 314
Akraiphia: 269
Alba Fucens: 543[406]
Alban Mount: 69
Alcalà la Real: 542[396]
Alcala: 328[53]
Alcudio: 560
Alexandria: 14, 16, 24, 24[19], 36, 39[50], 39[54], 48[13], 56, 56[2], 84, 118, 296,

328[52], 339[120], 340, 481, 484, 487[74], 491, 496[134], 497[141], 519, 527, 530, 532, 569, 570, 604, 613[19]

Alexandria Troas: 476

Amiens: 524, 559, 559[508]

Amiternum: 554

Amphipolis: 3

Anagnia: 476

Anazarbos: 577[627]

Ancyra: 521[280], 573, 586

Andemantunnum: 144

Anicium: 442[33]

Ankara: 582[652]

Anticaria: 328

Antioch: 52, 56, 477, 519, 619

Antipolis: 132[244], 497

Apamea: 347[186], 348[192], 395[35], 433

Aphrodisias: 49, 445, 492, 515[256], 518[267], 529, 551[462]

Apollinopolis Heptakomia: 515[256], 583, 586

Appian Way: 341

Apta: 476, 526

Apulum: 498[147], 600

Aquae Flaviae: 580[642]

Aquae Sextiae: 613[19]

Aquileia: 346[180], 439, 478[16], 481, 504, 511, 586

Aquincum: 303, 303[19, 20], 346, 381, 539[384], 602, 606, 613, 611

Aquitania: 101, 143, 390, 391, 407, 407[40], 416, 417

Ara Ubiorum: 436

Arae Flaviae: 298, 299, 436

Arba: 498[147]

Arelate: 130[234]

Argentorate: 222

Argos: 47, 521

Arles: 109[82], 110, 134, 519, 522, 559, 583, 584[666], 619

Armenia: 298

Arnsburgerhof: 599

Arrabona: 602

Arsinoe: 488, 494, 501, 548, 550, 557, 561, 562, 567, 568, 583

Asia: 259, 297, 297[21], 494[125], 495, 496[136], 551[463]

Asia, province of: 28, 28[49], 47, 48, 50, 77, 127, 129[221], 158, 188, 198[18], 271, 569, 572, 577, 578, 586

Asia Minor: 5, 9[29], 18[80], 22, 46, 48, 81, 132, 185, 524[294], 531, 531[337], 547, 551, 552
Aspendus: 434
Asturia: 142, 143, 230[45]
Asturica: 223[20], 353, 355
Asturica Augusta: 143, 143[313]
Athens: 9, 10, 12, 21, 22, 25, 26, 27, 28, 33, 36, 47, 48, 57, 59, 123, 240, 241, 314, 341, 515[256], 548, 552, 567, 567[550], 569[570]
Augustodunum: 445, 571[580]
Auzia: 571[580]
Avaricum Biturigum: 442
Avenches: see Aventicum
Aventicum: 228, 523, 524, 535, 543, 559[508]
Avignon: 560
Azaila: 535, 541

Babylon: 9
Bactria: 9
Baetica: 149, 158, 160, 164, 187, 198[18], 219, 220[3], 221, 222, 223[19], 226, 226[31], 227, 227[31], 228, 230, 235[70], 237, 238, 238[83], 242, 261, 261[23], 262, 265, 268, 269, 273, 274, 277[46], 279, 284, 286, 298, 300, 311[19], 355, 356, 360, 389, 394, 395, 502, 578[632]
Banasa: 597[17]
Bargylia: 22
Bath: 406
Beausoleil: 131[238]
Belgica: 101, 143, 390, 391, 407, 407[39-40], 413[60], 416, 417, 417[69], 423, 432
Beneventum: 439, 440[21], 524[299]
Beni Barbar: 542[396]
Beroia: 562
Besançon: 131[238]
Betriacum: 85[12]
Béziers: 540[387]
Bibracte: 100
Bigerriones: 611[12]
Bilbilis: 524, 583, 619
Birdoswald: 418, 596, 598
Bitburg: 408
Bithynia: 77, 297, 573

Black Forest: 298
Bolsena: 247[48], 491[96]
Bonn: see Bonna
Bonna: 445, 601, 602, 605
Bordeaux: 110
Bosa: 244[26], 356[22]
Bosphorus: 286
Bosporus: 147[333]
Bourdigala: 443[36]
Bourges: 110, 381, 407
Bovillae: 162[78], 491[105], 537, 563, 616[37]
Bracara Augusta: 143, 143[313], 328[53], 439, 439[18]
Bremenium: 596
Brescia: 89[45], 512, 531[335], 614[21]
Brigetio: 498
Britain: 93, 103, 131[238], 201, 202, 216[96], 217[106], 286, 287, 288, 297[17],
    320[18], 389, 389[9], 391, 399, 407, 408, 409, 410, 413, 413[60], 416[65], 417,
    420, 431, 432, 467, 500, 525[304], 557[497], 594
Brixia: 491[104], 546
Brough-on-Humber: 431[57]
Brundisium: 76, 80, 172, 503, 513
Bubon: 522[285]
Buccino: 524[299]
Bulla Regia: 262, 264, 265, 451[34, 37], 522, 523[290], 583
Burgh-by-Sands: 418
Byzacena: 579[638], 583[664], 587[686]

Cabo Torres: 439, 439[18]
Caere: 510, 576
Caerleon: 418, 605
Caesarea Philippi: 147, 147[334]
Caesarea: 123[183], 124, 129, 147, 438, 521, 577, 582, 619
Caesarea: see also Iol Caesarea
Caesariensis: 282, 284, 285, 287, 293
Callaecia: 141, 142, 142[302], 143
Calles: 491[103]
Campania: 609
Camulodunum: 103[39], 123[186], 195, 197, 199, 200, 200[28], 201, 202, 203,
    213, 213[87], 215, 216, 216[96], 217, 217[106], 218, 255[96], 282, 287, 305,
    308[3], 309, 390, 436, 519, 524[297], 558

Cannstatt: 599
Cape Finisterre: 142
Capena: 491[104]
Caria: 16, 531
Carrara: 153
Carthage: 128, 258, 260, 261, 262[29], 266, 268, 503, 524[294], 526, 558, 578, 580
Casae: 603
Castlesteads: 340, 418, 598
Castra Lambaesitana: 599
Castulo: 164, 166[108], 221, 226[31], 227, 227[31], 228, 236
Cavillonum: 443
Centuripe: 613[18]
Ceos: 48
Cestrus: 522[285]
Chalcis: 46, 47, 51[28]
Channel: 417
Chateauneuf-les-Boissons: 131[238]
Cherchel: 523, 542[395], 583, 618
Chesterholm: 428[33]
Chichester: 423, 428
Chios: 49
Chisiduo: 246, 424, 568[561]
Chusira: 268[64]
Ciciliano: 614
Cigognier: 536, 559, 571[582]
Cilicia: 47
Cirta: 267, 498
Claros: 596
Clunia: 143[311], 177, 524
Coela: 425, 433, 611[13]
Colchester: see Camulodunum
Coligny: 499
Collipo: 498
Cologne: see Colonia Agrippinensis
Colonia Agrippinensis: 137, 139, 145, 287, 498
Colonia Agrippinensium: 604
Colonia Iulia Felix Lucus Feroniae: 524[298]
Commagene: 13, 18, 19, 20, 21, 24, 24[20], 26, 39, 551
Condate: 101, 104

Conimbriga: 164, 521[281], 524, 559[507]
Corbridge: 595
Corduba: 166[108], 219, 220, 220[3], 221, 227[31], 238, 279, 279[58], 281, 321[21], 394, 558, 580[642]
Corinium: 597
Corinth: 46, 270[8], 283, 423, 425, 461[43]
Cornus: 244
Corsica: 328
Cos: 270[7], 453
Cottian Alps: 299[31]
Croix-Rousse: 100
Ctesiphon: 329
Cuicul: 263, 264, 265, 498[148], 597, 600
Cumae: 91[55], 132[245], 490, 509, 510, 513, 516, 517
Cures: 491[104]
Cyme: 49[20]
Cyprus: 548
Cyrenaica: 515
Cyrene: 36, 122[181], 514
Cyzicus: 163[85]

Dacia: 301, 303, 478
Dalmatia: 145, 287, 299[34], 302, 442[31]
Danube: 93, 301, 313
Delos: 23, 47, 429[42], 549, 609
Delphi: 548[438]
Dianium: 276
Didyma: 17, 573
Didymoteichon: 536[368]
Divodurum: 417[69]
Divona: 335[92]
Djebel Dokhan: 599
Djemila: 520[273]
Doclea: 145, 302[15], 329
Dougga: 451[37], 452, 522, 523[290], 583
Dura: 489[86], 499, 593, 594, 595, 597
Dura-Europus: 488

Ebchester: 401
Egypt: 9, 13, 14, 14[59], 16, 17, 24, 24[19], 30, 37, 38, 40, 60, 130[231], 198, 297,

395, 492, 492[109], 493, 493[116, 119], 494, 495, 499, 500, 501, 530, 548, 550, 551, 562, 566, 570, 590
Elephantine: 199[23], 495[128], 562, 571[587], 589, 590
Eleusis: 548, 574, 574[602, 604]
Elizmendi: 357
Emerita: 123, 125, 156, 158, 163, 165, 166[105], 168, 178, 180, 181, 183, 184, 198, 198[19], 236, 278, 278[52], 279, 279[58], 281, 281[69], 503, 520, 526, 528, 529, 558, 559, 566, 582[655], 583
Emesa: 348[192]
Emona: 287, 480
Ephesus: 23, 23[10], 47[6], 48, 50, 76, 77, 123, 126, 188, 278, 346[180], 492, 496, 496[133], 496[138], 514, 515, 515[256], 521, 531, 548[444], 551, 552, 557[500], 560, 563, 564[540], 568, 569[570], 573, 577, 618
Epidaurum: 145
Epidaurus: 571
Eriza: 477
Este: 524[299]

Falerii: 381[29], 576
Fano: 560[509]
Fendeille: 572
Ferento: 524, 524[299]
Fidenae: 491[104]
Forum Clodii: 91[55], 380[22-23], 381[29], 399[10], 490, 500, 510, 514, 516, 517, 518[264], 576, 585, 611[12]
Forum Gallorum: 490[93]
Fourvière: 100, 110, 112, 245[39]
Fucine Lake: 537
Fulda: 535[365]
Furnos Maius: 257, 262

Gabii: 525
Galatia: 129, 130[233], 297, 579[635], 582[652]
Gallecia: 222, 229[43]
Gallia Belgica: 144
Gallia Narbonensis: 224[22], 240, 241, 242, 243, 245, 245[32], 246, 247, 248, 250, 255, 298
Gangra: 130[233]
Gaul: 97, 98[8], 142, 146, 299, 318, 347, 391, 572
Gauls: 93, 103, 356, 389, 399, 501

Gebel Tukh: 496[135]
Geneva: 428, 434[81]
Germania Inferior: 139, 230[47], 249, 354
Germanies: 389, 390, 391, 399, 407, 408, 413[60], 416, 417, 432
Germany: 103, 138, 146, 222, 354, 354[9]
Gigthis: 568[560]
Gissey-le-Vieil: 443
Glanum: 583, 584[666], 619
Gorsium: 246, 303, 303[19, 20, 21], 304, 305, 306, 558
Gortyn: 495, 496[134], 611[12]
Gragnano: 532[341]
Greece: 43, 48, 531[337], 547, 562
Greetland: 407
Grosskrotzenburg: 599
Grumentum: 615
Gulf of Hammamet: 452
Gytheum: 47, 123, 278, 492[113], 514, 552, 564, 565, 566, 582, 617, 618

Hadrian's Wall: 452, 571[580]
Hadrimetina: 325
Haluntium: 453[47]
Heddernheim: 433, 498[148], 599
Henchir Suik: 607
Herculaneum: 161[69], 286[28], 523, 576
High Rochester: 596
Hippo Regius: 542
Hispania Citerior: 135, 135[265], 142, 142[307], 146, 155, 156, 157, 158, 164, 200, 201, 223, 223[19], 226[31], 227[31], 249, 269, 274, 276, 277, 277[46], 278, 278[48], 279, 284, 355[14], 358
    see also Tarraconensis
Hispania Ulterior: 142
Hispellum: 576
Hither Spain: see Hispania Citerior, Tarraconensis
Hohe Pforte: 606
Housesteads: 597
Hypaepa: 271, 586

Iasos: 16
Igabrum: 227[31]
Ilion: see Ilium

Ilium: 21, 25, 26, 33, 36
Illyricum: 73, 145, 487[74]
Intaranum: 444
Interamna: 463[56]
Intercisa: 604
Iol: 104, 147
Iol Caesarea: 148, 282, 285, 287, 288. 288[40], 578
Ipagrum: 611[12]
Ipsca: 541
Ireland: 99
Issos: 494[124], 501[166]
Istros: 562
Italica: 136, 183, 184, 368, 478, 523, 523[294], 580, 583, 619
Italy: 55, 73, 78, 90[48], 91[55], 103, 110, 175, 181, 247, 475, 481, 490, 492, 495, 509, 513, 515, 545, 557
Iulipa: 615[33]

Jarrow: 313
Jebel Mansour: 451
Jerusalem: 230
Judaea: 147, 181, 286
Jugoslavia: 503

Karanis: 496[135]
Kemerarasi: 617
Khargeh: 477[12]
Kirby Hill: 431[57]
Kirkby Lonsdale: 397, 420
Köngen: 498
Ktesiphon: 599

Lacipo: 524
Lagina: 531
Lambaesis: 429, 434, 467, 499, 540, 541, 550, 604
Lanchester: 418
Langres: 144, 434
Laodicea: 328[52]
Lapethus: 496[134]
Lauriacum: 605
Laus: 612

Lavinium: 51, 51[35], 52[35]
Leiria: 498
Lepcis Magna: 141[298], 167, 265, 291[56], 337, 338, 339[118], 340, 341, 346, 378, 450, 451[34], 468, 521, 522, 523, 523[290], 529, 541, 547, 583, 600, 611[12]
Lesbos: 48, 51
Lete: 47
Liburnia: 145, 299[34]
Lixus: 287
London: 409, 410
Lower Germany: see Germania Inferior
Lower Moesia: 302
Lower Pannonia: see Pannonia Inferior
Luceria: 454, 615
Lucus Augusti: 143, 143[313]
Lucus Feroniae: 423
Lugdunensis: 101, 131[236], 143, 390, 391, 407, 407[39], 416, 417, 438, 442, 445
Lugdunum: 51, 97, 98, 99, 100, 103, 104, 107, 107[69], 110, 112, 113, 117, 118, 122, 122[177], 125, 126, 129, 131, 132, 133, 134, 134[255], 134[260], 138, 142, 143, 144[315], 145, 148, 155[37], 167, 167[118], 176, 178, 182, 198, 199, 200, 200[32, 33], 201, 217, 232, 245[39], 251[69], 253, 255, 273, 277[46], 278[52], 280, 281, 281[69], 305, 306, 307, 308, 310, 311, 312, 312[24, 25], 314, 315, 316, 316[53], 317, 319[15], 321, 323[28], 324, 325, 325[34], 328, 329, 331, 332, 334, 347, 348, 348[195], 349, 362, 363, 363[12], 365, 390, 392, 393, 436, 437, 437[9], 494, 498, 498[147], 500, 500[163], 501, 504, 517, 519, 521, 524, 524[297], 526, 541, 557, 559, 565, 566, 571, 572, 578, 579, 579[635], 580, 581, 581[652], 582, 583, 584, 588
Luna: 491[104]
Lusitania: 55, 156, 157, 158, 163, 164, 166, 166[107], 178, 183, 198, 201, 236, 242, 269, 274, 278, 278[48], 279, 288, 298, 311[19], 355, 558[502], 578[632]
Luxeuil: 131[238]
Luxor: 496[134]
Lycia: 271, 286, 298
Lyon, Lyons: see Lugdunum

Macedonia: 13, 47, 233, 259, 562
Mactar: 167[116], 265, 563
Magdalensberg: 139, 140, 141, 167, 168, 247[48], 304[22]

Magnesia: 270
Mahemdieh: 496[136]
Mainz: 86[22], 138, 466, 560
Malaca: 395
Mantua: 582[652]
Marengo: 536, 543
Maritime Alps: 299[31]
Marsal: 132[244], 497
Marseille: see Massilia
Maryport: 418, 595, 598
Massilia: 103[47], 172, 248[54], 497, 503, 513
Matisco: 442
Mauretania: 92, 104, 147, 282[1], 286, 287, 478, 529[325], 536
Mauretania Caesariensis: 259, 578
Mauretaniae: 298
Mediolanum Santonum: 133, 325[34], 362[12]
Mediomatrici: 442
Megara: 548[438]
Mellaria: 219
Mérida: 522, 523, 523[290], 619
Mesopotamia: 323[29]
Messene: 186, 187, 514, 528
Milan: 434, 512[235], 612
Miletus: 23, 495[131]
Minnodunum: 428
Minoa: 496[134]
Minturnae: 520[275], 523[292]
Minturno: see Minturnae
Moesia: 146, 233, 302
Mogontiacum: 453, 453[50], 599, 601, 603, 604
Mograwa: 265, 438
Moirans: 324
Monaco: 536[368]
Mons Caelius: 158
Monte Louro: 142
Motella: 496[136]
Msaken: 525[303], 536
Mt. Eryx: 546
Mulva: 166
Munda: 56, 57, 58[15], 114, 175

Municipium Latobicorum: 606
Mutina: 114[119], 116[138]
Mylasa: 47, 48, 141[298], 521[280]
Mytilene: 47, 48, 51, 171, 172, 177, 178, 186, 188, 189, 496, 497, 548, 564[542]

Naples: 78, 87[26], 91[55], 133[250], 510, 513, 539[382], 546[430], 556, 570, 572[592], 575, 583[663], 584
Narbo: 110, 174, 188, 196, 238, 245, 245[32], 246[40], 247, 248, 248[56], 249, 249[61], 250[65], 251[71], 252, 254, 255, 256[97], 277, 278[52], 321[21], 379, 379[18], 380, 380[22], 385, 388[5], 410, 424, 450, 476, 479[23], 482, 497, 500, 501, 502, 504, 505, 507, 508, 509[219], 510, 514, 515, 516, 517, 518, 519, 521, 522, 522[286], 524[297], 525, 526, 531, 550, 557, 558, 565, 566, 580, 581[652], 582[655], 583[665], 584, 588, 610, 611, 611[12], 612, 613, 617, 618
Narbonensis: 93, 135, 149, 223[19], 238, 261, 261[23], 262, 268, 273, 277[46], 286, 300, 314, 315[44], 355[14], 364[22], 388, 389, 399, 579[638]
Narbonne: see Narbo
Narona: 438, 612[14]
Nasium: 417[69], 423, 428
Nassenfels: 131[238]
Naucratis: 24[16], 493[117]
Naulochus: 79, 115, 117, 176
Neapolis: 510[221]
Nemausus: 131[238], 132[244], 134, 245, 252, 253, 306, 308[1], 315, 330[65], 479[23], 480, 497, 504, 509, 511, 519, 523, 524[297, 299], 525, 526, 527, 540, 559, 578, 584, 587, 614[23], 618
Nemrud Dag: 18, 19, 551
Neoclaudiopolis: 496[136]
Nescania: 394, 449, 502, 526, 529
Neuilly-le-Réal: 535, 545
Neustad: 433
Nicaea: 77, 126, 564[542], 573[598]
Nicomedia: 126, 129, 200, 367, 521[280]
Nicopolis: 386
Niederbieber: 606
Nîmes: see Nemausus
Nizy-le-Comte: 523
Noega: 142, 142[302]
Noeta: 142[302], 143

Nola: 163[84], 433, 438
Noricum: 139, 140, 167, 287
Novae: 604
Novaria: 434[77], 612
Numidia: 112, 346[176], 579[638], 583[664], 587[686]
Nysa: 572[590]

Obenburg: 599
Oenoanda: 478[22], 479[23], 513[242], 551[465], 564[541], 617
Oescus: 244[26], 302
Okehampton: 195[4]
Old Carlisle: 424
Old Penrith: 431[57], 434
Olisipo: 166[105]
Olympia: 274[27], 521, 522[285]
Ombos: 496[134]
Oppidum Novum: 287
Orange: 522, 583, 584[666], 618
Osterburken: 599
Ostia: 85[13], 141, 167, 327[49], 346[181], 425, 433, 491[103, 104], 492[106, 107, 108], 512, 523[292], 537, 539, 556, 561, 567, 586, 615
Oxyrhynchus: 493, 494, 501, 530, 549

Padua: 353
Padum: 524[299]
Paguignan: 247[47, 49]
Palatine: 576, 590[697]
Palestine: 561
Palmyra: 593
Pannonia: 138, 145, 146, 287, 302, 304, 306
Pannonia Inferior: 302, 303, 304, 305
Pannonia Superior: 302
Papcastle: 606, 607
Paphlagonia: 130[233]
Paris: 441
Pednelissus: 565
Pergamum: 12[43], 13, 22, 47, 50, 102, 126, 129, 159, 172, 187, 199, 215, 271, 313[31], 367, 461[43], 489[88], 495[132], 513[243], 514, 516, 517, 521[280], 562, 567, 569, 571, 573, 574, 577, 586
Périgueux: 363[12], 366[28], 524

Persia: 42, 60
Perusia: 438
Petelia: 586
Pézilla: 253
Pharsalus: 47
Philadelphia: 496[134]
Philae: 199[23]
Philippi: 48, 87[30]
Philippoupolis: 573
Phrygia: 578
Picenum: 112
Piraeus: 549
Pisa: 490, 524[299]
Pisaurum: 449, 452, 525[299], 613[20]
Pisidia: 565
Poetovio: 445, 504, 525, 537, 540
Pola: 167, 308[1], 437
Pompeii: 52[36], 91[55], 110, 166[109], 175[27], 310[14], 376, 438[11], 479[23], 503, 504, 508[213], 511, 532[341], 554, 611[12], 615
Pompeiopolis: 47
Potenza: 112
Praeneste: 103, 491[104], 499[154], 547
Priene: 23[10], 522[285]
Proconsular Africa: see Proconsularis
Proconsularis: 149, 238, 259, 260, 261, 261[23], 262, 262[24,] 266, 267[57], 268, 273. 277[46], 286, 293, 298, 299, 299[33], 300, 323, 345, 346, 389, 501, 529[325], 583[664], 587[686]
Prusias: 48[13]
Ptolemais: 32, 16, 514
Ptolemais Hermiu: 496[134]
Ptuj: 503, 509, 511, 517, 525
Puteoli: 87[26], 92[56], 330, 331[73], 424, 438, 481, 525[299], 569, 570, 576, 583[663]

Raetia: 432
Ravenna: 512
Remesiana: 302[11]
Rennes: 524, 547
Rhamnonte: 548
Rhine: 93, 345, 500[162]

Rhineland: 390
Rhodes: 33, 49
Rhône: 100, 308, 314³⁹, 365, 390, 572
Rhône Valley: 308
Rindern: 110
Risingham: 452
Rome: 52, 53, 54, 55, 57, 60, 61, 67, 69, 75, 76, 78, 84, 90⁴⁸, 91, 91⁵⁵,
    103, 110, 111, 120, 122, 123, 125, 128, 148, 162, 163, 173, 175,
    177⁴⁶, 182, 183, 183¹⁹, 184, 197, 203, 205⁴⁷, 230, 241, 286, 287,
    296¹³, 312, 329⁶⁰, 330⁶⁸, 336, 338, 341, 344, 348, 356, 378, 409, 425,
    428, 428³⁸, 447, 452, 474, 475, 481, 482, 483, 484, 486⁷¹, 487, 488⁸²,
    489, 490, 493, 493¹¹⁹, 504, 505, 506¹⁹⁷, 507, 510, 511²²⁶, 513, 515,
    520, 522, 523²⁹³, 525, 526, 530³³³, 544⁴⁰⁹, 545, 546, 557, 576, 583⁶⁶³,
    585, 594, 596, 598, 600, 602, 603, 610, 611¹³, 614²³, 615
Rumilly: 242¹⁴
Ruscino: 524
Rusicade: 267, 267⁶¹, 498, 503, 526, 529
Rusucurru: 287

Sabratha: 523²⁹⁴, 524²⁹⁸, 529, 589⁶⁹²
Safar: 542³⁹⁵
Saint-Quentin: 408⁴³
Saint-Tropez: 254
Saintes: see Mediolanum Santonum
Sala: 287³⁶
Salona: 601
Salpensa: 395
Samaria Sebaste: 147, 147³³⁴
Samos: 7, 48, 521²⁸⁰, 548
Santarem: 157
Saône: 308, 365, 390
Sardinia: 267⁵⁷, 299, 299³³, 356²²
Sardis: 548
Sarmizegetusa: 302, 302⁸, 346, 498¹⁵⁰
Sárpentele: 303, 304
Sarrok: 597
Savaria: 287, 303, 346, 439
Scardona: 145, 299³⁴, 302, 302¹⁵
Seleuceia: 17
Selinus: 520²⁷³

Sicily: 103, 484
Side: 552
Simitthus: 262, 264, 265
Sinope: 329
Sitifis: 536
Siwa: 8, 10
Skelani: 498
Smyrna: 49, 159, 189, 514, 571, 577, 577[627]
Solômos: 283
Somerdale: 396, 408
Soriano del Cimino: 511
Soriano: 525
Spain: 93, 132[238], 150, 178, 226, 236, 238, 259, 269, 299, 316, 354, 357,
    587
Spain, north-west: 146, 356[19], 519
Spains: 356
Sparta: 9, 10, 269
Spello: 491[101]
Spoletium: 616
Stobi: 453[47]
Stratonicea: 568
Straubing: 597[18]
Sulci: 244
Syedra: 328
Syene: 199[23], 589
Syracuse: 46, 122[181]
Syria: 15[65], 594
Syros: 496[133], 586
Székesfehérvár: 303, 304

Tác: 303[21]
Talmis: 527[313], 603
Tanagra: 552
Tarentum: 110
Tarracina: 437
Tarraco: 103[39], 110, 121[167], 123, 125, 129[227], 132[244], 134[255], 135, 136,
    136[272], 144[315], 146, 151, 154, 155, 156, 157[46], 158, 163, 165, 168, 171,
    172, 174, 175, 176, 177, 177[46], 178, 179[58], 180, 180[2], 181, 183, 188,
    198, 198[19], 242, 247, 247[50], 253, 254, 255, 256[97], 268[63], 271, 272[20],
    273, 275, 276, 277, 277[46], 278, 278[52], 279, 279[58], 280, 281, 281[69], 298,

305[34], 306, 309, 316, 328[51], 346[176], 357, 358, 378, 392, 427, 449, 463[64], 476, 497, 500, 503, 504, 505[187], 513, 517, 518, 519, 519[268, 270], 520, 520[273], 523, 524, 524[297], 526, 541, 557, 558, 559, 559[505], 563, 565, 566, 571, 580, 581, 581[652], 582[655], 583, 600, 611[12], 615, 619

Tarraconensis: 142, 155, 158, 163, 164, 166[107], 167, 178, 187, 198, 226[31], 242, 243, 265, 266, 268[63], 275, 278[48], 279[55], 288, 298, 311, 355, 360, 391, 395, 442[31], 578[632]

see also Hispania Citerior

Tchonemyris: 496[135]

Tebessa: 499

Tebtunis: 132[243], 488, 493, 494

Teos: 16, 23, 37, 186, 567

Termessus: 548[440]

Termessus Minor: 551[465], 553,

Testur: 398[6]

Teutoburg forest: 138

Teverina: 524[299]

Thamugadi: 357

Thapsus: 56, 57, 114, 115

Thespiae: 188

Thessalonica: 171

Theveste: 501

Thinissut: 452

Thrace: 21[2], 287

Thracian Chersonese: 3

Three Gauls: see Tres Galliae

Thubursicu Numidarum: 228[35]

Thugga: 229[39], 439

Thysdrus: 499, 524[294]

Tibur: 434[77], 491[105], 615

Ticinum: 310[14]

Tifernum: 525

Timgad: 523[293, 294]

Tingi: 282[4], 287, 287[36], 288[42], 587

Tingis: see Tingi

Tingitana: 282, 285, 287, 288, 292, 293

Tipasa: 287, 537, 540

Tolosa: 240

Tomis: 532, 565

Tor Tignosa: 52
Toulouse: 241, 241[9], 540[387], 583
Traianopolis: 496[136]
Tralles: 175
Trebula: 585
Trebula Suffenas: 586, 613[19], 614
Tres Galliae: 143, 167, , 187, 199, 200, 223[19], 227, 244, 277[46], 286, 288, 307, 319, 349, 356, 361, 363, 365, 399, 407, 408, 416, 430[46], 500, 575, 578, 579, 580, 581
Trier: 407
Trion: 134[255], 281[69]
Tripolitania: 378, 579[638]
Troesmis: 302
Troy: 56
Tucci: 166[108]
Tunis: 110, 476[9]
Tupusuctu: 497[141, 143]
Turiaso: 153[20]
Tusculum: 466, 491[104]

Uchi Maius: 542[396]
Ulmetum: 498
Ulpia Traiana: 601
Unter-Haidin: 503
Upper Danube: 345
Upper Germany: 230[47]
Upper Moesia: 302[11]

Vaison: 523, 583
Valence: 324
Valentia: 324
Valeria: 357
Veii: 491[103]
Venusia: 615[33]
Vercellae: 54, 434[77], 612
Vercelli: 511, 529
Verecunda: 395[35]
Verulae: 492[107]
Verulamium: 287
Vicus Aesculetus: 508

3. LITERARY AUTHORITIES

Accius
    646 R: 383[40]
    E92 R: 383[40]
Acta Sanctorum
    21: 579[635]
Acts of Marcellus
    1: 587
    2: 587[687]
Acts of Paul and Thecla
    26-39: 477
Acts of the Apostles
    17, 23: 452
Aelian
    VH 2, 19: 10
        12, 51: 44
Aeschylus
    Hicet. 980-83: 38[45]
Anthologia Palatina
    9, 307: 171
Appendix Perottina
    12, 6: 429
    28, 7: 429
Appian
    BC 2, 102: 59[25], 79, 545
        2, 106: 60, 61[42], 62, 65[73], 76[18]
        2, 146: 65
        2, 148: 67, 75, 311[22], 326[40]
        5, 132: 78, 79
    Pun. 136: 260[18]
Aristotle
    NE 7, 1, 2: 1145a, 22f: 3
    Pol. 3, 13, 1248a: 42
    Rhet. 1361[a], 28-37: 33
Arnobius
    Adv. Nationes 4, 1-12: 460[39]
Arrian
    Anab. 3, 3, 2: 8
        4, 4, 1: 34

4, 8, 1: 34
4, 11, 2 ff.: 33[5]
7, 23, 2: 9, 25[22]

Athanasius
Contra gent. 10, col. 21C: 7[5]

Athenaeus
4, 149D: 493[117]
5, 195A: 550
5, 198D, F: 125[197]
12, 537F: 34
197C-203B: 550[453]
266D: 3
289: 44

Augustine
De civ. D. 4, 21: 460[39]
21, 6: 567[550]

Augustus
RG 1-4: 117
3, 1: 111
4, 2: 89[46]
7, 3: 89[42]
9, 2: 90[48]
10, 1: 84[7], 570
10, 2: 89[41]
11: 206
12, 2: 206, 207, 209[70], 212[83], 172[9]
19, 1: 90[50]
19, 2: 88
24, 2: 83[4]
34, 2: 107, 109, 174[24]
35, 1: 108[75]

Aulus Gellius
10, 15, 17: 476
10, 15, 32: 476
14, 7, 7: 211
15, 21: 10[36]

[Aurel. Vict.]
De Caes. 3, 8: 334[84]
11, 6: 334

Ausonius
Mos. 478: 103[47]

Ordo Urb. mir. 19, 14-17: 252[73]

Caesar
  BC 3, 105: 175
  BG 6, 13: 101
    7, 63: 100
Cassiodorus, *Chron.*
  385D: 144
  396: 144
Cassius Dio
  15, 20, 2: 116
  39, 30, 4: 585
  43, 14, 6: 57[7]
  43, 14, 7: 66[79], 71
  43, 21, 2: 57[12]
  43, 44, 2: 74[7]
  43, 45, 2: 58
  43, 45, 3: 58[19]
  43, 46, 1: 66[79], 71
  43, 50: 260[18]
  44, 4, 4: 64[68], 78
  44, 4, 5: 61
  44, 4-6: 60
  44, 6, 1: 61[49], 70, 377
  44, 6, 3: 61, 68[94], 70
  44, 6, 4: 62
  44, 8, 1: 71
  44, 9, 1-2: 71
  44, 11, 2: 68, 69
  44, 50, 1: 377
  45, 1, 2: 80[52]
  45, 7, 1: 59[24], 64[63]
  47, 18, 2 ff.: 75
  47, 18, 4: 59[24], 64[63]
  47, 18, 5: 481, 530
  48, 43, 6: 175[31]
  49, 15, 5: 81, 211
  49, 43, 7: 285
  51, 1, 2-3: 81[69]
  51, 19, 2: 375[2], 516
  51, 19, 7: 84, 375[2]

56, 29, 2: 510[221]
56, 41, 1: 162
56, 46, 2: 159[62]
56, 46, 3: 161, 212[85]
56, 46, 4: 59[24], 161, 483[51]
56, 46, 6: 182
57, 8, 3: 377
57, 21, 3: 522
57, 24, 6: 163[85]
58, 2, 1-3: 160[69]
58, 4, 4: 522, 555
58, 8, 4: 159
59, 4, 4: 502
59, 7, 1: 161, 197
59, 7, 1 f.: 585
59, 13, 8: 556
59, 16, 10: 483[48], 555, 570
59, 21, 2: 580
59, 24, 7: 485
59, 27, 3: 565[545]
59, 28, 1: 159
60, 5, 2: 160[69], 485
60, 17, 1: 508
61, 20, 4: 570
62, 7, 2-3: 103[47]
62, 23, 3: 565[545]
62, 26, 4: 376[2]
63, 4, 2: 481
63, 20, 5: 570
63, 29, 6: 333
64, 1: 466
65, 1, 2[a]: 579, 580
65, 1, 3: 134
66, 15, 1: 29[58]
69, 10, 3: 313[33], 315[47]
72, 10, 5: 346
72, 17, 4: 555
72, 31, 1: 546
72, 31, 2: 555
72, 34, 1: 522[289]

75, 3, 2: 347
75, 4, 1: 555
75, 4, 5: 328[52]
77, 11, 1: 344
77, 16, 3: 338
78, 7, 4: 342[141]
79, 8, 6: 347[186]
Censorinus
    De die nat. 2, 3: 382[33]
              3, 1: 382[33]
            12, 2: 564[539]
Cicero
    Ad Att. 5, 21, 7: 127[206]
          12, 45, 2: 58[20]
          13, 28, 3: 58[16]
          13, 44, 1: 60[33]
          16, 15, 3: 65, 73
    Ad Fam. 11, 20, 1: 75
    Ad Luc. 3: 248[58]
    Ad Qu. fr. 1, 1, 26: 127[206]
           1, 1, 31: 47[7], 472
    Cat. 3, 2: 54
    De domo sua 39, 104: 384
             127: 212[84]
    De leg. 1, 1, 4: 125[199]
         2, 8: 303[21]
         2, 11, 28: 460, 465[79], 469
    De nat. deor. 2, 23, 61: 462[50]
              3, 88: 468[96]
    De off. 3, 20, 80: 534, 567
    Or. post red. ad Quir. 8, 18: 384
    Phil. 2, 85: 68, 69
        2, 110: 63, 74[13], 75
        2, 111: 60, 63
        3, 3: 90[50]
        3, 32: 384
        5, 23: 90[50]
        5, 43: 90[50]
    Pro Sest. 123: 209[72]
    Rep. 6, 13: 54

Verr. 2, 51: 46
   4, 67: 46
Clement of Alexandria
   Protrep. 4, 54, 6: 22
Clementis Recognitiones
   4, 13: 585[672]
Cod. Theod.
   5-7: 570[577]
   15, 4, 1: 522[289], 566[548]
Q. Curtius Rufus
   8, 5, 10: 513[241]
Cyprian
   Quod idola dii non sint 2: 92[59]

Demochares *ap.* Athen.
   6, 252 f.-253 a.: 375[2]
Demosthenes
   19, 280: 3
Diodorus
   16, 20, 6: 4
   16, 92, 5: 19[85]
   16, 95, 1: 19[85]
Dionysius of Halicarnassus
   2, 71, 3-4: 564
   7, 72, 13: 553
   7, 72, 15: 564[541]
   8, 55, 3: 211, 212[83]
   8, 55, 4-5: 211

Epictetus
   1, 19, 26-29: 477
Eupolis
   117, 6: 38
Eusebius
   HE 1, 44 f.: 578
      1, 47: 578
      4, 15, 5: 577[627]
      5, 1, 3-2, 8: 578
      5, 1, 47, cf. 44: 579[635]
      5, 1, 62: 135, 573

6, 41, 4: 528
7, 15: 533[352]
MP 1, 1: 37[40], 533[352]
1, 54: 533[352]

Frag. gr. Hist.
75, F.1: 12[49]
Festus (ed. Lindsay)
p. 146, 16 (= 157 M): 211[77]
p. 298, 25: 509[216]
pp. 304 f. (= 306), 7 f.: 210[76]
p. 424, 14: 438
p. 484, 32: 481
Firmicus Maternus
Math. 3, 5, 33: 571
Fronto (ed. Naber)
Princ. hist. p. 206: 306[41], 315
Ep. ad M. Caes. 4, 4, 1; p. 67: 476
4, 12, 4; p. 74: 330[68], 533

Gaius
Inst. 1, 4: 209[72]

Herodotus
6, 38: 3
Herodian
2, 10, 2: 327
2, 13, 6: 327
4, 2, 5: 570
4, 4, 5: 534[361]
5, 5, 6f.: 534
8, 6, 2: 553[475], 562[525]
8, 7, 2: 481
Homer
Iliad 22, 1.394: 38
24, 258: 42
Odyssey 8, 467 f.: 38
Horace
Ep. 1, 3, 17: 82[72]
2, 1, 15 f.: 377, 385

2, 1, 16: 377, 378
2, 2, 187: 382[33]
2, 2, 188 f.: 381[28]
Odes 1, 2, 43: 89[40]
1, 12, 49 ff.: 88[38]
3, 5, 1 ff.: 88[38]
3, 5, 2: 152[16]
3, 21, 20: 125[199]
4, 5, 31-36: 375
4, 5, 33 f.: 385
4, 5, 34 f.: 376[2], 377, 378, 384
Sat. 2, 3, 281: 610

Hyperides
Epitaph. col. 8: 41[66]
In Dem. 31: 10
Or. 1, col. 32: 59[27]

Isocrates
Ep. ad Phil. 3: 42

Josephus
Ant. Iud. 15, 8, 5: 147[334]
15, 9, 6: 147[334]
15, 339: 129, 438, 521
16, 137f.: 577
18, 55: 552
19, 75: 583
19, 87: 485[59]
Bell. Iud. 1, 21, 2: 147[334]
1, 21, 7: 147[334]
1, 414: 129, 438, 521
1, 415: 577
2, 169: 552
2, 194: 78[41], 547[435]
2, 409: 527
2, 414: 527
7, 71: 530[333]
7, 73: 585
7, 136: 554[485]

Juvenal
  Sat. 1, 42-44: 572[595], 573
       13, 233f.: 511[229]

Lactantius
  Div. Inst. 1, 15, 6: 92[59]
           1, 20: 460[39]
Leviticus Rabba
  34, 3: 561[517]
Livy
  1, 6: 303[21]
  1, 10, 5: 211
  1, 18, 6-10: 211[78]
  7, 30, 20: 384
  9, 46, 6-7: 212[84]
  10, 23, 1f.: 530
  27, 25, 8 f.: 141[298]
  30, 25, 1: 248[58]
  32, 25, 2-4: 40
  38, 56, 12: 545
  39, 46, 3: 585
  40, 52, 7: 253[85]
  Per. 139: 97, 131[235], 144, 244
Lucan
  Phars. 3, 399-425: 103[47]
            5, 510: 465
Lucretius
  3, 144: 384
Lydus
  De mag. 3, 8 : 563[535]
           3, 21: 563[535]
Macrobius
  Sat. 3, 3, 2: 438
        3, 7, 3: 438
Malalas
  Chron. 9, p. 216, 19-21: 547[433]
Marcianus
  Dig. 1:8, 6, 3: 216[100]
Martial
  *Ep.*3: 575[612]
     9, 101: 341

       12, 67: 531
       14, 163: 505[187]
Martyrdom of Apollonius
    7: 533[352]
    13: 527[315]
Martyrdom of Conon
    4: 533[352]
Martyrdom of Crispina
    1, 4: 528
    2: 533[352]
    2, 1: 528
Martyrdom of Dasius
    7: 534
    11: 533[352]
Martyrdom of Julius the Veteran
    2: 533[352]
Martyrdom of Pionius
    4, 24: 534
    8: 37[40], 533[352]
Martyrdom of Polycarp
    12: 527[314]
Martyrdoms of Agape, Irene and Chione
    3, 5: 527
Martyrdoms of Fructuosus, Augurius and Eulogius
    12: 281[68]
Martyrdoms of Perpetua and Felicitas
    7, 9 f.: 578[629]
Menander Rhetor
    Bursian p. 97; Spengel p. 370: 470[109]
Migne
    Patrol. 30 (11) col. 453: 579[635]
       30 (11) col. 461: 579[635]
Minucius Felix
    Oct. 8, 4: 480
       21, 9: 92[59]

Nonius
    173, 27: 383[40]

Obsequens
    70: 114[119]

Origen
  Contra Cels. 8, 67: 470[110]
  Exhort. ad mart. 33: 534
Ovid
  Amor. 3, 2, 43ff.: 553
  Fast. 1, 701: 423[6]
    1, 709 ff.: 208
    2, 634: 376[4]
    2, 637 f.: 375[1]
    3, 837 f.: 210[76]
    4, 951: 90[50]
    5, 145 f.: 384
    6, 810: 423
  Met. 8, 12f.: 467
    15, 858 ff.: 88[38]
    15, 865: 80
  Pont. 2, 2, 74: 425
    2, 8, 1-10: 532
    2, 8, 19 f.: 128[210]
    3, 1, 97 f.: 385[49]
    3, 1, 135: 425
    3, 1, 161-164: 385[49], 532
    3, 1, 163: 385[49], 532[343]
    3, 6, 16: 452[40]
    4, 6, 10: 385[49]
    4, 6, 20: 423
    4, 9, 105-110: 385[49]
    4, 9, 107 f.: 532
    4, 9, 109 f.: 532[344]
    4, 9, 111 f.: 532
  Trist. 2, 169-176: 467
    3, 1, 31-48: 108[75]
    3, 1, 47 f.: 108[74]
    3, 1, 78: 152[16]

Pacatus
  Paneg. 37, 3: 570[576]
    2[12]: 480
Panegyrici Latini
  6 (7), 2, 2: 469

6 (7) 5, 4: 467
10 (2), 11, 2: 400[20]
10 (2) 2, 5: 6[4]
37, 4: 480
Passion of St. Ignatius
2, 2, 1; p. 478 (Lightfoot): 469
Pausanias
1, 5, 5: 314
1, 8, 6: 28
1, 18, 6: 548, 549[446]
1, 24, 7: 548[438]
1, 26, 7: 567[550]
1, 40, 2: 548[438]
2, 1, 2: 260[18]
2, 20, 1-2: 186, 542[397]
4, 32, 1: 186, 542[397]
6, 11, 8: 3
10, 8, 6: 548[438]
Petronius
Cena Trimalch. 60, 7: 375[1]
                  60, 8: 376[4]
Phaedrus
5, 7, 25-7: 570[576]
5, 7, 38: 423, 429
Philo
In Flacc. 4, 23: 425
Leg. ad Gai. 22:151: 569[573]
               75-114: 186
               356 f.: 35
Plato
Rep. 540 B/C: 3
Pliny the Elder
NH praef. 11: 387
       2, 5: 460[39]
       2, 18: 387
       2, 94: 74
       3, 31: 247
       4, 111: 142
       5, 51: 286
       7, 162: 234[67]
       15, 137: 234[67]

17, 244: 175
33, 16: 253[85]
34, 14: 568
35, 12: 545
35, 14: 253[85]
Pliny the Younger
    *Ep.*2, 11, 2: 283
        2, 13, 4: 135, 224[22], 291
        3, 9, 4: 283, 284
        3, 9, 6-7: 283
        5, 20, 1: 283
        6, 31, 1: 334[86]
        10, 8f.: 525
        10, 35 f.: 497, 515
        10, 52: 517[262]
        10, 71: 216[100]
        10, 96, 5: 533, 543[404]
        10, 96, 5 f.: 565
        10, 96, 6: 534, 543
        10, 100 f.: 497, 515
        52 f., 102 f.: 528
    Paneg. 1, 3: 341[136]
          2, 3: 301
          11, 1: 297, 387[64]
          35, 4: 387[64]
          52, 1: 387[64]
          52, 2: 301
          52, 3: 243, 243[21], 543
          54, 1f.: 570[576], 575
          80, 4-5: 337
          89, 2: 301[4]
Plutarch
    Amat. 9:753 E: 59[26]
    Ant. 24, 4: 48
    C. Gracch. 18, 2: 53, 533
    Caes. 6, 1: 112[103]
        57: 260[18]
        57, 3: 62
        60, 3: 71
        67, 4: 66

Cat. Maior 19, 4: 545
Cic. 2, 1: 490
Demetr. 10, 12: 34
            11, 1: 25[22]
            12: 23, 41
            12, 2: 26
Dion 29, 1: 38
            46, 1: 4[9], 38
Flam. 16, 3-4: 46
            16, 4: 569[572]
            17, 1: 47
Lys. 18, 2: 7
            18, 4: 25
Marcell. 23, 7: 46
Marius 27, 5: 54, 375[2]
            32, 4: 112[104]
Mor. 219e: 10
Numa 6, 2: 469[108]
Otho 3, 1: 556
Sulla 6, 1: 112[104]
Polybius
    5, 27, 6: 13
    26, 1[a]: 17
Pomponius Mela
    3, 11: 143
    3, 13: 142, 143[310]
Porphyrion
    ad Horace, *Sat.* 2, 3, 281: 610
Porphyry
    De abst. 2, 24 (Budé): 37[39]
Posidippus
    apud Athen. 318D: 39
Propertius
    4, 1, 23: 509[216]
    4, 6: 81, 87[32]
Prudentius
    Cathem. 5, 149-56: 567
    Contra Symm. 1, 245-250: 520[274]
                    1, 247: 506[197]
                    1, 248: 527
                    1, 250: 520

Peristeph. 6: 578[630]
Pseudo-Acron
  ad Horace, *Sat.* 2, 3, 281: 610
Ptolemy
  Geogr. 2, 6, 3: 141
          2, 11, 15: 298
          2, 13, 3: 140

Quintilian
  De inst. orat. 6, 3, 77: 121[167], 146, 154[25], 171, 181, 503, 526
          6, 3, 79: 137
          8, 5, 15: 137

Scribonius Largus
  Compos. 60: 334[84], 424[11]
          163: 334[84], 424[11]
  Ep. ded. 13: 424[10-11]
Seneca
  ad Polyb. 13, 2: 424[10]
  Apoc. 8, 3: 196
  De cons. ad Marc. 22, 4: 522
  De ira 3, 18, 1: 54, 534
  De tranquill. an. 14, 9: 424[11]
  frg. 36: Haase, p. 24: 566
Servius
  ad Aen. 1, 330: 470[115]
          1, 446: 211
          3, 81: 475[3]
          4, 262: 479[27], 480[29]
          5, 45: 152[16], 201[38]
          6, 777: 53
          7, 612: 480[28]
          8, 664: 475
          12, 139: 426
  ad Ecl. 4, 10: 82[72]
          9, 46: 57[11]
SHA
  Ael. Ver. 7, 1: 521[281]
  Alex. Sev. 28, 6: 521[281]
          43, 6: 520[278]

Ant. Pius 6, 7: 555
      9, 2: 252
      12, 5: 466
      13, 3-4: 212[85]
Carac. 5, 7: 562[525]
Commod. 9, 2: 520[274]
Gall. Duo 8, 1: 564[537]
      8, 6: 554
Hadr. 10, 1: 314[39]
      12, 2: 306[41], 315[47]
      12, 3: 150, 305[34], 316, 328[51]
      13, 6: 306[41], 315[46], 521[278]
Marc. Anton. 3, 5: 533[350]
      7, 3: 466
      11, 4: 580
      18, 6: 533
      27, 6: 580
Max. et Balb. 17, 2: 534
Maxim. Duo 24, 2: 534, 553[475], 565[546]
Pert. 15, 3-4: 328
Sept. Sev. 3, 4: 150, 328[51]
      3, 5: 347
      3, 9: 343
      6, 9: 329
      7, 8: 328
      22, 3: 468
      23, 5 f.: 466
Sev. Alex. 29, 2: 533[350]
      31, 55: 533[350]
Tac. 9, 5: 489[88], 573
Sidonius Apollinaris
Carm. 23, 40: 583[665]
      23, 41: 252[73]

Silius Italicus
    2, 475-525: 469[108]
Solinus
    27, 11: 260[18]
Statius
    Silv. 5, *praef.*: 423, 429

Theb. 10, 632-635: 468
      10, 780f.: 469[108]
      12, 493f.: 469[108]

Strabo
    4, 3, 2: 101, 102, 122, 131[235], 200, 581[651]
    5, 4, 7: 510[221]
    7, 7, 6: 81[69]
    17, 1, 54: 199[23]
    17, 3, 12: 147[335]
    17, 3, 15: 260[18]

Suetonius
    Aug. 5: 212
       7, 1: 533, 545
       7, 2: 107[69]
       18: 81[69]
       26, 3: 172
       29, 3: 82
       35, 2: 585
       47: 266
       52, 1: 46, 92[58], 126, 188, 198, 834
       53, 2: 570
       57: 505[191]
       57, 2: 570[576]
       58: 424[13]
       59: 79[44], 546
       59, 3: 583
       60: 147[333]
       70: 81
       79, 2: 90[50], 424[10]
       91, 2: 88, 505[188]
       92, 1: 175[33]
       94, 4: 80[52]
       94, 11: 175
       98, 2: 92[56], 481, 532, 569[573]
       98, 2, 5: 87[26]
       98, 5: 510[221]
       100, 4: 159[62]
    Caes. 10, 1: 211
       11: 112[103]
       76, 1: 61[42], 65[73], 74[7], 76[18]

84, 2: 65
88: 74
Claud. 1, 3: 500[162], 502
    2, 1: 97, 131[235], 500[163], 578[632]
    9, 1: 573
    11, 2: 160[69], 510[221], 555[490]
    45: 158
Domit. 4, 4: 478, 572
    13, 2: 334
Gaius 14, 3: 565[545]
    15, 1: 556
    16, 4: 483[48], 555, 570
    20: 134, 137, 572
    21: 197
    22: 141[298]
    22, 3: 563
    24, 2: 377
    27, 3: 377
    35: 134[260]
Galba 4, 3: 466
    11: 333
    18, 2: 466
Nero 18: 217
    20, 3: 570
    25, 1: 570
    57, 1: 563
Tib. 13, 1: 543[399]
    17, 2: 116[134]
    26: 521
    26, 1: 159[56], 543
    27: 427
    65, 1: 544[411]
Titus 2: 544
    4, 1: 543[399]
Vesp. 4, 3: 262[25]
    7: 296
    8, 4: 262
    9: 202[40], 217, 297
    12, 23, 4: 295[1]
    23, 4: 295

Vitell. 2, 5: 528[318], 533
Symmachus
   Rel. 3: 530[332]

Tacitus
Agric. 13, 5: 214
Ann. 1, 10: 92[55], 201[34]
     1, 14: 160[69], 163
     1, 39, 1: 137
     1, 39, 2: 137, 138
     1, 39, 4, cf. 8: 138
     1, 42 f.: 138
     1, 43: 138[282], 214
     1, 54, 1: 162[77]
     1, 55: 150[2]
     1, 57, 2: 139, 475
     1, 58, 2: 139
     1, 73: 85[13], 159, 537, 613
     1, 78: 150, 173, 198, 213[89], 284, 316
     2, 17, 2: 384
     2, 41: 214, 466
     2, 49: 197, 213[87]
     2, 64, 2: 330[66]
     2, 83: 161[69]
     2, 83, 1: 556
     2, 83, 2: 162
     2, 87: 427
     3, 44: 101, 581[651]
     3, 63: 214
     3, 64: 215
     3, 64, 2: 163[84]
     3, 64, 4: 162[78]
     3, 70: 533
     3, 72, 5: 522
     4, 2, 4: 522
     4, 15: 150[1], 159, 198[18], 284
     4, 36: 163[85], 215
     4, 37: 126, 150[1], 198, 215, 284
     4, 37 f.: 198[18]
     4, 37, 1: 158

Velleius Paterculus
   2, 27, 6: 114[120]
   2, 43, 4: 112[103]
   2, 91, 1: 107[69]
   2, 123, 1: 510[221]
Vergil
   Aen. 8, 704 ff.: 87[32]
   Ecl. 1, 6-8: 77[33]
       1, 7: 92[56]
       1, 7 f.: 531
       1, 40-41: 77[33]
       1, 42 f.: 78[37]
       1, 43 f.: 531
       4, 8-10: 80[56]
       5, 65 f.: 80[58]
   Georg. 1, 24 f: 79[46]
       1, 24-42: 79
       1, 42: 79[48]
       1, 339-350: 531[339]
       1, 503 f.: 79
       3, 12-39: 582[652], 619
       3, 13-25: 79
       3, 16-25: 590[698]
Vitruvius
   3, 2, 7: 153
   4, 8, 7: 212[82]
   5, 1, 6 f.: 560[509]
   5, 1, 7: 174
   5, 1, 7 f.: 91[55]
   Prol. 1: 424[10]

Xenophon of Ephesus
   1, 2, 2-5: 551

Zonaras
   11, 16, p. 47, 3-7D: 579
Zosimus
   2, 12, 1: 553[475]
   4, 59, 3: 530[332]
   5, 38, 2: 530[332]

4. INSCRIPTIONS

APF
   5 (1913), pp. 156 f., no. 1: 38[48]

BullEpig
   1944, 82: 241[8]
   1958, 496: 313[31]
   1969, 495: 23[9]
   1971, 307: 569[568]
   1971, 142: 159[59]
   1983, 174: 137[275]

CIG
   2282: 79[43]
   2715a: 568
   3062: 567[552]

Durrbach, *Choix de* Délos
   171: 549[450]
   172: 549[450]
   175: 549[450]
   176: 549[450]

Forsch. in Ephesus
   4, 3
      24: 76[26]

Hesperia
   10 (1941), pp. 72 ff., no. 32: 241[8]

I Crete
   4
      272: 496[136]
      300: 495
I Didyma
   148: 572
I Erythrai
   64: 23[15]

I Ephesus
    1a 27: 492[112], 549[444], 572[590]
IG
    2²
        3277: 137[275]
        3289-3385: 548
        3407: 548[440]
        4193: 226, 240
    3
        805: 270, 425
        1085: 426
    5,1
        305: 269
        463: 270[7], 425
        503: 269
        504: 269
        553: 269
        554: 269
        555: 269
        556: 269[3]
        1172: 426
    7
        1773: 572[588]
        2234: 426, 440
        2711: 199[27]
        2713: 269
    12,2
        44: 172
        656: 177
    12,5
        663: 496[133], 586
    12, Suppl.
        124: 587
        Addenda suppl. *ad* 2, 9; p. 208: 177
    14
        2495: 584
        2525: 571[580]
IGBulg
    47: 497[144]

30: 503
39: 513
95: 177
144: 423[6]
180: 426
353: 496, 514, 562[529], 571, 573, 574, 587
353d: 516
362: 308[1]
566: 327[49]
623: 496[136]
751: 496[136]
1017: 496[134]
1431: 571
1608: 271, 425[14]
1608c: 586
1615: 496[134]
1756: 548

I Olympia
56: 510, 556
I Pergamon
374: 496, 514
Sardis
7, 1
8: 548
I Stratonikeia
2, 1
662: 531[336]

Le Bas-Waddington
496: 23[15]

Maiuri, *Silloge Rodi e Cos*
466: 453[49]
MAMA
4
309: 496[136]

OGIS
3: 22
11: 23[10], 186

760: 48
790: 270, 270[6], 425
804: 270[6]
813a: 271
814: 269
1101: 549

Wilcken, *Chrestomathie*
41: 495[128], 562[527], 571[587], 589
96: 488[81]
113: 492[109]
490: 492[109]
491: 515[256], 583
Wilcken, *Griechische Ostraka*
152-155: 199[23], 548[442]

AEpig:
1874, 129: 491[104]
1888, 57: 266[51]
1891, 142: 429
1895, 204: 323[29]
1897, 100: 272[20]
1902, 15: 288[39]
1902, 37: 247[52]
1903, 138: 253[85]
1903, 146: 498
1903, 273: 247[51]
1904, 38: 247[48]
1904, 95: 602
1905, 45: 499[154]
1908, 138: 253[87]
1908, 149: 272[20], 355[14], 364[22]
1909, 184: 580
1910, 133: 604
1911, 119: 323[29]
1911, 184: 524
1912, 19: 499
1913, 1: 539
1913, 124: 498

1913, 134: 539[382]
1914, 41: 293[69]
1914, 114: 433[70]
1915, 95: 157[51], 166[105]
1915, 96: 537
1916, 13: 264[35], 267
1916, 29: 600
1916, 75: 264
1916, 120: 329
1917-18, 10: 433[76]
1917-18, 44: 500[161]
1917-18, 111: 428[32], 428[34], 487[77]
1921, 19: 289[45]
1922, 70: 498
1924, 61: 229[39]
1925, 23: 226[27], 264
1925, 24: 226[27], 264
1925, 75: 167[117]
1926, 116: 428[36]
1927, 2: 423[3]
1928, 113: 234
1928, 147: 497[144]
1929, 156: 597
1930, 150: 399[15]
1933, 2: 548[440]
1934, 7: 545[421]
1934, 8: 545[421]
1934, 88: 571[587]
1936, 60: 496[135], 599
1936, 95: 487[74]
1937, 112: 395
1938, 43: 525[303]
1938, 149: 286
1939, 81: 359[36]
1939, 113: 453[47]
1940, 26: 502[174]
1940, 62: 124[88], 492[106], 539, 556, 567, 586
1941, 46: 579[638], 583[664], 587[686]
1941, 79: 294
1941, 105: 533[345]

1942-43, 37: 599
1944, 110: 498
1945, 123: 405[36], 408
1946, 2: 254
1946, 53: 247[51]
1946, 198: 174[22], 401[22]
1946, 201: 157[48]
1947, 53: 73[3], 576
1947, 69: 226[28], 241[8]
1948, 56: 359[34]
1948, 97: 488[77]
1948, 239: 445
1949, 40: 226[27], 264, 267
1951, 52: 360
1951, 62: 246, 251
1952, 159: 496[134]
1953, 24: 487[75]
1954, 104: 130[234], 248[57]
1954, 164: 491[104]
1954, 239: 247[48]
1957, 55: 563, 566
1957, 77: 542[395]
1957, 204: 400[18]
1957, 251: 278
1957, 295: 357[26]
1957, 338: 398[9]
1958, 134: 288[39], 357
1958, 244: 453[45]
1959, 78: 133
1959, 81: 133
1959, 308: 500[161]
1961, 53: 583[664], 587[686]
1962, 225: 399[14]
1962, 228: 599
1963, 3: 328
1964, 154: 491[103]
1964, 177: 226[27], 293[69]
1964, 177a: 262, 264
1965, 195: 380[22], 399[10]
1965, 341: 324

1966, 177: 157, 278[47]
1966, 181: 219, 321[21], 395, 404
1966, 183: 166, 242[14]
1966, 187: 353, 356
1966, 252: 324, 325[34], 363[14]
1966, 355: 451
1966, 509: 450[29]
1967, 94: 166[108]
1967, 187: 278[47]
1967, 195: 278[47]
1968, 321: 138[283]
1968, 422: 303[16]
1968, 588: 587[686]
1968, 591: 587[686]
1969-70, 405: 547[433]
1969-70, 110: 491[103]
1969-70, 214: 278[47], 355
1969-70, 388: 399[14]
1969-70, 548: 478[17]
1969-70, 592: 329
1969-70, 651: 439
1969-70, 747: 294
1971, 29: 425[15], 487[77]
1971, 33: 232, 488[78]
1971, 34: 231
1971, 183: 219
1971, 248: 499
1971, 395: 302[9]
1971, 442: 461[43]
1971, 477: 619
1972, 154: 586, 614
1972, 174. 156
1972, 204: 546[430]
1972, 284: 453[45]
1972, 432: 303[21]
1972, 433: 303[21]
1972, 699: 349[198]
1973, 138: 396[37]
1973, 236 303[17]
1973, 342: 408

1973, 343: 361[4]
1973, 436: 303[17]
1973, 494: 572[588]
1974, 274: 396[37]
1974, 345: 434, 612
1974, 369: 279
1974, 376: 279[55]
1975, 115: 488[78]
1975, 829: 548[440]
1976, 144: 73[3], 576
1976, 285: 279[55]
1976, 446: 606
1976, 458: 514
1976, 502: 599
1976, 698: 248[58]
1976, 737*bis:* 450[29]
1976, 782: 597
1977, 656: 302[9]
1977, 689: 302[9]
1977, 855: 450[29], 451
1978, 286: 540[385]
1978, 295: 423, 432[59]
1978, 402: 225[25]
1978, 526: 599
1978, 551: 599
1978, 778: 461[43]
1979, 388: 417[71]
1979, 403: 321, 323, 363[14], 365, 366
1980, 615: 225[26]
1980, 623: 133, 362[12]
1980, 634: 136[272]
1981, 504: 524
1981, 624: 323, 365, 366
1982, 520: 368
1982, 681: 618
1983, 643: 404[32], 415
Alföldy, *Flamines Provinc. Hispan.*:
    13: 247[50]
    38: 271[15], 272[18]
    55: 271[15], 272[18]

73: 271[15], 272[18]
Allmer-Dissart
2
    99: 581[649]
    100: 581[649]
Britannia
    8 (1977), p. 429, no. 16: 415
    9 (1978), p. 474, no. 6: 417, 419[76], 431[57]
    10 (1979), p. 346, no. 7: 417[71]

CIL
1
    XI, p. 244: *Fasti Amiternini:* 330[66]
2
    23: 440[24]
    41*: 157[48], 164
    46: 440[24]
    122: 278[47], 355[14]
    194: 166[105]
    471: 442[31]
    473: 157, 312[26]
    480: 183
    895: 225[26]
    1074: 587[684]
    1194: 253[87]
    1471: 579[638], 582[656]
    1516: 398[9], 611[12]
    1569: 542
    1643: 542[396]
    1663: 579[638], 582[656], 583[664], 587[685]
    1944: 225[25]
    1956: 583[664], 587[685]
    1963: 396
    1964: 292[66], 396
    1978: 433[76]
    1979: 547[433], 587[685]
    2008: 449
    2009: 394, 399[14]
    2038: 225[26], 232, 328
    2039: 225[26], 232, 328

2040: 225[26], 232, 328
2070: 399[15]
2221: 219, 221, 244[29], 346
2344: 219, 220, 244, 244[29], 395, 404
2349: 238[84]
2426: 234[65], 298[29], 328[53], 330[67]
2473: 580[642]
2477: 236
2479: 233
2573: 537[373], 540
2637: 353, 356
2641: 226[31]
2703: 439, 439[18]
2782: 177
2952: 357
3183: 357
3271: 164, 164[93], 221, 222, 224, 226[31], 228, 234, 236, 237, 239,
      275[32], 279
3278: 166[108], 226[31]
3279: 166[108]
3329: 272[20]
3350: 225[26], 232, 328[53]
3395: 227[31]
3412: 272[20]
3555: 438
3584: 276
3585: 276
3832: 453[45]
3840: 233, 233[61]
4061: 225[25]
4083: 600
4085: 449
4092: 558
4093: 153
4188: 156
4191: 272[20]
4199: 272[20]
4202: 153[21], 247
4205: 272[20]
4212: 276

4217: 272, 272[18], 272[20], 274, 274[31]
4219: 354[11]
4222: 272[20]
4223: 164, 272[20], 276
4224: 177[45]
4225: 272, 276, 278. 355
4226: 272, 272[20], 276, 279
4228: 272[20]
4230: 280, 541, 548
4235: 272[20]
4239: 272, 272[20]
4243: 272[20]
4247: 272[20]
4248: 244[29], 277, 357
4249: 272[20]
4250: 272[20], 276
4251: 276
4258: 272[20]
4280: 155[35], 280[64]
4289: 615[32]
4290: 615[32]
4293: 615[32]
4297: 615[32]
4303: 615[32]
4304: 615[32]
4306: 615[32]
4307: 615[32]
4514: 275[36]
4616: 225[25], 230
4721: 238[84]
5026: 440[24]
5182: 439
5232: 498
5264: 236, 278, 528[321], 535[363], 536[369], 558
5439: 479, 490
5488: 587[685]
5510: 238[84]
5514: 587[685]
5523: 579[638], 580[642], 582[656]
5617: 233

3390: 446, 449[23]
3427: 449[23]
3438: 539[384]
3487: 380[22], 381, 411[54], 611
3524: 606
3626: 303[17]
4038: 329[55], 537
4107: 615
4170: 346
4364: 602
5443: 357
5531: 446[2], 449[19]
5788: 500[161]
5935: 441
5973: 597[18]
6170: 302[13]
6992: 433
7090: 233
7267: 233
7380: 433, 611[13]
7429: 244[26]
7434: 386, 399[14]
7435: 386, 411, 420
7506: 302[13]
8086: 449[22]
8257: 302[11]
8663: 498[146], 601
10496: 303, 346
10570: 303[17]
10789: 606
10873: 504
10875: 504[183]
10914: 446[2]
10918: 439
10975: 446[2]
11082: 602
11976: 597[18]
12036: 496[136]
12350: 407[42]
12762: 302[15]

12766: 302^{15}
13827: 329
13828: 302^{15}
14120: 496^{134}
14147^5: 199^{23}
14219^{10}: 498
15208: 605

4

3882: 380^{22}, 401^{22}, 611^{12}
5285: 376

5

18: 167^{115}, 308^1, 437
852: 439
875: 360^{38}
985: 586
2090: 248^{58}
2533: 524^{299}
3259: 231, 328
3332: 253^{87}
3341: 225^{26}
3936: 233, 310^{14}
4087: 446^5, 462^{55}
4315: 546^{430}
4316: 546^{430}
4317: 546^{430}
4449: 491^{104}
4482: 512
4484: 357
4966: 328
5465: 612
5736: 232, 328^{53}
5749: 612
5844: 612
5856: 227
6349: 612
6431: 310^{14}
6518: 612
6648: 612
6657: 434^{77}, 612
6658: 434^{77}

6991: 357
7212: 381[27]
7259: 299[31]
7907: 299[31]
7917: 229[39], 299[31]
8056: 420
8922: 612

6

42: 487[77]
43: 487[77]
44: 487[77]
100: 603
200: 487[76]
209: 598
210: 598
218: 488[77], 537
224: 602
226: 428[38]
235: 237
236: 412[55], 433[73]
240: 433[73]
251: 487[74]
253: 434[77], 488[78]
283: 487[74]
307: 434, 537[375]
338: 433[73]
343: 448, 487[75]
360: 424[9]
414 a + b: 488[77]
445: 328[54], 487[74], 509
446: 487[74]
447: 487[74]
449: 232, 328[54]
451: 232, 328[54]
452: 232
461: 428[35]
471: 434, 537[375]
479: 253[87]
539: 407[41], 452
540: 452

541: 433[72], 611[13]
542: 433[72]
543: 433[72], 546
544: 402
622: 487[76]
643: 546
671: 537[375]
692: 328[54]
716: 488[78], 605
791: 487[77]
811: 487[74]
852: 487[74]
853: 487[75]
855: 487[77]
862: 487[77]
872: 64[68]
909: 161[74]
927: 537, 563
932: 236, 546
934: 217
954: 327[49]
956: 434[79]
958: 434, 537[375]
971: 487[77]
1027: 487[77]
1033: 345
1035: 338[117]
1054: 487[77]
1063: 488[78], 600
1090: 288[41]
1119b: 487[77]
1599: 546
1872: 539
1936: 538
1984: 236
2010: 433[75]
2028b: 207
2120: 334[86]
2130: 488[77]
2170: 545[421]

2799: 488[77]
2835: 488[78], 603
3514: 358
3654: 358
3679: 440[24]
3682: 598
3756: 535[363], 536[369], 539
4222: 160[69]
5539: 409
5818: 233
6992: 395[35]
8494: 232
8686: 539
8943: 409
9015: 233
9047: 233
9053: 233
9053a: 233
9797: 561[522], 565
10251a: 387[61]
12892: 440[24]
21415: 233
29681: 491[103], 576, 585, 613, 614[26]
29691: 488[78],
29722: 319[17]
29847a: 233
30712: 487[76]
30808: 537[375]
30901: 425[15], 447
30957: 508
30961: 488[77]
30983: 433[73]
30985: 433[73]
30995: 537[375]
30998: 278[49], 536[369]
31125: 487[77]
31232: 338[117]
31267: 284[15]
31403: 467
31404: 467

2388: 253[87]
2394: 357
2395: 357
2399: 357
2465: 323[29]
2554: 540[386]
2555: 540[386]
2557: 323[29], 604
2563: 394[30], 429, 434
2586: 540[386], 541
2618: 448
2643: 450[27]
2705: 320[18]
4191: 210[73]
4199: 395[35], 433, 433[73]
4252: 293[69]
4323: 603
4584: 542[395]
4641: 449
4674: 449[22]
4764: 468[95]
5177: 393, 398[9], 399[14], 411[52]
5290: 468[95]
6038: 261
6339: 253[87], 500[161]
6353: 448
6942: 498
6948: 357
6979: 498
6981: 253[87]
6983: 253[87]
6984: 253[87]
6985: 500[161]
6986: 500[161]
7009: 411[50]
7010: 411[50]
7014: 253[87]
7095: 461[47]
7119: 244[28]
7966: 500[161]

7986: 267, 293[69]
7987: 267, 293[69]
7988: 498, 500[161]
8203: 393[26]
8210: 225[25]
8331: 498[148]
8351: 597
8390: 448
8409: 536, 537
8458: 260
8476: 411[51]
8780: 500[160]
8808: 395[34], 402
8834: 92[59]
8837: 497[141]
8927: 285
8930: 288[41]
8991: 323[29]
9014: 500[160]
9018: 571[580]
9037: 288[41]
9040: 288[41], 398[6]
9047: 288[39]
9257: 285
9317: 327
9342: 286
9362: 288[39]
9368: 288[39]
9409: 288[40]
9699: 288[39]
9797: 536[369], 542[395]
10178: 451
10564: 225[25]
11167: 253[87]
11193: 450[29], 451[34]
11205: 253[87]
11912: 265[45], 438
11998: 579[638], 583[664], 587[686]
12001: 450[27], 568[560]
12006: 579[638], 587[686]

12018: 587[686]
12027: 257
12028: 257
12029: 257
12030: 257, 257[3]
12039: 257, 257[3], 258, 259[8], 261
12061: 411[51]
12094: 449[22]
12122: 268[64]
12228: 449
12377: 450[27]
12464: 253[87]
12758: 232
14343: 583[664]
14381: 225[25]
14395: 395[34], 399[14], 400[18], 411[52]
14465: 449[22]
14546: 449[22]
14611: 226[27], 262, 264
14731: 293[69]
14791: 449[22]
14874: 449, 449[22]
15421: 411[51]
15512: 449[22]
15644: 411[51]
16472: 293[69]
17143: 537
17159: 92[59]
17408: 542
17620: 451
17829: 583[664], 587[686]
17831: 587[686]
17835: 448
17837: 449[22]
17896: 478[17]
17950: 542[396]
18050: 323[29]
18071: 320[18]
18072: 540[386]
18240: 467

26606: 583[664], 587[686]
26607: 583[664], 587[686]
26615: 258[7]

9

423: 615[33]
783: 454
808: 615
1541: 225[25]
1545: 383
1556: 439, 452[43], 524[299]
1566: 233
2441: 253[87]
2595: 247[48]
2842: 253[87]
3019: 233
3088: 227
3609: 357[26]
3688: 253[87]
3887: 537, 538[379], 563
3960: 537[375]
4209: 232
4957: 491[104]
5136: 64[68]
5438: 253[87]
5533: 234
5811: 111[101]

10

112: 118[148], 225[27], 615
114: 586
131: 310[14]
202: 568
205: 615
378: 383
415: 524[299]
513: 161[74]
823: 438
830: 166[109]
837: 166[109]
838: 166[109]
840: 166[109], 310[14]

1545: 253[87]
1922: 438
1923: 438
3040: 439, 525
3083: 576[620]
3200: 616[35]
3303: 91[55], 233[63], 380, 388[5], 399[10], 410, 490, 510, 537, 576, 586, 611[12]
3613: 576[620], 614[27]
3616: 510
3806: 491[103]
3872: 225[25]
3876a: 491[104]
3885: 233
3936: 491[104]
4170: 86[16]
4639: 229[40]
4815: 616
5265: 576
5763: 225[25]
6071: 434[79]
6163: 248[58]
6306: 395[34], 452, 613[20]
6308: 449, 452
6315: 452
6316: 452
6940: 248[53], 254[93]
6955: 226[27]
7270: 524[299]
7431: 524
7556: 536[369]

12

81: 299[31]
103: 231
169: 132[244], 497
252: 407[41]
261: 248[57]
392: 243, 243[22], 243[24], 244[29], 250, 251, 254, 256
530: 613
697: 579[638]

1114: 476
1120: 357
1121: 579[638]
1236: 226[27]
1566: 247, 450[27]
1585: 579[638]
1782: 312[24], 393[26]
1797: 314[39]
1851: 319, 319[14], 319[17], 320[17]
2224: 398[6]
2373: 443
2516: 242[14]
2595: 446[2], 449[19]
2596: 394, 428, 434[81]
2653: 450
3074: 504[184]
3075: 504[184]
3076: 504
3077: 504[184]
3082: 504
3156: 330[65]
3175: 481
3180: 310[14]
3183: 584
3207: 310[14]
3232: 584
3312: 540
4146: 399[14]
4323: 243, 321[21], 346
4332: 391[21], 399[14], 450
4333: 146, 174, 246, 379, 385, 388[5], 401[22], 410, 424, 482,
      519[268], 610, 611[12]
4342: 252, 255
4354: 248[57]
4363: 251
4371: 248[57]
4393: 225[26], 249, 251, 253, 254, 256
4426: 228[38], 251
4435: 251
4445: 583[665]

4447: 479[23]
4448: 479[23]
5115: 476
5374: 247
5864: 544[412]
5905: 132[244], 497, 587
5953: 407[41]
5964: 251
6024: 253
6038: 102, 220, 240, 277, 278, 502, 528, 540, 580

13

38: 226[27]
256: 325[34]
257: 325[34]
389: 380[22], 401[22], 407[40], 611[12]
520: 393[27], 428[34]
546: 435
548: 312[25], 325[34], 363[14]
566: 443[36], 443[37], 445[45], 452[43]
587: 432[58]
588: 535[363]
920: 535[363]
939: 363[12]
946: 401[22]
949: 397[3], 401[22], 407[40]
959: 535[363]
1036: 133, 362[12], 363[17]
1042: 363[13], 363[17]
1043: 363[13], 363[17]
1044: 363[13], 363[17]
1045: 363[13], 363[17]
1048: 225[25], 225[26], 325[34]
1049: 309, 364
1124: 442[33], 444[40]
1179: 541[390]
1189: 441
1194: 232
1318: 398[6]
1320: 397[3]
1330: 397[3]

1362: 317
1366: 535
1376: 363^{14}
1377: 363^{14}
1379: 399^{10}
1384: 363^{14}
1421: 535^{363}
1497: 408
1514: 442, 444
1541: 321^{22}, 335^{92}, 363^{13}, 363^{17}
1575: 442^{33}
1632: 319^{16}
1664: 105
1667: 581^{649}
1668: 137^{275}
1670: 101^{26}, 432^{58}
1674: 311, 363^{12}, 363^{18}
1675: 310, 363^{12}
1676: 450^{28}
1680: 227, 318
1684: 325^{34}
1684a: 324, 325^{34}, 365, 366
1684b: 136^{267}, 325
1687: 227
1688: 244
1691: 309^{9}, 321, 323
1691a: 309
1691 a + b: 322, 365
1691c: 136^{267}
1694: 364, 364^{19}
1697: 321^{22}
1698: 244
1699: 362^{11}
1700: 136^{267}, 244, 362^{11}
1701: 136^{267}
1702: 309^{9}, 321, 323, 325, 365
1703: 227^{32}
1704: 136^{267}, 321, 363^{12}
1706: 244, 309, 309^{9}, 311, 316, 323, 335, 364, 392
1709: 244

1710: 244, 320, 321, 365, 389
1711: 319^{17}, 321
1712: 227, 309^9, 318, 319, 319^{14}, 319^{17}, 365
1714: 309, 309^9, 322, 364
1716: 309^9, 322, 364
1717: 317
1718: 309, 315, 321^{22}, 323, 335, 364
1719: 363^{13}, 363^{18}
1722: 244, 364^{19}
1728: 446^2
1742: 407^{39}, 407^{41}
1749: 450^{27}
1752: 393
1753: 393^{26}
1754: 348, 393^{26}
1769: 541
1780: 450^{27}
1788: 314
1805: 582^{654}
1821: 225^{25}
1919: 582^{654}
1921: 582^{654}
1926: 319^{17}, 320^{17}
1927: 312^{25}, 363^{14}
1974: 319^{17}
2002a: 432^{58}
2020: 498^{147}
2181: 325^{34}
2501: 399^{14}
2532: 407^{39}
2583a: 444^{40}
2583b: 442, 444^{40}
2606: 450
2608: 443^{37}, 444
2609: 443^{37}, 444
2636: 443^{37}, 444^{39}
2656: 443^{37}, 445
2812: 443^{38}, 444^{41}
2831: 443
2840: 443, 443^{37}, 444

2862: 443
2863: 443, 443[38]
2887: 443[37], 444[39]
2891: 443[37], 444[39]
2892: 443[38], 444[41]
2895: 443[38], 444
2898: 443[37], 444
2899: 443[37], 444[39]
2900: 443[37], 444[41]
2901: 443[38], 444
2902: 443[38]
2903: 443[37], 444[39]
2904: 443[37], 444[39]
2906: 443[38], 444[41]
2921: 443[38], 444[41]
2940: 321[22], 363[13], 363[17]
3026a: 441
3063: 449, 450[25]
3071: 450[25]
3073: 450[25]
3074: 450[25]
3096: 450[25]
3104: 443[38], 444[41]
3107: 407[39], 407[42]
3144: 364
3148: 432[58]
3149: 432[58]
3150: 432[58]
3151: 432[58]
3154: 407[39], 407[42]
3162: 135[261], 136[267], 361[1], 410
3184: 450
3197: 450[28]
3200: 363[14]
3363: 432[58]
3450: 523
3488: 449
3527: 407[39], 407[41]
3570: 441[27]
3639: 407, 407[41]

7918: 319[16]
7996: 428[34]
8007: 445
8016: 605
8017: 602
8019: 429, 605
8035: 601
8038: 432[58]
8165: 319[16]
8207: 604
8244: 319[16]
8253: 432[58]
8493: 433
8619: 601
8626: 432[58]
8638: 210[73]
8701: 210[73]
11042: 366[28]
11070a: 444[40]
11174: 320, 323, 365
11223: 443[37], 444[39]
11224: 443
11225: 443[37], 444[39]
11226: 443[37], 444[39]
11233: 443[37], 444
11239: 444[41]
11239a: 443[37]
11240: 443[37]
11241: 443[38], 444[41]
11280: 450[27]
11518: 432[58]
11728: 433
11758: 603
11759: 607
11810: 319[16]
11967: 354[8]
12057: 505[190]
3100[16]: 450[25]

14

32: 253[87]

4556: 538
4570: 538
5326: 546
5327: 538[377]
5328: 538, 538[377]
15
3863-3873: 254
16
20: 230
23: 230, 354[8]
28: 230, 234
158: 359[34]
CIL Suppl. Ital.
1
883: 612

EA
1 (1983), pp. 141-152, no. 1: 159[59]
EphEp
7
505: 398[6]
946: 397, 420
1941: 402
8
104: 238[84]
201: 328
210: 328 f.
269: 615
280: 439
356: 233
804: 328
2213: 238[84]
9
252: 615[33]
390: 272[20]
742: 398[6]
767: 491[104]
FB Baden-Württemberg
1 (1974), p. 536, no. 2: 599

Henzen, *AFA:*

  XXXV: 506[195]

  XXXV f.: 162[81]

  XLI-XLIX: 484[58]

  XLII: 207[58], 209[70]

  XLV, 15: 182[16]

  XLVI: 484[57]

  LIV: 506[198]

  LV: 506[198]

  LVII, 8: 424[12]

  LVII, 24: 424[12]

  LIX: 506[198]

  LXI f.: 506[193]

  LXI-LXXXIX: 484[56]

  LXII: 91[55]

  LXIII: 485[62], 506[199]

  LXVII: 485[62], 507[205]

  LXIX: 91[55], 485[62]

  LXIX-LXXII: 506[199]

  LXX: 506[193]

  LXXI: 507[205]

  LXXIV, 14: 182[16]

  LXXV: 485[62]

  LXXVI: 506[193]

  LXXVII: 485[62], 507[205]

  LXXI: 485[62]

  LXXXI, 4: 182[16]

  LXXXII: 485[63]

  LXXXIV f.: 485[63]

  XC: 507[205]

  XC-XCVI: 485[64]

  CXVI ff.: 424[7]

Howald-Meyer

  54: 416

  81: 416

  203: 228

  204: 228

IAM

  2

84: 597[17]
344: 597
345: 613[17]
377: 540, 613[17]
490: 538[375], 540, 613[17]
491: 538[375]
491e: 613[17]
492: 538[375]
493: 538[375]
494: 538[375]

ILAfr

300: 579[638], 587[686]
303: 579[638], 583[664], 587[686]
304: 579[638], 587[686]
458: 262, 264, 293[69]
517: 583[664]
519: 439
530: 587[686]
546: 450[29], 451[37]
547: 451[37]
550: 451[37]
636: 289[46]
646: 289[45]

ILAlg

1

95: 579[638]
533: 411[52]
1028: 398[9]
1290: 226[27]
1295: 228, 241[9]
2055: 579[638]
2130: 587[686]
3041: 499
3066: 579[638], 587[686]
3991: 395[34], 411[53]

2

10: 583[664]
36: 267
71: 267
709: 583[664]

ILGN

    3: 229[39], 299[31]

    17: 400[20]

    347: 401

    429: 251

    558a: 225[26]

    634: 243[22], 364[22]

    635: 225[26]

ILIug

    199: 302[14]

ILLRP

    200: 85[12], 446[5], 462[35]

    409: 64

    410: 64

ILM

    56: 290, 290[50], 292

    57: 290

    116: 225[26], 285, 289, 290, 291[57], 293

    129: 225[26], 292, 293

    130: 225[26], 292, 293

    131: 292, 293

    135: 289[43]

ILS

    73: 64[68]

    73a: 64[68]

    89: 616[35]

    103: 284[15]

    106: 439, 525

    108: 490

    109: 233, 439, 452[43], 524[299]

    110: 167[115], 437

    112: 174, 246, 379, 388[5], 401[22], 410, 424, 482, 519[268], 610, 611[12]

    115: 442[32]

    117: 233

    119: 453[47]

    139: 490

    154: 233[63], 380, 388[5], 399[10], 410, 490, 510, 537, 576, 586, 611[12]

    158: 611[12]

    162: 265[45], 438

    163: 232

1613: 232
1643: 233
1777: 233
1786: 409
1810: 233
1838: 409
1855: 386
1856: 386, 411
1929: 538
1995: 234
2107: 537
2381: 540[386], 541
2445: 540[386]
2446: 540[386]
2647: 237
2711: 276
2714: 272, 276, 355
2714a: 272, 276
2718: 476
2933: 461[47]
3175: 440[24]
3206: 541
3230: 597
3230a: 597
3230b: 597
3302: 504[183]
3361: 428[35]
3440: 537[375]
3453: 237, 442
3528: 231
3542: 328[54]
3543: 537[375]
3544: 546
3613: 328[54], 509
3615: 508
3617: 232, 328[54]
3619: 232, 328[54]
3620: 232
3622: 231, 328
3626: 537, 538[379], 563

3663: 237
3668: 412[55]
3687*bis:* 547
3811: 467
4009: 232, 328[53]
4130: 312[24], 393[26]
4132: 393
4133: 393[26]
4134: 393[26]
4135: 393[26]
4136: 393[26]
4386: 278[49], 536[369]
4454: 587[686]
4537: 310
4611: 443
4613d: 441
4657: 443
4675: 442
4702: 444
5010: 545[421]
5025: 236, 237[77]
5052: 614[27]
5072: 579[638], 583[664], 587[686]
5146: 380[22], 401[22], 611[12]
5160: 539, 535[363], 536[369]
5163: 136[269], 580
5173: 561[522], 565
5372: 401[22]
5400: 587[686]
5434: 438
5471a: 278[49], 536[369]
5472: 468[95], 587[686]
5474: 542
5477: 468[95]
5490: 498
5713: 583[664], 587[686]
5796: 233
5973: 238[84]
6087: 479, 490
6088: 215, 396

1288: 579[638], 587[686]
1416: 587[686]
1501: 395[34], 411[53], 452
1647: 293[69]

InscrIt

13, 1

1:*Fasti Antiates Maiores*: 301[5]
5:*Fasti Ostienses*: 486[69], 493[119]

13, 2

3:*Fasti Pinciani*: 491[95]
8:*Fasti Caeretani*: 204
10:*Fasti Maffeiani*: 111, 491[95], 491[99]
17:*Fasti Praenestini*: 86[19], 86[24], 184, 210[76], 214, 378, 388[1], 483[48], 491[97], 491[98], 491[99], 585[671]
18:*Fasti Vallenses*: 204[46], 491[95]
22:*Fasti Verulani*: 204
25:*Fasti Amiternini*: 204, 204[46], 330[66], 491[98], 491[100]
26:*Fasti Antiates Ministrorum*: 204, 491[98], 491[101]
29:*Fasti Pighiani*: 491[95], 585[674]
42:*Fasti Furii Filocali*: 489[89]
42:*Fasti Furii Philocali*: 568[588]
43:*Fasti Polemii Silvii*: 489[89]
44:*Feriale Cumanum*: 86[18], 87[30], 91[55], 116[138], 132[245], 204, 207[61], 490, 490[92], 509[219], 517[263]
46:*Feriale Campanum*: 490
47:*Menologium Rusticum Colotianum*: 585[671]
48:*Menologium Rusticum Vallense*: 585[671]

IRT

117: 579[638]
273: 395[34], 454[30]
292: 323[29], 600
315a: 411[53]
319: 167[116]
321: 167[116]
322: 167[116]
323: 167[116]
324: 378, 611[12]
324a: 388[5], 398[9], 410[49]
325: 451
326: 451

327: 451
601: 579[638]
607: 544[412]
I Sardegna
    42: 597
    45: 225[26]

JRS
    27 (1937), pp. 248 f., no. 12: 404[32]
    47 (1957), p. 230, no. 19: 405, 415, 422
    49 (1959), p. 136, no. 6: 390[18]
    52 (1962), p. 192, no. 8: 415
    53 (1963), p. 161, no. 7: 414
    55 (1965), p. 221, no. 3: 414, 421
    59 (1969), p. 235, no. 1: 400, 403, 414

MZ
    66 (1971), p. 144, Bild 2

Orelli
    686: 402
    1961: 401
    2489: 402

Pflaum, *Fastes Narbonn.*
    pp. 103-105, no. 2: 241[8]
    p. 208, no. 6: 247[47]
    p. 251, no. 3: 251

RCHM
    London 3 (1928), p.173, no. 16: 410[48]
RGKBer
    17 (1927), no. 204: 399[14]
    27 (1937), no. 162: 319[16]
    40 (1959), no. 8: 407[40]
    40 (1959), no. 23: 232
    40 (1959), no. 145: 599
    40 (1959), no. 163: 604
RIB
    5: 409, 422

21: 410
89: 410^{45}, 417
91: 217, 410^{45}, 417, 423
146: 412, 414
152: 389, 390^{18}, 403, 406, 414, 419
181: 396, 399, 404, 408, 415
193: 399^{11}, 415, 419
223: 401
235: 398^{6}, 399^{11}, 415, 419, 421
247: 399^{11}, 415, 419
274: 399^{11}, 415, 419
309: 404^{28}, 415, 422
326: 420
327: 400, 400^{20}, 406, 414, 418, 419, 420, 605
328: 605
333: 234
430: 234, 320^{18}
458: 401, 402, 403, 404, 418
459: 399^{11}, 408, 414, 419
611: 398^{6}, 399^{11}, 397, 415, 419, 420
623: 403^{27}, 414, 421
627: 400, 403, 404, 407, 414, 419
636: 234
640: 403^{27}, 414, 421
656: 398^{6}, 399^{11}, 415, 419
657: 404^{28}, 415, 420, 422
707: 398^{9}, 399^{11}, 415, 417, 419, 431^{57}
740: 234, 320^{18}
746: 234, 320^{18}
812: 596
815: 404, 415, 418, 421, 422
815-836: 596
824: 390, 404, 409, 413, 415, 418, 421, 422
825: 390, 409, 413, 415, 418, 421, 422
840: 596
842: 390^{18}
843: 390^{18}
844: 390^{18}
882: 606
883: 607

897: 394, 417
913: 405[34], 421
915: 419, 421, 594
916: 417, 431
918: 399[11], 400[20], 400, 415, 419
919: 394, 400, 402, 403, 405, 414, 417, 418, 434
940: 405, 415, 421, 422
949: 400, 403, 414, 418
976: 401, 414, 422
978: 401, 403[25], 414, 418
979: 403[25]
990: 390[18]
1041: 415, 419
1056: 399[11], 415, 419
1073: 390[18]
1074: 385, 400, 403, 405, 414
1083: 404[28], 415, 418, 420, 422
1100: 400, 403, 405, 409, 414
1127: 390[18], 417
1128: 390[18]
1138: 390[18]
1149: 234
1153: 234
1202: 401[21], 414
1225: 400, 402, 403, 406, 407[41], 409, 414, 420
1227: 399[11], 415, 419
1234: 234, 320[18]
1235: 401[21], 414
1270: 596, 601
1327: 399[11], 402, 415, 419
1330: 398[6], 398[9], 399[11], 415, 419
1337: 390[18]
1452: 407[41], 420
1466: 390[18], 406
1579: 597
1584: 398[6], 399[11], 415, 419, 421
1585: 398[6], 399[11], 415, 419, 421
1586: 398[6], 399[11], 415, 419, 421
1587: 399[11], 415, 419, 421
1588: 399[11], 415, 419, 421

1593: 403[27], 414, 418, 421
1594: 385, 402, 403[27], 414, 418, 421
1596: 399[11], 400, 400[20], 408, 415, 419, 420
1612: 320[18]
1692: 400, 403, 404[30], 414, 420
1700: 415, 417, 417[66], 422[82]
1706: 401, 403[25], 414, 418, 422
1731: 390[18]
1778: 390[18]
1786: 398[6], 399[11], 415, 419
1791: 571[580]
1874-1896: 596
1882: 403[27], 414, 421
1904: 403[27], 414, 418, 421
1909: 234, 320[18]
1910: 234, 320[18]
1922: 410[45]
1978: 390[18], 417
1983: 400, 401, 402, 403, 404[29], 414, 418, 420, 598
1987: 403[27], 414, 421
1991: 403[27], 414, 418, 421
1995: 390[18]
2040: 401, 402, 403, 404[29], 414
2042: 399[11], 400, 400[20], 408, 414, 415, 418, 419, 421
2063: 403[27], 414, 421
2066: 394, 401, 403[25], 414, 417
2071: 452
2092: 390[18]
2100: 390[18]
2103: 404[28], 415, 422
2200: 390[18]
2217: 415
2223: 234, 320[18]
2230: 234
2256: 320[18]
2264: 405, 415, 421
RIT
48: 174[22], 379, 380[22], 388[5], 504, 611[12]
53: 558
79: 179[58], 559

84: 280[63]
162: 272[17]
173: 177[45]
240: 280[63]
250 a-b: 155[35], 280[64]
251: 155[35], 280[64]
264: 153[21], 247[50]
288: 271[15], 272[18]
289: 271[15], 272[18]
301: 271[15], 272[18]
316: 271[15], 272[17], 272[18]
369: 504[187]
385: 615[32]
408: 615[32]
409: 615[32]
415: 615[32]
418: 615[32]
423: 615[32]
425: 615[32]
426: 615[32]
432: 615[32]
433: 280[63]
805-813: 280[63]
922: 254[89]

RIU
  1
     249: 602

Smallwood, *Documents Gaius, Claudius and Nero*:
  2: 207[58]
  370: 104[49], 198[20], 495[127]
  371: 198[21]

West, *Corinth*
  8, 2
    15: 461[43]
    110: 461[43]

5. COINS

Head, *BMC Ionia*
  p. 89, nos. 293-294: 496[138]

Wroth, *Catalogue Galatia, Cappadocia, Syria*
  p. 72, nos. 212 ff.: 123[183]
  pp. 80 f., nos. 270 ff.: 123[183]

Beltrán, *Numismática antigua*
  61-62: 152[14]
  63: 151[10]
  65: 153[20]
  353: 151[8]
Burgos, *Catálogo general 5*
  1569-1570: 156[45]
  1571-1574: 180[1]
  1579-1582: 180[1]
  1583-1584: 156[45]
  1737-1738: 151[8], 520[273]
  1739: 171[2]
  1741: 171[2]
  1743: 151[8]
  1746: 151[8]
  1744: 171[2]
  1751: 171[2]

Cohen, *Descript. hist.*
  1
        pp. 95 f., nos. 236-241: 104[50]
        pp. 192 f., nos. 28-42: 104[50]
        pp. 256 f., nos. 81-82: 104[50]
        p. 296, no. 256: 104[50]
        p. 400, no. 422: 276[39]
        p. 400, nos. 424-427: 295[3]
Crawford, *RRC*
  p. 99, Table xvii: 76[21]
  480, 2 a-c: 68[92], 70[111]
  480, 21: 62[57], 152[17]
  506: 225[25]

153-155: 147[337]
157-161: 148[339]
157-165: 104[48], 286[30]
162-165: 148[339]
189-192: 92[59]
398: 286[30]
427-428: 286[30]
464: 286[30]

Mattingly-Sydenham, *RIC*
1
    p. 113, no. 35: 485[59]
    p. 117, no. 37: 485[59]
4
    pp. 46-51: 347[188]
    p. 53: 347[188]
    p. 113: 328[52]
    p. 127: 328[52]
    p. 136: 328[52]
    p. 161: 328[52]
    p. 183: 328[52]
    p. 186: 328[52]
5, 2
    p. 355: 467[91]
    pp. 395 f.: 467[91]
    p. 403: 467[91]
    p. 407: 467[91]
    p. 413: 467[91]
    p. 421: 467[91]
    p. 465: 467[91]
    p. 481f.: 467[91]
    p. 502: 467[91]
    p. 527: 467[91]
    p. 527, no. 752: 468[98]
    p. 558: 467[91]

Mattingly, *BMC*
1
    pl. 1, no. 2: 122[180]
    pl. 7, nos. 3, 10: 122[180]

pl. 20, no. 20: 121[172]
pl. 21, nos. 1-4: 121[172]
pp. 79 f.: 117[145]
pp. 82-84: 117[145]
pp. 92 f., nos. 548-560: 104[50]
pp. 94-96, nos. 565-588: 104[50]
p. 104, no. 638: 82[70]
pp. 127 f., nos. 62-64: 104[50]
p. 134, no. 102: 555[490]
p. 140, no. 142: 506[197]
p. 153, no. 41: 485[59]
p. 164, no. 1: 464[66]
p. 196, no. 227: 104[50]
p. 197, no. 229: 520[276]
pp. 271 f., nos. 360-365: 122[177], 182[11]
p. 279, note *: 104[50]
p. 328, no. 119: 464[68]
p. 331, nos. 131 ff.: 464[68]
p. 352, no. 241: 465[80]
p. 360, nos. 261-262: 464[68]
p. 361, no. 265: 464[68]
p. 377, no. 57⁺+: 468[93]

2

p. 70, no. 356: 276[39]
p. 121, no. 565: 295[3]
p. 136, no. 620: 295[3]
p. 180, + : 276[39]
pp. 187 f., nos. 774-776: 276[39]
p. 246, no. 138: 465[76]
pp. 281-285: 486[66]
pp. 414-415: 486[66]

3

p. 146, no. 709: 520[276]
p. 394, no. 1091: 520[276]

4

p. 310, no. 1869: 520[277]
p. 350, no. 2051: 520[277], 506[197]
p. 816, no. 616: 469[103]

5

p. 31, no. 67: 337[103]

p. 136, no. 550B: 337[105]
p. 210: 328[52]
p. 219, no. 341: 339[122]
p. 222: 328[52]
p. 247: 328[52]
p. 256, no. 507: 339[122]

Carson, *BMC*
6
      p. 193, no. 785: 468[101]

Robertson, *HCC*
1
      pp. 38-40: 117[145]
      pp. 44-47, nos. 230-244: 104[50]
      p. 46, no. 237: 119[158]
      p. 46, no. 240: 119[158]
      p. 83, no. 17: 485[59]
      p. 107, no. 94: 104[50]
      p. 141, no. 113: 182[11]

Sutherland-Kraay, *Ashmolean Catalogue*
1
      337-338: 121[112]
      337-361: 104[50]
      339-342: 121[172]
      340: 124[190], 124[195]
      347: 121[112]
      371 ff.: 121[172]
      371-403: 104[50]
      374: 119[158]
      405-408: 104[50]

Vives, *Moneda hispánica*
4
      p. 64, no. 39: 180[1]
      p. 65, nos. 46-49: 180[1]
      p. 66, nos. 58, 61, 64: 180[1]
      p. 66, nos. 59-60: 156[44]
      p. 67, no. 77: 156[45]
      p. 68, nos. 80-81: 156[45]

p. 93, no. 14: 153[20]
p. 131, no. 7: 171[2]
p. 131, nos. 9, 12, 13: 151[8]
p. 131, no. 10: 171[2]
p. 131, no. 14: 171[2]
pp. 131 f.: 152[14]
p. 132, no. 16: 151[8]
p. 132, no. 21: 171[2]

6. PAPYRI

BGU
2
   362: 488[81]
   646: 492[109]

Hunt and Edgar, *SP*
2
   405: 549[447]

P. Amsterdam
22: 492[109], 530[331]
P. Baden
4
   101: 548
P. Giss.
1
   3: 515[256], 583
P. Lond.
1912 (*P. Jews*): 495[127]
P. Oslo
3
   77: 132[243], 488[79], 607
   94: 550[457]
P. Oxy.
7
   1021: 492[109]
10
   1265: 550[457]
12
   1449: 59[25], 549[447], 549[449], 550[451], 550[457]

13
    1612: 573[598]
27
    2465: 36
    2476: 564
31
    2553: 132[243]
37
    2820: 199[23]
42
    3020: 4[10]

P. *Paris*
    69: 495[128], 562[527], 571[587], 589

Preisigke, *Sammelbuch*
    684: 496[136]
    982: 496[136]
    1015: 496[134]
    4383: 496[135]
    6672: 496[135]
    8277: 496[134]
    8443: 496[135]
    8807: 496[134]
    8831: 496[134]
    8908: 496[136]
    8909: 496[134]
    8912: 496[134]

7. BAS-RELIEFS

Bellido, *Esculturas*
    p. 402, no. 403: 503[175]
    p. 403, no. 404: 503[176]
    pp. 407 f., no. 408: 502[174]

Espérandieu, *Recueil*
    1
        432: 504
        462: 504, 479[23]
        465: 504
        467: 504

478: 480
674: 476

3

2655: 131²³⁸
2707: 476⁶

7

5361: 131²³⁸

8

6439: 505¹⁹⁰

10

710: 131²³⁸

8. GEMS

Henig, *Gemstones*
p. 216, no. 249: 131²³⁸
pp. 69f.: 131²³⁸

9. GREEK AND LATIN WORDS

ἄγαλμα: 23, 23¹⁰, 58, 59²⁴, 63⁶³, 65⁷³, 186, 341, 346¹⁸¹, 438, 521, 527, 534³⁶¹, 548, 549, 619,
ἀγορά: 3, 4, 21, 241, 552
ἀγών: 14, 47, 126, 618
ἀγωνοθέτης: 617, 618
ἄλσος: 103
ἀνάθημα: 61⁴², 437
ἀνδριάς: 23, 58, 59²⁴, 61, 78, 186, 199²³, ²⁷, 545, 548, 555
ἀνήρ: 42
ἀντίθεος: 42
ἀπεικόνισμα: 551
ἀποθέωσις: 40
ἀρετή: 3, 113
ἀρχηγέτης: 51
ἀρχηγός: 25
ἀρχιερεύς: 16, 241⁹, 246⁴⁴, 269, 271, 275, 283, 392, 395³², 425 f., 584
ἀρχιθέωροι: 25
ἀτέλεια: 32

ἀφιερόω: 206, 212[83]

βασιλεύς: 36, 36[29], 38[49]
βασίλισσα: 38[49]
βουλή: 241
βωμός: 3, 122

γερουσία: 545, 552, 562, 568

δεξίωσις: 19
δῆμος: 549
δωδεκάθεος: 80

εἰκονείδιον: 549[447]
εἰκών: 23, 58, 59, 59[24f.], 60, 61, 122, 123, 161[72], 186, 199[23], 441, 545, 546, 548, 548[438], 551, 552, 553, 553[475], 555, 562[529], 564, 566, 567, 619
εἰσιτήρια: 26
ἐκθέωσις: 40
ἐκφώνησις: 569
ἐνκωμιογράφος: 572
ἐξάρεον: 524
εὐεργεσία: 32, 185
εὐεργέτης: 11, 27, 46, 47, 48, 50, 297
εὔκοσμος: 562[529], 573
ἐπήκοος: 43[78]
ἐπίβασις: 493
ἐπιβατήριος: 27
ἐπίκλησις: 28, 29
ἐπιμανής: 17
ἐπιφανής: 17, 28, 189
ἐσχάρα: 3
εὔκοσμος: 574
εὐτυχία: 113
εὐχή: 38

ζάκορος: 561, 567

ἡμέραι Σεβασταί: 494 f.
ἡμίθεος: 57, 57[11]
ἥρως: 4[10], 51, 61[46]

θεά: 34¹²
θεῖος: 34, 42, 57¹¹, 344, 367, 430
θεῖος ἀνήρ: 388
θεῖος ἄνθρωπος: 469
θειότατος: 430, 430⁴⁸
θεολόγος: 571, 573⁶⁰⁰, 574, 574⁶⁰⁴
θεός: 14, 18, 28, 28⁴⁹, 34, 48, 129²²¹, 130, 189, 297²¹, 342, 437, 450²⁶,
    548⁴⁴⁰, 548⁴⁴²
θεοειδής: 42
θεοείκελος: 42
θεοὶ εὐεργέται: 48
θεοῦ υἱός: 76²⁴
θεοφάντης: 573
θεσμῳδός: 572
θεωρία: 582, 582⁶⁵⁸, 583
θεωροί: 25
θήκη: 563⁵³⁵
θηκοφόρος: 563⁵³⁵
θυμιατήριον: 564, 564⁵⁴¹

ἱδρῦσαι: 78⁴¹
ἱερεύς: 36²⁹
ἱεροθέσιον: 19
ἱερόν: 22, 122
ἱεροφάντης: 573
ἱερώτατος: 430
ἱμάτιον: 480
ἱσόθεοι τιμαί: 11, 14, 21, 32, 33, 46, 50, 57, 60, 84, 126, 131, 158, 186
ἱσόθεος: 34, 75, 84⁷, 161⁶⁹, 570

κανηφόρος: 15
καταιβάτης: 27
καταστερισμός: 20, 74¹²
κλίνη: 566
κοινόν: 48, 93, 126, 130, 188, 199²⁷, 271, 283, 284, 284¹⁸, 557, 582⁶⁵²
κοσμοκράτωρ: 339¹²⁰, 340, 342
κτίστης: 3, 4, 11, 14, 23, 47, 48, 51
κύριος: 297
κωμασία: 550, 589⁶⁹³, 590

κωμαστής: 550

λογιστής: 552

μερισμός: 548
μετάστασις: 18

ναός: 103, 315[47], 548
νέμεσις: 6
νέος: 30[69], 342
νεωκόρος: 22
νεώς: 346[181], 534[361]
νόμος: 19

οἶκος: 423, 423[6], 425, 429, 429[42]
οἰνοχόη: 36
ὀμφαλός: 100
ὁσιώτατος: 430
ὄχος· 58[16], 62

παραβώμιον: 569
πάροδος: 569
παρουσία: 26, 28
πέπλος: 34, 562
περίβολος: 106, 122, 122[177], 123
πολιοῦχος: 7
πόλις: 9, 11, 140
πόλος: 339[122], 477[15]
πομπή: 14, 24, 58, 125[197]
προγόνοι: 17, 17[73]
προεδρία· 32, 479, 617, 618
προθύτης: 565
πρόναος: 123, 179[58], 257, 258, 261, 522, 549
προσκυνήσις: 9, 185, 527, 534[361], 565[545]
προτομή: 545, 548, 552
πρῶτος: 241, 241[7]

ῥήτωρ: 573

σεβαστολόγος: 572, 573

Σεβαστός: 84⁸, 171, 269 f., 392, 548⁴⁴⁰
σεβαστοφάντης: 573, 573⁶⁰⁰
σεβαστοφόρος: 551, 551⁴⁶⁵, 552, 553, 618
σηκός: 3
σῆμα: 15
σημαία: 552
σκιάς: 125¹⁹⁷
στρατηγός: 562, 589, 589⁶⁹², 590, 590⁶⁹⁷
συμβουλευτικός: 60³⁴
σύμβωμος: 129, 131
συνέδριον: 552
σύνθρονος: 19
συνιδρύω: 79
σύνναος: 19, 22, 23, 58, 59, 61, 61⁴², 62, 79⁴³, 129, 160⁶⁹, 438, 441, 485,
    548⁴⁴²
σωτήρ: 11, 27, 46, 47, 48, 50, 297

τιμή: 21, 33
τέμενος: 3, 22, 122, 211, 213⁸⁷, 548, 524, 526, 619
τύχη: 49²⁴

ὕβρις: 6, 41
ὑμνοδιδάσκαλος: 569
ὑμνολόγος: 571
ὑμνωδεῖον: 562⁵²⁹, 574
ὑμνωδοί: 568, 569⁵⁶⁹, 574
ὑπέρ: 34, 34¹⁸, 35²⁴

φιλοσάραπις: 342¹⁴⁹
φυλή: 25

χαλκούργος: 561

ψηφίζω: 212⁸³
ψήφισμα: 271

ᾠδεῖον: 523²⁹⁴

abolla: 286²⁸

acerra: 511, 525

acroterium: 112, 122[180], 147, 152, 156

actuarius: 605

adiutor: 600

adlectio: 244[26]

adlectus: 244, 244[29], 246

adolescens: 529

adulatio: 544

adventus: 69, 84, 208[65], 507, 515, 553, 563, 570

aedes: 200, 250, 252, 253, 254, 312, 335, 426, 525, 525[303], 541

aedes principiorum: 534[361]

aedes publica: 88[37]

aedicula: 183[22], 312[27], 507[197], 520, 525[303], 537, 540, 554, 557, 616[37]

aedilis: 291[57]

aedituus: 247, 561

aera: 259[11]

aeternitas: 474

ala: 359

allector: 539

amphitheatrum: 133

annus: 227[33], 257, 258, 259, 261, 265

antistes: 247[52]

apex: 125, 125[199], 173, 475, 476, 476[6], 480, 511

apiculum: 475

apodyterium: 140

aqua Alexandriana: 603

ara: 98, 107, 122, 138, 139, 143, 144, 145, 302, 303, 305, 308, 322, 323, 324, 330, 331, 332, 333, 346, 348, 349, 362[11], 366

area: 211, 303, 303[21], 304, 305, 306

arena: 134, 559

arensis: 363, 363[12], 366[28]

aspergillum: 154, 173, 504, 526

auctoritas: 109, 296

augur: 71

aureus: 152[17], 173[14], 175, 337

auspicia: 466

auxilia: 290, 602

baioli: 606

basilica: 315⁴⁷, 523²⁹⁴, 524, 524²⁹⁷, 547
beneficiarius: 590⁶⁹⁷, 600, 603
beneficiarius consularis: 541, 604, 606
beneficiarius legati: 604
biga: 554
bos femina: 507
bos mas: 506, 507
bucrania: 154, 163, 173, 174, 175, 181, 503, 526

caduceus: 88³⁹, 347, 457
caelestes honores: 387
chalcidicum: 378
camillus: 503, 526, 527
campus: 582⁶⁵²
candelabrum: 539, 568⁵⁶⁰
capite velato: 383³⁷, 503, 526
carpentum: 160⁶⁹, 162⁸²
cavea: 523, 575⁶¹²
cella: 140, 141, 141²⁹⁸, 153, 161⁷², 167, 519, 521, 521²⁸², 522, 536, 544, 547, 549, 560, 566, 567⁵⁵⁰
cena: 80
censor perpetuus: 511²²⁶
centenarius: 325
cippus: 438, 476, 502, 526
civitas: 135, 136, 139, 140, 145, 289, 310, 318, 325, 361, 363, 581
clementia: 109, 109⁸⁷
clipeus: 555, 570
clupeus virtutis: 86¹⁶, 110, 111, 117, 128, 174, 175, 181
coactor: 538
cognomen: 357, 457
collegia iuvenum: 561
collegium: 490, 540
coloni: 497¹⁴¹, 502, 517, 531
colonia: 196, 267, 364
comes: 296, 382, 386, 465, 467, 468, 469, 470, 471,
comitia: 76
comitia consularia: 484
concilium: 93, 100, 102, 134, 136, 139, 141, 148, 150⁷, 155, 163, 220³, 241, 244, 248, 259⁸, 278, 281, 284, 288⁴², 289⁴⁷, 302⁸, 304, 348, 502¹⁷³, 578

conditor: 54[51]
consacrare: 206
consecrare: 203
consecratio: 197[16]
consecratum: 216
consensus: 244[28]
consentire: 244[29]
conservator: 337
consors: 449
constituere: 203, 206, 209, 209[72], 212
constitutio: 203[45], 204, 205[47], 206, 207, 208, 209, 210, 211, 212[82]
constitutum: 203, 213, 216
consul: 71
consules ordinarii: 445
contio: 65
contubernalis: 59, 60[34]
conventus: 140, 143, 143[313], 144, 145, 273, 273[20], 287, 298, 356, 356[19], 360
cornicularius: 606
corona: 478
corona aurea: 68
corona civica: 61, 106, 107, 108, 110, 111, 112, 119, 154, 173[14], 175, 181
corona obsidionalis: 61, 108[71]
corona quercea: 496[136]
corona radiata: 160
coronatus: 478
creatus: 139, 244
crustulum: 586
crypta: 524
cryptoporticus: 524
cultores: 490[92]
cuneus: 607
cura: 247, 248, 254[93], 509, 605, 614
curator: 222, 230, 247, 247[49], 248[53], 253, 254
curia: 132, 136, 141, 155, 280. 280[64], 523[294], 557
cursus: 222, 277, 279[55], 355, 358[30]

D.N.M.Q.E.: 388, 391, 400, 401[21], 411
damnatio memoriae: 189

decennalia: 507[206], 554
decuriae: 312[24]
decurio: 498, 599, 607
dedicatio: 197[16], 203, 203[45], 204, 205[47], 207, 208, 210, 379[19], 614
dedicatum: 216
delectus: 244
denarius: 62, 64, 68, 531, 561, 574
dendrophori: 394
deus: 78, 152, 152[16], 201[38], 334, 334[84], 426, 450, 452, 453
deus parens: 53
devotus: 345, 388, 391, 393, 398[9], 399, 400, 416, 417, 418
di: 338
di manes: 51
dictator: 71
dies Augusta: 495[127]
dies fastus: 204[46]
dies festi: 47
dies gymnasiorum: 499
dies imperii: 26, 297, 329[62], 484, 485, 487, 487[76], 487[77], 489, 491, 492[108], 495, 496, 498, 498[148], 499, 500, 517, 517[262], 528, 586
dies natalis: 26, 84[6], 208, 210
dies solemnis: 538, 539, 611, 613
disciplina: 417
diva: 301[5], 313[30], 485, 515, 582
divae: 429[41], 483, 486, 489, 507, 517, 555, 555[490], 589, 594
divi filius: 76, 77, 87, 88[39], 90, 327[49]
divi parentes: 51
divi: 178, 242, 251, 251[69], 265, 270, 274, 274[31], 275, 275[36], 276[6], 279, 297, 297[20], 301[4], 306, 310, 311, 312, 312[26], 313, 314, 315, 326, 327, 328, 335, 337, 377, 391, 392, 394, 395[32], 396, 419, 425[18], 429, 429[41], 430, 432, 451, 483, 486, 489, 501, 507, 517, 518, 555, 555[490], 589, 593, 594
divina: 424, 427
divinitas: 424
divinus: 344, 367, 424[10], 426, 429, 430, 431, 433
divus: 57[11], 61[46], 83, 141, 152[16], 156, 158, 160, 160[64], 161, 163[83], 201[38], 202, 214, 215, 217, 230, 235[70], 270, 270[6], 292, 297[16], 298[28], 301[4], 312[26], 426, 426[21], 427, 431, 432[59], 485, 493, 512, 515, 518
dodecahedra: 568
domesticus: 447, 449[19]

dominus: 334, 334[84-86], 344
domus: 423
domus publica: 60, 60[38]
dona militaria: 354, 358, 359, 360,
donum: 539
dorsale: 527
duodecimviri: 313, 356
duplicarii: 596
dupondius: 151, 180, 296, 506[197]
duumvir quinquennalis: 247[49], 292[66], 498
duumvir: 247[49], 291

edictum sacrum: 563
editor muneris: 559
effigies: 533, 534[361], 546, 556
electus: 244
elogium: 52
epulae: 584[670], 586
epulones: 584[670]
epulum: 587
equites singulares: 600
evocatus: 498
ex usuris: 606
exareon: 524
exta: 121, 503, 526
exuviae: 62, 553, 555

fabri: 249, 250, 251, 252, 253
fanum: 54, 335, 426, 567[550]
fasces: 484, 490, 491, 517
fasti: 118, 142, 204, 208, 297, 483, 489, 491[96], 508
fastigium: 64
felicitas: 55, 114, 116, 117, 470
felix: 55, 457, 470, 473
ferculum: 58[16], 553, 554
feriae: 206, 207, 207[60]
feriae publicae: 574
feriale: 490, 491[96], 492, 495, 499, 500, 509, 593, 594, 595, 596, 597, 598
fiscus: 222, 235
flamen: 63, 65, 75, 76, 110, 125, 132, 154, 156, 157, 157[51], 161, 163, 165,

165[104], 166, 166[109], 178, 201, 223, 224, 225, 226, 226[31], 228, 228[36], 229[39], 241, 241[9], 242, 242[13], 243, 243[24], 244, 246, 246[44], 247, 248, 249, 250, 251, 254, 254[93], 256, 257, 261, 263, 264, 265, 265[42], 266, 266[55], 267,267[57], 268, 269, 272[20], 275, 276, 277, 277[44], 278, 279, 288, 291, 292, 292[66], 293, 299, 302, 311, 312[25], 312[26], 321[21], 324, 325, 325[34], 328, 346, 346[180], 355, 356, 360, 363, 363[14], 392, 395, 425, 426, 475, 476, 476[9], 478, 478[22], 479[23], 479[27], 480, 480[33], 482, 486, 504, 504[186], 528, 579, 587, 612

flamen Augustalis: 161, 161[74], 162, 162[76], 163, 164, 165, 276, 276[40]
flaminalis: 368
flamines maiores: 165[103]
flamines minores: 165[103]
flaminica: 166, 166[105], 166[107], 166[108], 178, 183, 242[14], 251, 288, 292, 293, 293[68], 425, 480[33], 559, 587
flamonium: 243[24], 245, 258, 587[686]
foculus: 121, 503
focus: 121, 122[180], 125[197]
fortissimus: 473
forum: 303

galerus: 125, 475, 476, 476[6]
gaudia publica: 108[76]
genius familiaris: 383[37]
genius loci: 603, 606
genius: 60, 84, 84[10], 84[11], 85, 91[55], 120, 133, 286, 347, 375, 375[2], 376, 376[2], 376[4], 377, 377[6], 377[10], 377[11], 379, 380, 380[23], 381, 381[27-29], 382, 382[33], 383, 383[41], 384, 385, 386, 386[58], 388, 388[2], 400[18], 418, 419, 420, 433[70], 441, 472, 503, 506, 507, 510, 512, 516, 537[375], 594, 604, 605, 606, 610, 611, 613, 613[20]
gens: 448, 451
guttus: 526
gymnasium: 499, 579[638]

hasta: 476[9]
herma: 434
honores: 64
hostia: 505, 512[237], 516
hypaetrum: 524

imaginifer: 124[194], 535[361]

imago: 124[188], 124[194], 160[64], 242[19], 329[55], 346[181], 441, 452, 522[288], 525[303], 517, 527, 532, 533, 533[346], 533[348], 534, 534[361], 535, 536, 537, 537[373], 538, 539, 539[382], 540, 540[385], 540[387], 541, 542, 542[395], 543, 546, 556, 556[495], 562, 563, 586, 614, 616[37]

imago clipeata: 538, 543[400], 546[430]

imago laureata: 553

imaguncula: 533

imperator: 71, 74[7], 119[158], 235, 236, 237, 240[2], 240[3], 329, 333, 334, 348[195], 467, 473, 490[93], 508, 533

imperium: 46, 207

IN H.D.D.: 417, 431, 432, 432[59], 433, 440[24], 444, 603, 604, 605, 606, 607

incolae: 502, 517, 531

incolumitas: 428

inferiae: 162[78]

infula: 475[3]

ingenui: 610

intermundia: 7

interpretatio Romana: 100

invictus: 114, 116, 473, 473[126], 474

iudex: 267

iustitia: 109, 109[85]

labarum: 553[473]

laboriosus: 427

labratum: 553, 563

lacus: 519

laena: 479, 479[27], 480, 511

lararium: 85[13], 532[341]

laterculus: 541

lauratum: 553

lectisternium: 566, 566[548], 584

lectus: 566

legatus: 136, 304

legatus Aug. pr. pr.: 601, 602, 605

legatus iuridicus: 150[5]

legatus legionis: 601, 602

legatus pro praetore: 497[141]

legitimus honor: 40

lex curiata: 75

lex data: 102, 240
libamina: 573
libertini: 502, 610
libertus: 232
librarius praefecti: 601
lictores: 479
limes publicus: 601
lituus: 70, 379, 504, 526
locus: 518
lucerna: 568[561]
lucodunos: 100[19]
lucus: 104, 110, 143, 171[3]
ludi: 47, 574, 575, 614[21]
ludi scaenici: 583, 584[667]
ludiones: 564
lupercus: 69
lustratio: 526

macellarii: 315[44], 581
maiestas: 296
manes: 381
mantele: 527
manus: 424, 424[10]
mater castrorum: 494
mathematici: 343
maximus: 473
memoria: 508[208]
mens: 424, 424[10]
mensa: 122, 123
metropolis: 302[8]
meus: 447, 449[19]
miles: 601
mimographus: 558
modius: 339, 340
mola salsa: 527
mons lucidus: 100[19]
mulsum: 586
munera: 574
municeps: 303[21]
municipium: 56, 143[311], 226[31], 228, 257, 264, 287, 290, 291, 291[56], 299,

306

natalis: 84, 84¹⁰, 91⁵⁵, 118, 132, 132²⁴⁴, 163, 297, 372², 375², 380, 380²³,
    381²⁹, 483⁵³, 484, 484⁵⁷, 487, 487⁷⁶, 487⁷⁷, 488⁷⁸, 489, 489⁸⁵, 491,
    493, 494, 495, 495¹²⁷, 496, 497, 497¹⁴¹, 497¹⁴⁴, 498¹⁴⁶, 498¹⁴⁷, 499,
    500, 501, 505, 506, 507, 509, 510, 516, 529, 557, 569, 572⁵⁹³, 578,
    578⁶³², 585, 586, 588, 589, 597¹⁸, 599
natalis aquilae: 605
negotiatores: 609
nobilissimus: 330
nomen: 319, 319¹⁷, 357
nomen gentilicium: 448
noster: 321, 329, 449¹⁹
novum sidus: 79
numen: 90, 146, 177⁴⁶, 217, 345, 376, 377, 377¹¹, 378, 379, 380, 380²²,
    380²³, 381, 381²⁷, 382, 383, 383³⁸, 383⁴¹, 383³⁸, 384, 384⁴³, 385,
    385⁵², 386, 387, 387⁶¹, 388-396, 397-422, 432, 454, 455, 462, 466,
    470, 472, 594, 611¹³, 613, 613²⁰
nuncupatio votorum: 601

ob cives servatos: 112
ob honorem aedilitatis: 498
ob salutem: 500
officium: 253
olla: 527
oppidum: 142³⁰²
optimus: 473
ordinator: 413
ordo: 220, 244, 246, 257, 292, 498
origo: 220, 220³
ornamenta: 159⁵⁶
ornamenta sacerdotalia: 244²⁶
ornamenta triumphalia: 29

pagus: 101, 102, 103⁴⁷
palmata: 480
parens: 107
parens patriae: 54⁵¹, 67, 73, 108, 108⁷⁵
pater: 301⁴
pater patriae: 87, 88³⁸, 108⁷⁵, 473, 484, 506, 508

patera: 153[19], 379, 504, 511, 520[273], 526
paterfamilias: 84[11], 335, 376, 376[4]
patria: 133, 248, 249, 291, 361, 582[652]
patria potestas: 87
patrimonium: 230, 233[60]
patronus: 228
pertica: 261
phalera: 152, 153[23], 156, 157[46]
piaculum: 527
pietas: 109, 109[85]
pileus: 475
pius: 473
plebs: 379, 380, 613[20]
podium: 134, 152, 196, 200 , 251, 308, 315, 559, 581, 581[651]
pomerium: 64
pompa: 123, 553, 554, 564, 564[541]
pompa funebris: 160[64]
pontifex: 166[109], 328, 425
pontifex maximus: 53, 56, 60, 71, 78, 99, 102, 125, 161, 484, 491, 496[136],
    508
popa: 503, 511, 526
populus: 614
porticus: 523, 523[292]
portorium: 386
posuit: 542
praefectus: 230, 289
praefectus annonae: 53
praefectus castrorum: 605
praefectus i.d.: 267
praefectus legionis: 605
praefectus morum: 71
praefectus murorum: 247
praefectus praetorio: 505[190]
praenomen: 74[7], 235, 236, 264[35], 319
praepositus: 607
praesens: 343
praetorium: 595
primores civitatis: 162[77]
primum: 99
primus pilus: 601, 602, 605

princeps: 48, 83, 87, 89, 90[47], 109, 148, 171, 173, 387, 388, 424, 424[10], 484, 575
princeps iuventutis: 492[109]
principia: 124[194], 522[288], 544
pro salute: 35, 393, 449
pro salute et incolumitate: 393[27]
pro salute et incolumitate imperatoris: 507
pro salute imperatoris: 90[48], 515
pro salute mea: 90[48]
pro valetudine mea: 90[48]
procurator: 288
profectio: 529
propitium: 385
providentia: 182
providentissimus: 474
provincia: 243, 250, 267, 268, 354[11]
provincialis: 410
publicani: 50
pulvinar: 62, 64, 90[48], 90[50], 527
pulvini: 122[180]
purpurea: 479[25]

quadrifrons: 337, 529
quadriga: 57, 554
quaestor: 541
quaestor pro praetore: 514
quindecemviri sacrorum: 378
quindecimviri sacris faciundis: 81

reditus: 339[118], 428
regia: 89[44]
regnare: 70
regnum: 71[112]
religio animi: 187
res expetendae: 460
reversus: 248[58]
rex: 44, 69, 70, 71, 566[548]
ritus Romanus: 525, 527
rogatio: 76

sacellum: 523
sacer: 427, 431, 432
sacerdos: 131, 132, 132[240], 136, 138, 144, 165, 166, 166[105], 166[108], 166[109], 167, 201, 228[35], 243[24], 244, 244[27], 246, 246[44], 247[52], 254, 257, 260, 263, 264, 265, 266, 266[55], 267, 267[57], 268, 273, 302, 302[15], 303, 304, 306, 308, 309, 310[14], 313, 317, 319, 320, 322, 324[32], 325, 329, 335, 346, 348, 357, 360, 362, 363, 364, 366, 366[28], 395, 425, 426, 563, 610, 612
sacerdotalis: 246, 257, 263, 264[35], 299, 302, 303, 303[17], 319, 319[16], 346
sacerdotium: 135, 197, 243[24], 261, 311, 356[24], 357, 359, 360, 361, 365,
sacrarium: 162[78], 212
sacratissimus: 430
sacrum: 438, 439, 442-445
saeculum: 340
salus: 89, 217, 286, 348[195], 428, 449[23], 461, 541, 544[409], 600, 603, 605
sanctissimus: 430
sanctitudo: 383
sarcophagi: 30
scaena: 522, 523, 523[292]
scaenae frons: 619
schola: 250, 251, 539, 540, 556, 613, 614
schola speculatorum: 606
sella curulis: 520[273]
sellisternium: 555, 566[548], 574, 584
semisses: 104
senatus consultum: 136
servator: 54[51], 107
servus: 232, 320[18]
servus provinciae: 410
sestertius: 124, 296[13], 485[59]
sidus: 74, 79
signum: 112, 534[361], 539, 541, 542, 554, 563, 613[20]
simulacrum: 63, 64[63], 65[73], 74[13], 242[19], 520, 521, 534[355], 534[361], 542, 543, 544, 547
sodales: 328
spina: 308, 308[5]
sportulae: 613[19]
statio: 539[381]
stator templi: 247[51]

statua: 79[44], 124[188], 242[19], 441, 533[348], 534[361], 537, 539, 539[382], 540[387], 542, 543
statua acrolitha: 542
strationes: 586
subaediani: 250, 253
sufes: 291, 291[56]
suffimentum: 530
suggestus: 124[194]
summa honoraria: 498, 542
suovetaurilia: 122
supplicatio: 87[30], 133, 207, 207[60], 483, 502, 502[170], 505[190], 508, 517, 525, 528, 562
suus: 447, 449[19]

taurobolium: 393, 394
templenses: 303[21]
templum divorum: 518, 520
templum: 65, 144, 244, 246, 250, 252, 253[87], 305, 308, 322, 323, 331, 349, 426
tensa: 58[16], 62, 160[64], 553, 555
tesserarius: 601
tibicen: 526
titulus: 219, 220
toga praetexta: 376[4], 478, 478[23], 479, 480, 579
toga purpurea: 68
toga: 479, 504
toga virilis: 488[77], 490, 498, 517, 548, 602
togatus: 529, 529[324]
trabea: 479, 480, 480[28]
tria nomina: 136
tribunicia potestas: 253, 290, 484, 517
trinqui: 580
triumphator: 69
tumulus: 502
tunica: 563
turibula: 121
tutela: 382
tutulus: 481
tympanum: 163[83]
unanimitas: 575

unguentum: 561[522]
universa: 244[28]
urbs: 356
urceus: 379, 504, 526

vacca: 506, 507
valetudo: 90[48]
valva regia: 522, 560
velitis iubeatis: 76
venatio: 255, 308, 316[53], 574, 577
verna: 320[18]
vestibulum: 547
vexillarii: 606
vexillatio: 603
vexillum: 442, 561
vicennalia: 493, 569[567]
vici: 54, 483[51], 504
victimarius: 503, 509, 511, 512, 512[237], 526
victor: 111, 114, 116, 473[126], 474
victoria: 428
vicus: 85[13], 533
vigor: 424[10]
viri clarissimi: 590
viri egregii: 590
viritim: 290
virtus: 109, 117, 174, 406, 460
vis divina: 383
vitta: 475, 475[3], 481, 527
volens: 385
vomitorium: 557, 559
vota: 90[47], 430, 484, 490, 496, 496[138], 498[150], 514, 607
vota extraordinaria: 507
vota pro salute rei publicae: 89
vota pro incoluminate principis: 497
vota publica: 498[150]
votum: 500[161]

IV. CORRIGENDA

(see earlier above, Vol. I, 1: New Addenda and Corrigenda)

The following list is limited to errors that have resulted in misinformation. Harmless misprints are omitted.

errata	*corrige*	
p. xi, l. 15	February, 1985	Edmonton, Alberta
p. 17, l. 27	Polybius 26, 1ᵃ	
p. 29, note 56	*Ptolemaic Alexandria*	
p. 29, note 57	996-1084	
p. 37, note 33	Robert	
p. 38, note 48	*APF*	
p. 50, l. 8	conception of Rome	
p. 55, l. 1	*compita*	
p. 62, note 54	*G & R* 4 (1957), 46-53 at 52	
p. 79, l. 22	*Georgics* 3, 13-25	
p. 84, l. 11	CD 51, 19, 7	
p. 91, note 51	... below, p. 128, notes 215 f.	
p. 91, note 55, l. 14	*genius* of the emperor rather than directly to him, a form of cult which she takes to have been	
p. 97, note 1	See further Addenda, p. 187	
p. 120, l. 7	*compita* in Rome	
p. 126, l. 22	Suetonius	
p. 129, l. 16	Caesarea	
p. 140, l. 11	Livia	
p. 143, l. 10	on the Rhine	
p. 154, ll. 7-10	... will have been under the present seminary, to the north-east of the Roman precinct. (See below, Vol. II,1, p. 519, note 270)	
p. 154, note 27	at the *compita*;	
p. 172, l. 11	*IG* 12, 2, 44	
p. 186, l. 15	Pausanias 4, 32, 1	
p. 197, l. 7	by the Palatine	
p. 212, note 84	*Ad. Nat.* 1, 10	
p. 219, l. 21	*Cattio Sabino*	
p. 228, note 35	L. Calpurnius Augustalis	

errata	*corrige*
Pl. XIX: caption	... holding box for incense
Pl. XXXI: upside down	reverse
p. 241, note 8	*BCH* 90 (1966), 144-155
p. 289, l. 3	Ocratina
p. 296, note 15	by the Palatine ... For Caligula's incorporation of the *templum novum Divi Augusti* into the imperial Palatine complex - as a result of which inscriptions refer to the temple as *in Palatio* - see now D. Fishwick, "On the Temple of Divus Augustus", *Phoenix* 46 (1992), forthcoming
p. 305, l. 14	Marcomannic
p. 322, note 26	*Titolature* (above, note 9) 75 f.,
p. 328, note 52	CD 75, 4, 5
p. 332, note 76	... (1981) 175-184
p. 334, note 84	Scribonius Largus, *Compos.* 60, 163
p. 341, l. 6	on the Appian Way
p. 424, note 10	; Scribonius Largus, *Ep. ded.* 13 (Claudius);
p. 424, note 11	... 60, 163; *Ep. ded.* 13 ff. ...
p. 479, note 25	... preserved upright (ʿ) is the ...
p. 484, note 57	... *AFA* XLVI, 51, confirmed by *AEpig* (1983) no. 9, ll. 64-67... 113-128; D. Fishwick, "On the Temple of Divus Augustus", *Phoenix* 46 (1992), forthcoming
p. 485, l. 7	... joint temple by the Palatine, cf. Addenda, p. 296, note 15 (above).
p. 486, l. 5	stood by the Palatine
p. 506, note 196	... in A.D. 38); confirmed by *AEpig* (1983) no. 95, ll. 64-67.
p. 509, note 216	; Festus p. 253 (Olms = Lindsay p. 298,25);
p. 528, l. 25	(*Epp.* 10, 52f., 102f.).
p. 525, l. 12	... just as at the *compita* of Rome, ...
p. 537, note 371	See below, note 396
p. 541, l. 3	... *Divi Hadriani* ...
p. 541, l. 19	= *ILS* 3208
p. 558, l. 20	statues of Hadrian ...